ERRATUI

Page 184, final paragraph, line 3. The number of C.C.F. cadets in 242 schools should read 'about 25,000'.

Cadets – The impact of war on the Cadet Movement

Dr Larry J. Collins served as a cadet with the A.C.F. before enlisting as a Junior Leader with the Royal Signals in 1957. He left the army in 1966 to train as a teacher of physical education and history at Madeley College where he graduated with a B.Ed. in 1970. In 1974, after gaining an M.A. from Leeds University, he taught at Worcester College of Higher Education. A change of career occurred in 1980 when he entered the theatrical profession. A return to academia resulted in a Ph.D. in theatre history being completed in 1994. The military connection was resumed in 1986 when he was commissioned into the R.A.F.V.R.[T] where he served with the A.T.C. in Essex. In 1991, on moving to Hertfordshire, he transferred to the A.C.F. and whilst there he also served with the C.C.F. A further move in 1994 meant a transfer to Somerset A.C.F. and in 1996 to Shropshire, where he resides today. Larry J. Collins is still serving with the A.C.F. and now writes full time. In June 2000 he was awarded the MBE for services to the Army Cadet Force.

Previous publication: *Theatre at War, 1914–18* [Macmillan].

CADETS

The Impact of War on the Cadet Movement

L.J. Collins

Jade Publishing Limited,
5, Leefields Close, Uppermill, Oldham, Lancashire, OL3 6LA.

This first impression published by Jade Publishing Limited 2001.

© L.J. Collins 2001
All rights reserved.

ISBN 1 900734 03 6   Cadets – The impact of war on the Cadet Movement. (Pbk).

Printed in Great Britain

Typeset by
Nonpareil, Greenfield, Oldham, Lancashire.

British Library Cataloguing in Publication Data
Collins, L.J., 1942–
Cadets – The impact of war on the Cadet Movement
1. Military Cadets – Great Britain – History
I. Title
355.5'0941

ISBN 1-900734-03-6

    This book is sold subject to the condition that it shall not, by way of trade or otherwise, be lent, re-sold, hired out, or otherwise circulated without the publisher's prior consent in any form of binding or cover other than that in which it is published and without a similar condition including this condition being imposed on the subsequent purchaser. No part of this publication may be reproduced, stored in a retrieval system, or transmitted, in any form or by any means, electronic, mechanical, photocopying, recording, digital or otherwise, without the prior written permission of the publisher.

Contents

	Page
Acknowledgments	ix
Foreword	x
Introduction	1

Chapter
1. 1860–1910	7
2. From Boer War to the First World War	31
3. The inter-war years	45
4. Propaganda, recruitment and expansion	63
5. Pre-service training	101
6. Assisting the war effort	153
7. Rewards and awards, and looking to the future	167
Post-war postscript	181
Bibliography	187
Index	193

Illustrations

There are 28 plates between pages 100 and 101. All copyrights are acknowledged and permission was sought, and granted, to reproduce the pictures shown in this work.

The front cover illustration is of cadets of the A.T.C., S.C.C., and the A.C.F., prior to parading before H.M. the King on 4 July, 1942. It is reproduced by kind permission of the Imperial War Museum (Ref. H21154).

Acknowledgments

My acknowledgments of assistance are numerous. It would, of course, have been impossible to complete this book without the help and co-operation of staff at the different national cadet headquarters. Commander P. Higgins, R.N. kindly granted me permission to examine the Navy League files and S.C.C. magazines, and Lieutenant Commander (S.C.C.) J. Fletcher, R.N.R. provided additional material. I wish also to thank Maria Davies of the S.C.C. H.Q., for whom nothing was too much trouble. Brigadier R. B. MacGregor-Oakford, C.B.E., M.C., of the A.C.F.A., and the assistant editor of the *Army Cadet* journal, Elizabeth Walker, B.A., were most helpful. Indeed, so were Wing Commander F. T. West, R.A.F. and the P.R. team of Denise Hornsby and Tania King at H.Q. Air Cadets. Colonel R. P. D. Brook put the Cadet Training Centre library, Frimley Park, at my disposal and Lieutenant Colonel (Retd.) J. N. Arnold helped in the location of material.

Pictorial evidence was viewed and some reproduced thanks to the Departments of Photographs and of Film at the Imperial War Museum. Assistance was also sought and obtained from the British Film Institute, the National Maritime Museum, the National Army Museum, the Royal Air Force Museum, the Castle Museum of Shrewsbury, and Major (Retd.) J. Hobbis Harris.

Many thanks go to all those ex-wartime cadets who provided me with valuable information by completing a questionnaire. Unfortunately, there are too many to mention individually. An especial thanks to Captain (Retd.) F. J. M. Mair, M.B.E., who sent me a quantity of important vintage training pamphlets. Certain people were particularly helpful not only in providing research material, but also welcoming me into their homes, their schools or their units. The list includes Mr A. M. Robinson of the 'Die Hards of the 40s' [ex-Middlesex Regiment cadets], ex-C.P.O. S. Tilley of Northampton S.C.C., the Secretary of the Old Yeovillians' Association, the archivists of Shrewsbury School and the Old Ellesmerian Club. I am also grateful to Lieutenant Commander (S.C.C.) I. R. Wallace, R.N.R. from T.S. *Inskip* for his interest and hospitality, and to Major M. Bryant, A.C.F. for the chance to look at his archive collection. Thanks also to the H.Q. staff of the various cadet and county unit headquarters who allowed me to scan their archives. Lastly, and most importantly, I am indebted to Mrs Adrienne Forbes for her encouragement, and for her diligent proof-reading skills.

Foreword

by Professor E.R. Holmes, C.B.E., T.D.
(Director of Reserve Forces and Cadets, 1997–2000)

It gives me particular pleasure to write the foreword to Larry Collins's fine study of the Cadet Movement, and does so for three reasons. Firstly, because I am a military historian by profession, and as such know that this book fills an identifiable gap in the literature. The Cadet Movement has long deserved a proper academic history, not simply because it made an important contribution to the armed forces in two world wars (most notably the second, for most of which there were, at any one time, nearly half a million boys in military uniform), but also because it is a fascinating reflection of social attitudes to the armed forces. Secondly, I am myself an ex-cadet, and so have personal experience of what cadet service can do in terms of imparting confidence, a sense of worth and – though you would not guess it from the state of my study – the ability to organise oneself properly. Finally, I have served in the Territorial Army for more than 35 years, joining as a private soldier and retiring this month as a brigadier – the highest rank a Territorial can attain. In my last appointment I was Director of Reserve Forces and Cadets in the Ministry of Defence and thus had the opportunity of seeing today's Cadet Movement first-hand: and what a wonderful experience that has been.

From its very start there have always been two threads woven together in the Cadet Movement. One, which catches the eye most dramatically, and was most important through much of its history, has been its role as a pre-service training organisation, teaching boys skills, and developing attitudes, which would make it quicker and easier to train them when they entered the armed forces as adults. As Larry Collins explains, during the Second World War all three services took great care in the harmonisation of cadet qualifications with the requirements of adult service, a process which helped enable those with particular aptitudes to be identified early on and which saved valuable time in the training process.

But the second thread within the cadet structure, which has undoubtedly been the most important for at least the past forty years, was recognised well over a century ago: cadets form the services' youth movement. A group of sailors, on returning home from the Crimean War, were so disturbed by the 'laziness and apparent degradation' of the boys they saw on the streets that they formed a Lads' Brigade at Whitstable in 1856. Cadets have always been much more than miniature Regulars or Territorials: they have been young citizens too. The Cadet Movement has long done its best to make young men (and now, quite rightly, young women as well), feel valued and valuable; to rise above the depressing horizons to which economic circumstances have often confined them; and to develop as individuals in a climate of shared endeavour. The Cadet Movement is a great social and racial mixer, and as such helps break down those stereotypes which have proved so divisive in the past. But I would say this, wouldn't I, because I can remember what cadet service did for me. After a long and not wholly unsuccessful career as an academic, broadcaster and reserve officer I still rate becoming RSM of my cadet contingent as one of my proudest achievements. In terms of confidence building, if you can drill a large body of cadets, remembering the right words of command and not letting your nervousness show in your voice then, believe me, talking to a TV camera holds no terrors. And so, whether as brigadier or professor or simply as an ex-cadet, I warmly commend this valuable book.

Richard Holmes,
Ropley, Hampshire,
April, 2001.

INTRODUCTION

THE CADET MOVEMENT has its roots deep in military history, and evidence shows that boys regularly appeared in organised naval and army units whenever Britain went to war.

In medieval England knights had their accompanying pages, many of whom were boys. There is ample evidence to show that through the ages youths were regularly employed as drummers in British regiments, and could thereby be in the front line of an advancing army. It was not uncommon, writes Cockerill, for a boy as young as nine, or even seven, to be serving in the ranks, albeit as a servant or lackey.[1] Shrewsbury School had a volunteer cadet corps, albeit short-lived, as early as 1581.[2] In the seventeenth century King James I, whilst on a visit to the Isle of Wight, was 'much taken with seeing little boys skirmish'.[3] In 1702 Parliament voted into law the Act of Enlistment which required parishes to supply recruits for the army in return for a bounty. If they failed to do this they incurred a £5 penalty: as a consequence, according to one historian, 'vast numbers of boys enlisted'.[4]

A significant number of boys were employed as apprentices to farriers, tailors or in other army trades. In 1720 the Honorable Artillery Company had two boy drummers, two cadets (boy gunners) and five matrosses (assistant gunners), and by 1727 the total had risen to 48.[5] It was recorded in the *Britannic Magazine*, that when King George III opened Parliament on 22 November 1803, his attention was caught by the sight of 50 boys in blue and gold uniform, aged between 12 and 16, marching past carrying small muskets. Their own band of drums and fifes accompanied them.[6] In the same year colours were presented to the two companies of the re-formed volunteer Cadet Corps at Shrewsbury School on 26 September.[7] Indeed, during the Napoleonic Wars all Regiments of the Line had boy soldiers in their ranks. There are numerous other examples of boys serving in the army, and so a boy in uniform was not an unfamiliar sight.

The navy, too, unofficially 'encouraged' youths, via the press gangs, to serve their country. For the middle and upper classes entry to the wardroom for any young aspirant was, prior to 1794, via the 'Captain's Servant Entry'. This was a method whereby parents would ask a commander to take their son into his charge. This he would do if the boy was a relative or the son of an acquaintance, or if his parents paid an appropriate fee.[8] A number of young entrants for the Lower Deck came from the Royal Naval College at Portsmouth where ratings were as young as 12. During the wars with France in the eighteenth century boys as young as nine, 'or even as little as six' served below decks, many of whom were apprentices to Warrant Officers. This was strictly against the law as the minimum age for joining a ship was 13 – or 11 if a boy was the son of a naval officer.[9] After 1815, however, the Admiralty finally succeeded in abolishing this pre-pubescent entry.

There was also a private charity that trained boys for the Royal Navy as well as supplying apprentices for the Merchant Fleet. This was the Marine Society, founded in 1756 by the philanthropic 'social worker' Jonas Hanway. The society was intended, as recorded in the Sea Cadet Corps manual, to solve two contemporary problems. First, to rid the streets of 'the crowds of layabouts and vagrant youths' and, secondly, to help reduce the serious shortage of manpower in the Royal and Merchant Navies.[10] Once the youths had acquired the requisite skills on board the training ship they were sent to sea as volunteers, where, according to one source, they greatly outnumbered the pressed men.[11] Lewis, in his social history of the Royal Navy, sees Hanway's Marine Society acting as a sort of 'Dr Barnardo's Home for waifs and strays'; but concludes that only five per cent of its product actually went to sea.[12] Whatever the statistics, two things are clear: like the Sea Cadet Corps (S.C.C.) of today Hanway's school accepted youths from non-seafaring families – unlike the R.N. School – and, like the latter-day Cadet Movement it had an additional social aim.

Evidence shows that boys served on land and sea throughout the wars with France until Napoleon's military quests were finally ended at Waterloo in 1815. By this time the Industrial Revolution was well under way, and this had a profound effect on society, and, not least, on the embryonic Cadet Movement. And it is the history of the cadet organisations and their relationship to war that is the central concern of this book.

Research into the effects of war and service in the Armed Forces is a multi-million pound business. Millions upon millions of words have been written about war and the part played by our servicemen and women. Teachers and students in universities, colleges and schools devote time to studying the effect that war has had upon our lives. When studying the effects of war on the individual the concentration was, at least until the Second World War, on the man at the Front. Increasingly historians have looked at the role played by the 'auxiliary' and second-line services on the Home Front. Studies, reports and articles have been written about the Home Guard, the Royal Observer Corps, Civil Defence, the Fire Service, the Special Constabulary, the Balloon Squadrons of the Auxiliary Air Force, the Air Raid Wardens, Women's Land Army, W.V.S. and other lesser known national service organisations. In the summer of 1995 past members of these organisations, along with ex-regular and reserve forces members, celebrated the 50th Anniversary of the end of the Second World

War. It was a time when reunions – many of units now defunct – were held and the veterans reminisced. It was a time when the nation looked back, often with pride, at what was achieved during the years 1939–45. But what of the cadets, what did they do during the last world war? All the accounts dealing with the services listed are to do with adults. No one seems to have looked in any depth at youth in military uniform, and to examine the part they played during the periods the nation was at war.

Historical accounts are to be found at the headquarters of the three services, although the archives vary in both breadth and detail. One of the aims of this book is to redress this historical imbalance and to look at the role of the Cadets during the Second World War. This book is, however, more than an account of what happened in the years 1939–45. The part played by the Cadet Movement during the First World War and the preceding Boer War is reviewed. But the story starts, as it were, not with a war but with the threat of war in 1859, and the resulting formation of official cadet companies in 1860.

Very little was written about the cadets *per se* in the late nineteenth century, and despite the phenomenal growth of the Movement – particularly during the two succeeding world wars – later accounts are very scant. This is true albeit in propagandist terms much was written to encourage boys to don uniform, and in the early part of the nineteenth century drill was still an integral part of the elementary school curriculum. The cadet units based in the public and grammar schools that published an annual magazine have a continuous but generally not very detailed record of their cadet corps' existence. The volunteers who manned the town units would have had little time to keep records, particularly in wartime. Hence evidence from the individual units and their headquarters is piecemeal, and diverse.

The evidence obtainable from the three national cadet headquarters varies considerably. The Sea Cadet Corps' recorded history is confined to a few sheets of paper. The Army Cadet Force has periodically published a small up-dated history book. This provides a good general background with biographies of the 'good and the great' in the A.C.F. organisation, but says relatively little about cadet life at detachment level. However, unlike the other organisations, the Army Cadet Force Association does publish an account of its history. The Air Training Corps has a detailed but unpublished record, which is useful for those enthusiasts interested in uniforms, badges and buttons, and statistics. Despite this lack of collated historical data all three headquarters have dusty shelves and cardboard boxes containing back numbers of their respective magazines, all of which were first published during the Second World War. These provide a wealth of information, particularly about units and specific individuals. At the Sea Cadet Corps H.Q. there are back numbers of the Navy League's magazine and minutes of the Navy League's meetings.

Some oral and written evidence can be obtained from ex-cadets who served during the years 1939–45. There is comparatively little photographic archive material due, no doubt, to the difficulty of obtaining film and the paper restrictions pertaining to wartime.

The outside agencies, the Imperial War Museum in London, Maritime Museum at Greenwich, R.A.F. Museum at Hendon and the National Army Museum at Chelsea have surprisingly little in the way of either written or photographic evidence regarding the Sea Cadet Corps, Junior Training Corps, Army Cadet Force or the Air Training Corps. There are, of course, Hansard reports from the House of Commons and the Government reports on the Education and Youth Services. In fact, it was only the Education and Youth Service that considered the cadets as a whole, the Services, for the most part, concentrating on their own organisations; although there was some co-operation regarding training, and standardisation of entry requirements during the Second World War. There was also, owing to greater Government involvement, a need for co-ordination when it came to grants and funding. In terms of philosophy there was, indeed there still is, little difference between the cadet organisations. The military and social aims and objectives are almost identical. However, until now nobody has looked at the whole Cadet Movement.

The aim of this book, therefore, is to piece together in an understandable form the history of the Sea, Army and Air Cadets and to look at the relationship they had with one another and their parent services from 1860 to 1945. In doing so it is hoped that a missing piece in the jigsaw of military history will have been located and put in place, and that those who served with the Cadet organisations, particularly during wartime, will receive the recognition they deserve.

INTRODUCTION REFERENCES

1. A. W. Cockerill, *Sons of the Brave* [London: Leo Cooper, 1984], p. 5
2. J. Basil Oldham M.A., *A History of Shrewsbury School, 1852–1952* [London: Blackwell, 1952], p. 247–248
3. Army Cadet Force Association, *The Army Cadet Force Handbook* [London: A.C.F.A., 1962], p. 14
4. A. W. Cockerill, op. cit., p. 36–37
5. Ibid., p. 47
6. *The Britannic Magazine*, December 1803
7. J. Basil Oldham, op. cit., p. 248
8. Michael Lewis, *The Navy in Transition* [London: Hodder & Stoughton, 1965], p. 100
9. Ibid., p. 156
10. Ibid., p. 33
11. M.A.O. 8 [Sea Cadet Corps] 'History of the Cadet Movement', p. 1
12. Michael Lewis, op. cit., p. 33

Chapter 1 – 1860–1910

BY THE MIDDLE of the nineteenth century the United Kingdom had become the most powerful industrial country in the world. Britain ruled the largest empire the world had ever seen, and the word 'Great' was used with pride. This change from an agricultural to an industrial society did not benefit everyone. The large migration from country to town produced areas of densely populated urban squalor. The traditional establishments of church and school could not cope with this concentrated influx. And the concomitant source of cheap labour meant mass-exploitation of both adults and children. There was also a discernible lack of family supervision and a resultant change in the behaviour of many of the young. Some sailors returning from the Crimean War were so concerned about the apparent laziness and degradation of the youths on the streets that they decided to do something about it by starting a youth club. As a result a Lads' Brigade at Whitstable was founded in 1856. The boys were at first dressed in Victorian band uniforms – a band had been started in 1857 – but later a naval-style rig was adopted. By the turn of the century there were a few other similar independent units run on nautical lines which later became members of the Boys' Naval Brigade – the forerunner of the Sea Cadet Corps; although the Whitstable Brigade remained independent for some time and did not join the organisation until 1926.[1]

It was the threat of war that once again sparked national interest in the military. Despite the fact that Britain and France fought on the same side in the Crimea, statesmen and a group of publicists were becoming increasingly alarmed about the old adversary's growing military power. There was concern that Napoleon III might aspire to emulate Bonaparte. An invasion was thought a possibility, particularly as the French navy was being equipped with steam ships, and it was believed that the French had the capability of landing an army of 'up to 30,000 on British shores' in a single night.[2] It was felt that the Royal Navy would not have enough time to organise adequate opposition; added to which most of the army was abroad policing the Empire.

In response, the Secretary of State issued a circular on 12 May 1859, inviting Lord Lieutenants to form military (army) Volunteer Corps. They did and within a short period over 100,000 men had enrolled. This action inadvertently started what were later to become the Combined Cadet Force (C.C.F.) and the Army Cadet Force (A.C.F.). In 1860 several schools 'answered the call' by forming cadets units. Amongst the earliest were Eton, Harrow, Rossall, Felsted, Rugby, and Shrewsbury – for the third time – (*Plate 1*) and Hurstpierpoint, which were affiliated to the Volunteer Corps.

The Rugby Corps, as was the practice, shared the same title as the town corps, and were thus part of the 3rd Battalion Warwickshire Rifle Volunteers, although for the first two years it operated more like a rifle club.[3] These school-based corps became known as 'closed' units on account of membership being restricted to a particular institution. However, it was not long before 'open' units based on a particular locality followed suit. In May 1860, 35 cadets from one such company marched past Queen Victoria at the head of the Queen's Westminster Rifle Volunteers, at the first Volunteer Review in Hyde Park.[4] There is evidence of military cadets in Surrey dating back to 1809, when boys of 14 were admitted to the Honorable East India Company's Military College at Addiscombe. Today's unpaid volunteer Surrey cadets, however, can trace their beginning back to 1861 when the Surrey Rifle Volunteers started a cadet corps. Indeed, it is recorded that cadets of the 1st Surrey Rifle Volunteers were among 1,000 cadets on parade at Crystal Palace in September 1861.[5] During the next decade several more pubic and grammar schools in Surrey formed corps: Charterhouse School had R. S. S. Baden-Powell, the founder of the Boy Scout Movement, among its cadets. The pattern of expansion seen in Surrey was duplicated throughout the country. In Scotland an ex-police superintendent started a Company of Juvenile Volunteers for boys between 10 and 15 years of age: they eventually numbered 130. A year later in 1861 a unit consisting of four Scottish companies was formed. It called itself the British League of Cadet Corps, and in 1867 it was attached to the 3rd City of Edinburgh Rifle Volunteer Corps.[6] South of the border, in Yorkshire, in March 1862, 30 cadets from the Huddersfield Volunteer Battalion, dressed in red jackets and grey trousers, 'accompanied their parent battalion to a review in Doncaster, but were forbidden to take part . . . By September their strength had increased to sixty-five'.[7] One of the earliest War Office references to army cadets is contained in the Volunteer Regulations, published in 1863. Articles 279 to 286 officially authorised the formation of Cadet Corps by Volunteer battalions. It is likely that in 1863 the Huddersfield cadets officially received recognition, and, like all cadet units, were then allowed to wear the uniform of their parent battalion. The rules stipulated that cadets were to be 12 years old or more; rifles could be loaned to the unit, 'but small boys were not allowed to carry these . . . Officers were not commissioned but were honourably recognised'. By 1899 officers were granted commissions, and one captain and one lieutenant were allowed per unit of 50 cadets.[8]

The last quarter of the nineteenth century saw an unprecedented growth in all types of youth movements. The 1881 census shows that the population had almost doubled in the previous 50 years, and that more than 46 per cent were under the age of 20.[9] There was a significant shift of population from country to town; this brought large numbers of youths together and led to well-known problems; however, the bringing-together of large numbers of adolescent boys made it easier for youth organisations to recruit members. The problems of adolescent behaviour first addressed by the ex-sailors who fought in the Crimean War, and then by other service veterans, meant that youth organisations that were set up tended to be uniformed and with a military flavour. A number of social and moral reformers saw the possibility of using a kind of military training as a means of teaching boys a sense of discipline and citizenship. The reformers took their lead, in part, from the ideal of Christian manliness as encouraged in public schools. Hence several uniformed organisations were church-based, such as the Boys' Brigade (1883), and the Church Lads' Brigade (1901). Many units of these doctrinal, uniformed youth organisations were later to become affiliated to the army cadet battalions.

The recognition achieved by Volunteer Cadet Corps companies at some public schools encouraged other schools such as Dulwich College to start their own rifle corps. By 1886 the army cadet movement had grown to the extent that the regulations had been relaxed to allow the formation of cadet battalions independent of the Volunteer Force; this encouraged the considerable growth of 'open' units.[10] Manchester can claim the distinction of being the first self-administered battalion. Captain A. P. Ledward, an ex-captain in the 5th Manchesters, formed the 1st Cadet Battalion, The Manchester Regiment, in 1884. 'The initial strength was 3 officers and 40 cadets. By 1900 the strength had increased to 600.'[11] This was also a time when middle-class reformers and youth workers in working-class areas attempted to utilise the uniformed Cadet Movement for the betterment of the adolescent boy.

The work of the naval veterans of the Crimea in the handful of independent Boys' Training-Brigs of the eighteenth century is not well documented, and it is uncertain whether the activities really had a military (naval) content, or if they were youth clubs with a nautical syllabus. On the other hand, the work of the eponymous East London (army) Cadet Corps, formed in 1885, is recorded. This Corps was located at the Toynbee Hall University Settlement in Whitechapel. The aim was to instil public-school values in the working-class boy. Its formation was due to the enthusiasm of Sir Francis Fletcher Vane, ex-commander in the Militia and Volunteers and Toynbee Hall resident who later became London's first Boy Scout Commissioner.[12] Sir Francis claimed that 'through *esprit de corps*, patriotism will grow; true patriotism will lead to a just appreciation of the duties of citizenship, and the part which the Anglo-Saxon race is called upon to play in the cause of progress'.[13] Values displaying such overt racist sentiment would be unacceptable today, but 100 years ago, when Britain ruled most of the waves and much of the land, they would have seemed unremarkable.

Perhaps the best-known reformer who was instrumental in seeing the added social advantages of the Cadet Movement was Octavia Hill. Miss Hill is better known as one of the pioneers of the National Trust, although much of her time was spent running a Housing Association for the poor in East London. Following the example set by the East London Cadet Corps at Whitechapel, and along with William Ingham Brooke – who previously helped run the East London unit – she began a Volunteer Cadet Corps at Southwark in 1889. The inaugural meeting was chaired by no less a figure than the distinguished soldier, Viscount Wolseley. The Corps attracted 160 cadets, and many others were refused entry. It was not an uncommon practice for the larger public schools and universities to run Missions in the poorer areas in London. Knowing this, Octavia Hill wrote to Eton College and suggested a link between their Hackney Wick Mission and the Cadet Corps at Southwark; 'they accepted and helped pay for a smart red uniform which Octavia Hill felt would do much to cheer the dull Southwark Streets'.[14]

Colonel Albert Salmond became the Southwark Corps' commander and Octavia Hill the Honorary Colonel. The unit later amalgamated with six other London cadet corps and formed the 1st Cadet Battalion of the Royal West Surrey Regiment with a complement of 400 cadets. The company was the first to reach a size that, under the War Office regulations, meant it could be designated an independent affiliated battalion: hence it became the senior cadet battalion in the army. The unit still exists in the form of 1st (London) Cadet Battalion of the Queen's Regiment. Other units were formed by clergymen for the reasons stated by Octavia Hill, which were to 'see that exercise, discipline, obedience, *esprit-de-corps*, camping out, manly companionship ... will be to our Southwark lads the very best possible education'.[15] She believed it was important to try to influence a young boy by implanting these ideals before 'he gets in with a gang of loafers' and that 'it may make all the difference to his life'.[16] These objectives are still echoed by some adult individual members of today's Cadet Movement.

The Navy League, a 'non-political organisation' formed by retired Royal Navy officers in 1894 was eventually responsible for the formation of the Sea Cadet Corps (S.C.C.). The initial aims of the Navy League, as stated in the Minutes of 1895 were:

> (a) To spread information, showing the vital importance to the British Empire of the Navy supremacy upon which depend its trade, empire, and national existence.

(b) To call attention to the enormous demands which war would make upon the Navy, and to the fact that the Navy is not at present ready to meet them.

(c) To call attention from time to time to such measures as may be requisite to secure adequate preparation for the maritime defence of the Empire.

(d) To urge these matters on public men and, in particular, upon candidates for Parliament.[17]

In essence the Navy League was a pressure-group. Although the constitutional 'aims' are directly related to the work of the Navy League the subsequent formation of the League's Boys' Naval Brigade may be viewed as an extension of these objectives. The League members were much concerned about the low naval budgets set by the Government, lack of technical advancement in ship design and, as they saw it, the unpreparedness of the Royal Navy.[18] Navy League members, apart from lobbying M.P.s and thus irritating the First Sea Lord, attempted to promote the Royal Navy by talks in schools. It also urged both the Government and the Shipping Companies to establish training ships to train boys for the Merchant Navy – 'then 36% manned by foreigners'. The training of the Royal Navy's own cadets in *Britannia* had for some time received poor publicity. In 1882 *The Times* claimed that their training was inadequate and inappropriate, and the age of 12 was too young.[19] The Admiralty's response, writes Captain Wells in his social history of the Royal Navy, 'was a hands-off attitude, to the extent of regarding criticism as impertinent'. The Royal Navy was having little difficulty in recruiting boys either for the upper or the lower deck. Given the Admiralty's testy reaction to any newspaper's criticism, it is no surprise that the hierarchy regarded the Navy League with impassive indifference: an attitude which was to last for over 50 years.[20] Indeed, the relationship between the Admiralty and the Navy League has, at times, appeared mutually suspicious. This has not been to the advantage of the Sea Cadets.

A unit on the north coast, the Whitby Boys' Naval Brigade, was formed in 1896 and attracted 120 boys to its first parade. It was claimed by a local newspaper to be the first 'Naval Boys' Brigade in the UK'.[21] However, it did not last long. A handful of other similar units started elsewhere in the country, but unlike the army cadets they were independent and, alas, substantially undocumented.

THE BOER WAR AND ITS EFFECTS

If the preceding Victorian era saw the birth of the Cadet Movement then the ensuing Edwardian age witnessed its adolescent growth spurt. This was a period of reorganisation for the army, reform for the navy and war

11

against the Boers in South Africa, all of which had an effect on the Cadet Movement.

The Royal Navy at this time was going through a radical change, and some of the 'Old Salts' in the Admiralty were finding it difficult to come to terms with the new technology. The new metal warships required technically-minded sailors. Some of the hierarchy still thought in terms of sail power and unquestioning obedience; they did not understand why the newly-trained, technically-minded artificer and engineer officer was impatient with the Navy's obsolete ways and methods.[22] The R.N. had even less time for outsider critics such as the Navy League. From 1902 modernisation of the Navy came from the inside once the reformer, Admiral Lord Fisher was appointed. New subjects such as physical training and wireless telegraphy became part of the naval curriculum, subjects that would, eventually, be incorporated into the Navy League Boys' Brigade training syllabus. Admiral Fisher also extended training for boy artificers. Members of the League's Committee were therefore more concerned with training cadets for Britain's merchant fleet whose foreign employees equalled 48.4 per cent by 1908.[23]

An assessment of the training for boys was undertaken. The Marine Society had a training ship on the Thames and at Belfast; in addition there was a privately-run ship on the Hamble River. The Government subsidised the running of eight 'Industrial Ships', which despatched 3,000 to 4,000 boys to sea every year. It is recorded in the S.C.C. history notes that 'Most of these catered for orphans and their product was not highly thought of – with the exception of the *Warspite* cadets'.[24] This inadequacy of provision prompted the Navy League to decide to run its own training ships. In 1899 an old Thames barge was purchased and berthed at Windsor. A retired naval Petty Officer was put in command and the boys dressed in naval uniforms. Thus the unit at Windsor, opened in 1900, was the first Navy League Sea Cadet Corps unit, and since that time all independent units have become affiliated to the Navy League. By 1908 the T.S. *Windsor* was parading between 25 and 30 cadets, and during its eight-year history 130 boys had gone to sea.[25] Another training craft was located at Reading (*Plates 2 and 3*). At the inaugural meeting for the establishment of the latter in May 1908, General Sir John Moody said money was being spent at *Warspite* on providing training for boys 'brought up by the best class of parents' and that what was needed was training for 'honest boys' – by which he meant the poorer working class – as was the case at Windsor. The only other institutions serving such a purpose were the '*Indefatigable* at Liverpool, the NAVY LEAGUE HOME [for poor boys] at Liscard and the *Mercury* at Southampton'.[26] It was also the aim of the Reading Brig not only to further their education, but also to supply seamen for both the Royal

12

Navy and the Mercantile Marine. The Reading scheme was to be run by Rear-Admiral Fleet who asked for, and got, the £250 to buy a re-fitted barge, and the annual subscription of £60, as the Reading Brig got under way. The Reading Brig, like the one at Windsor, soon had all the accoutrements and activities associated with a sea cadet unit: boating, ropework, bugles, parades and a colour ceremony.[27] The League then became aware of the existence of 'another dozen or more Naval Brigades, Naval Brigs and similar organisations scattered around the country'.[28] One of the S.C.C. units that can trace its antecedents back to this time is the one located at H.M.S. *Nelson* in Portsmouth. It was formed circa 1900 by a Lieutenant Jack Thornback, and was known as the R.N. Barracks Boys' Brigade, later designated R.N. Cadet Corps.[29] The collation of these disassociated units into a recognisable coherent organisation was slow due – judging by the lack of entries in the Navy League's minutes – to the low priority of cadet training. However, eventually, enough nautical-based units agreed to affiliate with the Navy League and the Navy League Boys' Naval Brigade was formed in 1910. This was the predecessor of today's Sea Cadet Corps.

Whilst social considerations and training for the civilian mercantile navy was the concern of the Navy League regarding cadets, the army was following a different route. The social aims were not dissimilar but at times the military aims of the latter became paramount.

As a result of the British and Boers' expansion in Africa in the late 1880s, and the denial of rights for the Uitlanders (British immigrants) by the Boers and Britain's desire to protect her gold mining, there ensued a conflict of interests made manifest in a conflict of arms. This resulted in an initial defeat of the British at Majuba Hill in 1881. A second war began in 1899 and lasted until 1902. The South African wars had a profound effect on the military, and hence on the army cadets.

The public avidly followed the South African campaign, via the popular press, with feelings of increasing incredulity. The British had to fight a war where strategy and terrain favoured the enemy. The Boers were very good marksmen, well armed and highly mobile. Initially the British suffered considerable setbacks, and the reaction at home was, at times, hysterical. There was a 'retaliatory' rise in volunteers and these included cadets. In 1901, for example, the 1st Volunteer Battalion King's Shropshire Light Infantry was formed, comprising cadet companies from Shrewsbury School, Shrewsbury town, Bridgnorth and Ellesmere College (*Plate 4*), and a 2nd Battalion was formed later in the year.[30] In Somerset six schools formed the 1st Cadet Volunteer Battalion, Somerset Light Infantry.[31] Places that today would not have a cadet unit, or if they did it would be very small in numbers, attracted a large number of boys. At

Westerham, a village in Kent, a unit was formed in 1901 and grew to an establishment of three officers and 116 cadets.[32] This pattern was repeated throughout the country. Cadets attending the first Public Schools Camp came from Bedford, Bradfield, Haileybury and Sherborne Schools; whilst at camp they were invited to take part in 'the sham fight' at Aldershot, held in honour of the visiting German Emperor, Kaiser Wilhelm II.[33] Instruction at organised camps was an area of training that was to expand. By the end of the Boer War the number of school cadet contingents had increased from 41 in 1898 to 99 in 1902[34]; the exact rate of expansion for 'open' units is not known, but it was prodigious.

There was, at this time, one particular unit that warrants special mention in the history of the cadets, and that is London's 1st Cadet Battalion the King's Royal Rifle Corps. The K.R.R.C. cadets supplied volunteers for the Boer War, and 96 of its older cadets went to fight in South Africa as part of the City Imperial Volunteer Battalion. As a result they were singled out for a special award: Battle Honour 'South Africa 1900–1902'. This was bestowed at the 'express command of King Edward VII, and was later presented by H.R.H. The Prince of Wales (later George V) at the Guildhall in the City of London'.[35] Hence this battalion is the only cadet unit to be granted a battle honour, and is thus allowed to wear the miniature 60th Rifles' badge; its wearers are also entitled to be called Riflemen instead of Cadets.

In 1893, at a public meeting held at Paddington in London to support the local unit, General Sir George White, C-in-C Yeomanry and Volunteers, said that whilst the Navy was Britain's first line of defence, the Army the second and the Volunteers the third, 'he would add a fourth line in the shape of Cadet Corps'.[36] His words, as the K.R.R.C. cadets could testify, were prophetic. The Boer War proved to be the last great Imperial War of the British Empire, and the first and last time a cadet unit went into battle.

The impetus for service, and a naïve tendency on the part of some youths to see war as a 'romantic adventure' was encouraged by the plethora of patriotic stories in contemporary books and magazines; and of course, the continued work of the social youth leaders resulted in a significant increase in the formation of cadet units. The Balfour Act of 1902 ensured that Local Education Authorities provided County Secondary Schools, and their public scholarship method of entry created an opportunity for some boys to get an extended education. The Navy League sent speakers to both the public and secondary schools, but did not at this stage contemplate forming cadet units. Field-Marshal Lord Roberts, amongst others, toured the country on behalf of the Imperial Defence League and instigated the formation of army cadets units in various towns.[37] And a number of new secondary schools attempted to emulate the public schools, and created their own cadet companies. The expansion of the army cadet movement was not restricted to school and locality, it was extended to include places of work. The postal messengers of Derby were organised into a corps in 1905, and numbered 70 in total. In London Sir E. W. D. Ward, was the initiator and motivator behind the Corps for Junior Clerks in the Civil Service (*Plate. 5*). The unit began parading in 1903 in the courtyard of Somerset House with a turnout of six officers and 150 cadets.[38] This pattern of expansion was echoed throughout the British Isles; unfortunately most 'open' units did not keep records and it is therefore impossible to be exact about numbers.

The Boers were finally subdued and the war in South Africa ended in 1902 with the signing of the Treaty of Vereeniging, which led in 1909 to the formation of the Union of South Africa. The war greatly affected the Volunteers, and hence the army cadets. First, the Volunteers were no longer merely a home defence force as they had now, unprepared as they were, seen action overseas, and this raised questions regarding their efficiency; the Volunteers therefore became part of the general debate on the Army 'which was the consequence of the War'.[39] As a result of the deficiencies in the army revealed by the South African conflict, uniformed youth movements attracted closer attention from both the Government and the military; added to which there was an increasing fear of German aggression. In 1901 the German battle fleet was doubled in size; the Kaiser refused to enter into any alliance with Britain; and Germany's desire for expansion in Africa was seen as a threat to British and French interests.

A significant number of public and secondary schools had rifle clubs even though they had no cadet corps. These were to grow in size and number following the frequent observation that Boer children were taught to shoot when young. Shooting had been a part of training ever since the cadet movement's inception, indeed the Ashburton Shield for rifle shooting had been in existence since 1861, and there was an additional competition at Bisley for schools that had rifle clubs but no cadet corps. Rifle shooting therefore became an important activity in many schools: at Uppingham School every boy was required to pass a shooting test.[40] As a result of the Boer War more schools were to go a step further and convert their existing rifle clubs into full-scale cadet corps. The Newcastle-under-Lyme secondary school was an exemplar of this development. The school already had a rifle club and, following the lead set by ex-pupils who formed an Old Boys' Volunteer Company, the school governors sanctioned the setting-up of a cadet corps in 1908. All physically fit boys over the age of 13 were eligible to join. Its initial strength was 60 and 'every boy in the VIth Form capable of bearing arms' was a member. This was despite the fact that the cadets had to buy a uniform, which was not cheap, and pay a termly subscription.[41]

The level of physical fitness of the average working-class British male in the second half of the nineteenth century was lamentable. In 1866 the Army had rejected almost 50 per cent of all recruits on the grounds of physical defects. The Navy fared no better. In 1869, 4,410 out of 5,567 boys applying for service in the Royal Navy were refused entry.[42] There was no discernible improvement by 1899. In Manchester at the outbreak of the Boer War, out of 11,000 volunteering for enlistment in the Army, 8,000 were rejected and only 1,200 were 'accepted as fit in all respects'.[43] There was great concern at the abnormally high rejection rate. As many as 40 per cent in the country were judged to be unfit, and as a result the Committee of Physical Deterioration was established in 1904 to examine the problem. The only exercise some of the elementary school youngsters got – space permitting – was drill. Military drill had been part of some schools' programmes since the 1850s, but it was now argued that military drill should be started in all schools and continued for the post-school years in the Volunteer Cadet Corps.[44] The benefits, it was opined by the militarists, were threefold: first, drill improves the children's sense of duty, obedience and discipline; secondly, it prepares them for future military service; and thirdly, it improves their physical well-being.

There was a notable improvement in obedience and discipline mainly because drill aids control. As any person with military experience will know, marching is the most effective way of moving a body of people from one place to another in an orderly fashion. Thus elementary-school teachers used drill for this purpose and as a means of maintaining control. The drill period was also viewed by some as a break from the monotony of the classroom, and was the only exercise done by many children. However, the limited amount of drill a boy did at school might help if he joined the cadets, but would hardly prepare him for military service. The same applied to any additional physical exercise. Better living conditions, proper nutrition and medical services were much needed.[45]

What was attempted in the elementary schools and the cadet units ranged from military manoeuvres which the boys liked, to squad drill made, at times, 'unutterably boring by unimaginative and unintelligent instructors obsessed with a passion for repetition'.[46] Unfortunately, according to the physical educator P. C. McIntosh, the training of instructors in the army was restricted entirely to N.C.O.s, most of whom were ill-educated. They were often unsuited to dealing with children and teachers. The navy had a different system. The foundation of the Naval Physical Training School in 1902 – as part of Admiral Fisher's reforms –

also had its impact on schools. A number of navy officers after training abroad, adopted the Swedish Gymnastic system of exercises and instruction, and on leaving the service took posts in public schools, so at least the sons of the better-off benefited from more enlightened physical training. The army eventually adopted the Swedish system in 1907. Ex-naval officers who had been instructors in the navy probably preferred to accept posts in the public schools, where the other teachers were of similar social status, but the evidence suggests that they would have been equally effective in the State education system.[47] In State schools army instructors generally carried out instruction. There was a variation in standards and approach: some but not all army instructors were possessed of a rigid parade-ground mentality. In Manchester, it was reported that there was a 'high standard of drill of boys and girls', and that in the local schools teachers contributed to the cadet force which had 'enlisted 300 boys'.[48] And it was not all tedium in the schools. At the G.W.R. School in Swindon, for example, physical training included military manoeuvres where the boys formed squares, 'prepared to receive cavalry' and skirmished in the street, which they thoroughly enjoyed.[49] Drill for the elementary-school pupil was later to be augmented, and then superseded by Swedish Gymnastic Exercises, which took some cognisance of a boy or girl's physical development. These improvements and concern for physical training both in schools and cadet organisations ran parallel to those being implemented, initially in the Royal Navy and then in the Army.

Sports and games had been an integral part of public school education for many years. These schools valued sport, and regular participation in team games was said to be 'character building'; service with the cadet corps was seen as an extension of this training, although a small number of masters were concerned that the Corps' activities might rival those of the major games. At Clifton, for example, there was fear that participation in the Corps would detract from 'concentration on cricket'.[50] There were some who completely opposed the orthodoxy and disputed the value of games. One such was Rudyard Kipling who, following the Boer War 'disgrace', said that 'the flannelled fools at the wicket or the muddied oafs at the goals' ought to be undergoing a more realistic means of training'.[51] No doubt he would have approved of military training with the cadet corps.

Shrewsbury School was one of the first public schools to react to the consequences of the Boer War by reforming its defunct cadet corps. Practically every pupil became a member. The headmaster, Henry Whithead Moss, an enthusiastic patriot believed every boy should be prepared to serve his King and country. The training of the corps with its

17

'competition in shooting, the marches, the drills in uniform, the field-days and reviews by important generals, the summer camp, all became part of Shrewsbury life'.[52] Indeed, the headmaster wanted to go a step further and recommended a scheme for training army officers at the school, with scholarships for those who could not otherwise afford to stay on for the additional training. He envisaged a system of selection by examination and he concluded, 'thus boys of brain and character would then be available for the preservation of England's dominions in time of war. And the public school ideals would permeate through the ranks . . .'.[53] Edmund Warre, headmaster of Eton, was worried about the high number of casualties among officers during the first year of the war, and the shortage of officers among the Militia and Volunteers. In 1900, in an address to the Royal United Services' Institute, he voiced his concern, emphasised the support he had gained at the Headmasters' Conference for the extension of military training in schools, and asked the Government to enact the Conference's proposals.[54] It was not to happen then, but the connection between the public-school cadet and the future training and attainment of officer status was noted by the Liberal Secretary of State for War, the Rt. Hon. (later Viscount) Richard Haldane and his Committee which was in the process of examining the effects of the Boer War.

In 1906, as a result of the army's exposed deficiencies in the Boer War and the shortage of officers, the Haldane Committee recommended the disbandment of the Volunteers and a new Territorial Force was put in its place. The Territorial Force was to be organised on a county basis. The Committee reported a year later and its findings were implemented in 1908. The Committee, possibly mindful of what had been said by the headmasters in 1900, recommended the forming of an Officer Training Corps (O.T.C.). It was to be divided into two divisions, the Senior in the universities and the Junior in the public schools. Any public school that could produce a contingent of 30 or more cadets with a minimum of one officer could become part of the O.T.C., and 'over 100 immediately did so'.[55]

The school-based cadet corps experienced two periods of growth in the years 1900 to 1910. The first was at the turn of the century and immediately after the Boer War. This stemmed from the sense of outrage and the desire to help to govern the Empire. The second resulted from the reorganisation and re-definition of the role and function of the public school cadet corps. The public schools' elitist education stressed the importance of status, duty and service, and the formation of an Officers Training Corps underlined these values. Any new independent schools seeking acceptance among the school elite might well have viewed the formation of an Officers Training Corps as a means of assisting that process. The established public schools would, of course, wish to maintain their collective status and the lack of an O.T.C. unit may have been seen as leading to loss of rank as a school. The training for the O.T.C. was divided into two parts, Certificate 'B' for the universities, and Certificate 'A' for the school contingents. Successful completion of Cert. 'A', as it became known, plus a short attachment to a Regular Army Depot, was the prerequisite for a Commission in the Territorial Army.[56] This was a route into military service that many boys were to take, voluntarily or otherwise, in the very near future: the First World War was not too far away.

The new County Committees of the Territorial Force Association were given the task of general administration of all cadet corps outside the schools. This was to the units' advantage. The War Office was a bureaucratic machine several steps removed from the local unit but a county H.Q. was, in every sense of the word, more approachable. A number of counties, but not all, appointed a County Cadet Commandant that meant the cadets had a representative at the executive table. Some cadet commandants, however, were more concerned with their social position and became, in effect, little more than figureheads. Eventually the more enlightened and concerned gave proper support and leadership to the cadet corps.[57] Today most Army and Air Cadets units are still organised on a county basis; the Sea Cadets, being smaller, are organised in regions. Also in 1910, as part of the Territorial and Forces Act, all school and 'open' army cadet units outside of the O.T.C. were to be part of the Territorial Cadet Force.[58]

The first regulations for the Territorial Cadet Force (T.C.F.) were issued as a Special Army Order dated 21 May 1910, and stipulated that there should be no fewer than 30 cadets in a company. On the other hand, no company should contain more than 100 cadets, and a corps which enlisted more than 100 cadets was to be divided into two or more companies. Four or more companies formed a battalion. The number of officers was laid down by regulations. The County Territorial Associations were given the power to grant or refuse recognition of units, 'raise new units, to nominate Cadet Officers for appointment and to issue rules . . . subject to the approval of the War Office'.[59]

The challenge facing the Government following the Boer War was to create an organisation in which not only the Regular Army, and the Territorial Volunteers, but also any future servicemen – i.e. cadets – were better prepared to serve the country when the time came. As already noted, this was a challenge that was soon to be put to the test. As a result of the reorganisation, the cadets became more efficient under a local County Association but, at the same time, they were under greater control via regulations and conditions defined by the War Office. One method of control, and a means whereby standards could be raised was the selection of leaders. A gentleman desirous of being an officer would, if selected, be presented with a Certificate from the Lord Lieutenant of the County who, on behalf of the King, granted officer status to individuals. A candidate's selection would depend upon his capability at instructing in elementary military skills and his suitability at taking charge of young cadets. The Territorial Cadet Force (T.C.F.) officer's rank was honorary and therefore junior to those in the Regular and Territorial Forces.[60]

The age of enlistment for a cadet was subject to the approval of the County Association. It was usually 14 years of age, but could be as low as 12. However, when the cadet reached the age of 17 he was eligible for enlistment into the Territorials. If he wanted to remain with his cadet detachment after that age, he needed the permission of the County Association. Service with the cadets was seen as a stepping-stone to adult deployment. To show that cadet service had some bearing on adult training, a cadet who transferred to the Territorials within six months of leaving his cadet unit was excused all, or part of, the recruit's drill. Cadet service could also count towards the granting of the Territorial Efficiency Medal, again provided the individual joined within six months of leaving cadets, although service before the age of 15 was not counted.

Annual inspections by Regular or Territorial Army officers became standard practice for the O.T.C. and the T.C.F. A satisfactory annual report was particularly important for the latter, as a unit's survival depended on it. Units below the prescribed minimum in number, or deemed inefficient, could be closed. In addition each unit had to be financially self-supporting, although local revenue was augmented by an annual Government grant of £5 per company. County Associations were encouraged to establish reserve funds for the development of cadet units. The Government gave further concessions in the form of granting cadet organisations the use of War Office training areas. Transport, as well as equipment could be borrowed from the Territorial Army but any costs had to be borne by the cadet units. Cadet detachments also had the use of War Office firing ranges and could rent drill halls at low rates. In addition arms and ammunition could be hired or bought.[61] Haldane's Territorial Forces Bill proposed compulsory military training for boys at elementary school, but this was rejected following strong opposition by Labour and radical Liberal politicians. Nevertheless, the Government now had a greater degree of control over a voluntary youth movement than had ever been the case before.

The training undertaken by the army cadets was laid down in the War Office manual Infantry Training 1902. Drill was included in the core curriculum and was combined, especially when at camp, with the drill at battalion and even brigade level. There were also drill competitions. Fieldcraft included 'outpost work' and, for the cadet N.C.O., 'duties of a picquet commander' and the 'laying out of advance and rear guards'. There was instruction in first aid, shooting and signalling. In signalling, the aim was to transmit at six words per minute with flags and eight words per minute on the buzzer.[62] At Rugby School they had an annual 'competition in morse and semaphore'.[63] All units took part in shooting competitions, some of which were limited to either 'closed' units – as in the Ashburton Shield – or to 'open' units. Physical training in the school corps would, of course, be part of a separate timetable. Depending on facilities, the 'open' detachments could include gymnastics and games as part of their training schedule or alternatively they could incorporate these as part of a more informal club evening activity. Many units had bands that accompanied the contingents on public parades and route marches. The main means of transport for most people was the railway or horse-drawn buses. Hence it was not uncommon to march all or part of the way to weekend training areas and to annual camp.[64] Some contingents, such as the 1st Cadet Battalion The King's Royal Rifle Corps in Surrey, had a cyclists' section *(Plate 6)*. Indeed, the increase in youth organisations was due in no small measure to the bicycle, as this was the cheapest and, for the cadet who lived a long distance away, the most available method of getting to his H.Q.

Success at the annual inspection was not confined to the state of the stores and armoury. The unit was also expected to put on a good parade or display. Cadets were tested and assessed throughout the year and were graded as efficient or otherwise. In 1910 most units in the T.C.F. showed an 'average of eighty per cent of boys as efficient'.[65] Considering the size of individual detachments and battalions this was quite a feat. The 1st King's Royal Rifle Corps Cadet Battalion, for example, had an establishment of 29 officers and 922 cadets – twice the size of most of those at the larger public schools. The Corps was full and had a waiting list.

Whilst the army's Territorial Cadet Force was going through a period of expansion the sea cadet units were still disconnected, and independent. The Navy League was more concerned with promoting the Senior Service, both in and out of Parliament, but this began to change. Their propagandist message was conveyed in part by innumerable illustrated bioscopic lectures; many to schoolboys and youth club members, with the additional aim of setting up a branch of the Navy League in every town.[66] The League published a monthly journal with articles from ex-naval officers, headmasters and other civilians. One of them, who signed herself 'A Patriotic Englishwoman', declared that the efficiency of the Royal

Navy: 'is a personal matter to each English man and woman – it must not be regarded as a vague and little-comprehended question that can be airily handed over to the Admiralty and Parliament and given no further thought'.[67] Such sentiments, no matter how well meant, did little to promote relationships between the Admiralty and the League. It must be said, however, that the 'Englishwoman' may well have been an alias for a disgruntled ex-sailor. In addition to its propagandist remit, the League had the annual public duty of decorating Nelson's Column on Trafalgar Day. More important, with regard to the youth of the country, the League founded and ran a Sea Training Home for Poor Boys.

In 1910 a talk on 'The History of the British Navy' was given at Kensington to boys from the Church Lads' Brigade. At the end of the talk many wanted to know more about the navy. This created a problem, as the enthusiastic and competent speaker had created the desire but had no way of fulfilling the need. It is very doubtful if young boys would have wanted to join a Navy League Branch to attend talks and meetings. What they wanted was participation in matters naval and nautical. In February 1910, on a visit to Abingdon School, the Branch Secretary talked about the Windsor and Reading Brigs, and how Oxford was forming a similar unit. The aim of the talk was not only to promote the navy, but also to start a training brig on the river at Abingdon. The League was willing to make a grant towards initial expenses, and it was estimated that about £50 a year would be required. This is what the enthusiastic youngsters wanted to hear. Interestingly, the speaker felt the need to play down the jingoism, or 'gassing about the Empire' as he put it, but nevertheless he showed a map which highlighted British overseas territory, and emphasised the importance of naval supremacy from the point of view of protecting food supply. The point was made, presumably for the benefit of adults in the audience, that such a unit 'would be of great benefit to lads by discouraging loafing and the low moral tone which seemed on the increase everywhere'.[68] The financial assistance given by the League to an increasing number of nautically-orientated boys' clubs meant that the League was being drawn ever closer to forming a national organisation. The Paddington Navy League Boys' Club was a direct result of a lecture given at the Drill Hall of the Paddington Rifles on Trafalgar Day 1910. At the end of the meeting 40 boys expressed a wish to join the Navy League, and on 16 March the Brig was opened. The inaugural meeting was presided over by the mayoress, the League's branch secretary. Among the notable guests was Lady Cecile Goff, and a telegram of support came from the retired Admiral Lord Charles Beresford, himself an arch-critic of the naval reformer Admiral Lord Fisher. The new Paddington Brig was to meet at 19 00 hours for two hours, three times a week. The boys would, of course, have to become members of the Navy League for which they had to pay a subscription of one penny per month, and a further halfpenny per week for the use of the hall. This cost, not much by today's standards would, in fact, have been beyond the pocket of most working-class boys. It can therefore be assumed that the Paddington Brig was for the sons of the middle classes. Activities included 'signalling, knot-making classes, etc., and a Lieutenant Soames, ex-navy, was attending to instruct the boys in a range of naval matters'.[69]

In order to finance the increasing needs of the affiliated units, the League needed to raise additional funds. A way of doing this was to put on concerts. One such was a musical concert held at Kensington Town Hall in March 1910 (under the patronage of the Duchess of Somerset). The amount raised is not known, but apparently it was a success and receipts were given to the Navy League London Training Brig Fund.[70] The great need to raise funds to cover the cost of equipment, upkeep and rents continued to be a perennial problem given the detached relationship the Sea Cadets had from its adult Service.

After suggestions published in 1908, in *The Navy League* journal, from the Headmaster of Bath College who said everyone 'has a duty to the State' – and this included the youth; and the innumerable speakers from the League who emphasised patriotism and the navy; the economic assistance proffered by the League and the resultant affiliation of boys' naval clubs to the organisation, it was finally decided on 14 September 1910 to hold a meeting to discuss the setting up of a Boys' Naval Brigade. It was revealed that there was over a dozen 'Naval Brigades, Naval Brigs and similar organisations scattered around the country'.[71] They were invited to join the Navy League: those that agreed became a part of the Navy League Boys' Naval Brigade in 1910. Despite its obvious potential as a means of spreading the League's influence, it was, however, low on the list of priorities, and cadet matters were placed under a sub-committee in a small office a considerable distance apart from the main headquarters in Grand Buildings, Trafalgar Square. Nevertheless, the seeds of today's Sea Cadet Corps had been sown.

A glance at the chronological development of uniformed youth organisations shows that the 17-year period from 1883 to 1910 was a time of unprecedented growth and reorganisation. It reads:

    1860 Army Cadet Corps formed as part of The Volunteers
    1883 Boys' Brigade founded in Glasgow
    1891 Church Lads' Brigade and London Diocesan Lads' Brigade started (later amalgamated)
    1899 Boys' Life Brigade started (later amalgamated with the Boys' Brigade)

1899 First Public School Cadet camp
1900 First Navy League Sea Cadet Corps unit founded at Windsor
1902 Girls' Life Brigade founded
1906 Boy Scouts formed
1907 First Scout camp
1908 Public and independent school corps became Officer Training Corps
1910 Army 'open' and non-public school units became part of the Territorial Cadet Force (250 units)
1910 A dozen more naval units combined to form the Navy League Boys' Naval Brigade
1910 Girl Guides formed

There were both sea and army orientated 'unofficial' independent units that survived for various periods of time, going back beyond the dates listed. The table above is nonetheless a catalogue of the officially-recognised units. The Boys' Brigade argue that their organisation was the first uniformed Youth Movement; indeed, they were somewhat miffed when the Army Cadet Force celebrated its centenary in 1960. True, the Boys' Brigade was the first independent nationally organised youth movement. However, it was the army cadets, albeit as part of a larger organisation, who produced the first officially-recognised uniformed cadet units.

Many adults saw the disciplinary methods of the military-based youth organisations as a means of providing a social education: a way of imbuing the working-class boy with middle-class public-school values. Certainly the clergy, public school officers and social reformers who took an active interest in the uniformed youth organisations believed that social control through disciplined military training would benefit both the individual and society. Octavia Hill intended the cadet training to be an antidote to the 'ill educated, dirty, quarrelsome, drunken, improvident, unrefined, possibly dishonest, possibly vicious society from which cadets were recruited'.[72] Underpinning this crusade for socio-religious conformity was the military needs of the country. Edmund Warre, the Eton headmaster and 'able field officer of Volunteers' advocated compulsory military training.[73] It is no accident that ex-military men started all the better-known youth organisations. Ex-sailors ran the Navy League Boys' Naval Brigade; Volunteer officers ran the Territorial Army Cadet Force. Sir William Smith, a Lieutenant Colonel of the 1st Lanarkshire Rifle Volunteers, started the Boys' Brigade. General Sir Robert Baden-Powell, the best-known of youth leaders, began the Boy Scouts and inadvertently triggered off the formation of the Girl Scouts as well (later known as the Girl Guides). Baden-Powell wrote his famous

Scouting for Boys in 1908, the purpose of which was to 'assist Cadet officers and brigade leaders'. It is interesting to note that some years earlier Baden-Powell had been involved with the Boys' Brigade where he had tried out his ideas before publishing his famous training pamphlet. From 1907 until 1910 he commanded the Northumberland Division of the newly-formed Territorials. It is no surprise, therefore, that his *Scouting for Boys* was directed towards the Territorial Cadet Force. The mystery is, why did they reject it? Whatever the reason, Baden-Powell resigned from his position and devoted himself full-time to the Boy Scouts, declaring to Churchill in 1920 that 'You will find that the Scouts are likely to provide a fairly hearty contribution of men to the Territorials in the next few years'.[74] And, as the author of *The Cadet Story* wrote, 'A great opportunity was missed'.[75] Had the General and his idea been integrated into the army cadet movement things could have been different, and Haldane's idea of absorbing all the uniformed youth organisations into one movement would have had a better chance of succeeding.

The Secretary for War's aim was, not only to unify the uniformed organisations, but, for them to act as a training and recruiting agency for the newly created Territorial Force. In 1908 the County Associations, in order to pacify the Radical and Labour opposition in the House of Commons, were not allowed to support their local cadets financially from funds voted by Parliament, although this possibly did not prohibit the statutory annual grant of £5 per company.[76] However, the loan of equipment and permits to use War Office training grounds remained. The Secretary for War did tour the public schools on a recruiting drive and opened some new units, but the O.T.C. never met the establishment level that had been hoped for.[77]

From 1860 to the end of the Edwardian age, the armed services had to meet a steadily-increasing military commitment both at home and abroad, and the cadets were seen as part of this undertaking. Army recruiting rarely met its targets because soldiers were poorly paid, and poorly treated – although the barbaric practice of branding was abolished in 1871, and flogging in 1881. There was, however, as always, a rise in intake during periods of threat or colonial conflict, such as the South African War. The War Office, alas, took no interest in a soldier's recreation and hence the troops had nothing to do in their off-duty hours but drink, and the resultant bad behaviour added to the army's poor image. Indeed, 'many families regarded it as an utter disgrace if any of their members enlisted'.[78] Things were little better in the navy, where there was disgruntlement over pay, poor living conditions and unauthorised punishments. The resultant desertions amounted to 2,000 per year.[79] And yet, ironically, it was via military training that youth leaders attempted to control and reform the working-class youth. The object of the Navy League and T.C.F. cadet movements was to inculcate discipline, teamwork, obedience and a feeling of patriotism. And, given the impoverished background of many of the cadets, and the inadequate role-model of the military, it is to the credit of those militaristic social pioneers that the Cadet Movement succeeded.

Chapter 1 References

1. M.A.O. 8 [S.C.C.] 'History of the Sea Cadet Movement', p. 1
2. Hugh Cunningham, *The Volunteer Force* [London: Croom Helm, 1975], p. 5
3. Lt.-Col. H. J. Harris T.D. D.L., *Rugby School Corps, 1860–1960* [London: Spyer, 1960], pp. 1 & 2
4. A.C.F.A., *The Army Cadet Force Handbook* [London: A.C.F.A., 1949], p. 14
5. Lt.-Col. H. C. Hughes T.D. M.A., *The Army Cadets of Surrey, 1860–1960* [London: Spyer, 1960], p. 1–3
6. A.C.F.A., *The Cadet Story, 1860–1980* [London: A.C.F.A., 1982], p. 6
7. Capt. W. F. L. Newcombe, 'Some historical notes on Cadets' in *The Cadet Review*, No. 1, Vol. 1, 1945, p. 35
8. *The Cadet Story, 1860–1980*, op. cit., p. 8
9. J. Springall, B. Fraser, M. Hoare, *Sure and Steadfast – a history of the Boys' Brigade, 1883–1983* [London & Glasgow: Collins, 1993], p. 19
10. H. J. Hughes, op. cit., pp. 2 & 3
11. W. F. L. Newcombe, op. cit., p. 36
12. J. Springall, *Youth, Empire and Society* [London: Croom Helm, 1977], p. 72
13. J. A. R. Pimlott, *Toynbee Hall: fifty years of social progress, 1889–1934* [London: Dent, 1935], chapter 1
14. Gillian Darley, *Octavia Hill – A Life* [London: Constable, 1990], p. 245
15. Ibid., p. 244
16. Octavia Hill, *Letters to My Fellow Workers* [London: Martin, 1910], pp. 11 & 12 & C. Edmund Maurice [ed.], *Life of Octavia Hill as Told in Her Letters* [London: Macmillan, 1913], p. 492
17. Navy League Minutes, 'Constitution of the Navy League', 1895, p. A2
18. Capt. John Wells, C.B.E. D.S.C. R.N., *The Royal Navy – An Illustrated History, 1870–1982* [Stroud: Sutton, 1994], p. 39
19. Ibid., p. 40
20. M.A.O. 8 [S.C.C.] op. cit., p. 2
21. Ibid., p. 1
22. John Wells, op. cit., pp. 54 & 55
23. Parliamentary Papers No. 329 of 1902, 'Progress of British Merchant Shipping' in *The Navy League* journal, January 1908, p. 7
24. M.A.O. 8 [S.C.C.] op. cit., p. 2
25. *The Navy League* journal, July 1908, p. 224
26. Ibid., p. 224
27. M.A.O. 8 [S.C.C.] op. cit., p. 2
28. Ibid., p. 2
29. Lieut. H. D. Capper R.N., *Warrant Officers' Manual* [Royal Navy: 1910] para 103, p. 139
30. Author anonymous, 'A Brief History of Shropshire A.C.F.' [Shropshire A.C.F.: Unpublished, 1960]

31　Lt.-Col. Bill Currie, *The King's Cadets* [King Edward's School: Bath, 1994], pp. 11 & 12
32　*The Cadet Story, 1860-1980*, op. cit., pp. 12 & 13
33　*The Army Cadet Force Handbook* [1949] op. cit., p. 17
34　W. F. L. Newcombe, op. cit., p. 35
35　Capt. R. L. Collet, '100th Anniversary of the 1st Cdt Bn KRRC (60th Cadet Rifles)' in *The Army Cadet Journal and Gazette* Vol. LVII, April 1995, p. 40
36　A.C.F.A., *Army Cadet Force Handbook* [A.C.F.A.: London, 1962], p. 18
37　*The Army Cadet Story, 1860–1980*, op. cit., p. 13
38　Hugh Cunningham, op. cit., p. 127
39　Ibid., p. 12
40　W. David Smith, *Stretching Their Bodies – the history of physical education* [Newton Abbot: David & Charles, 1974], p. 90
41　Col. E. R. Clowes, 'Newcastle-under-Lyme Combined Cadet Force – a brief history' [unpublished notes: Newcastle-under-Lyme School, 1994] in letter to Wg. Cdr. West R.A.F.
42　Peter C. McIntosh, *Physical Education in England Since 1800* [London: Bell, 1968], p. 107
43　Interdependent Committee on Physical Deterioration: 'H.M.S.O. 1904 Evidence', pp. 13–14 & App. 1 in Peter C. McIntosh, op. cit., p. 148
44　W. David Smith, op. cit., p. 91
45　Board of Education, *Syllabus of Physical Training for Schools*, 1933 [London: H.M.S.O., 1933], pp. 6–7 and *Syllabus of Physical Training for Schools*, 1919 [London: H.M.S.O., 1919], pp. 3–5
46　W. David Smith, op. cit., p. 91
47　Peter C. McIntosh, op. cit., p. 149
48　T. C. Horsfall [Ed.] 'Proceedings of the Conference of Education and Health' [Manchester: Heywood, 1885], 214f
49　W. David Smith, op. cit., p. 91
50　Ibid., p. 40
51　Rudyard Kipling, *The Five Nations* [London: Methuen, 1949], p. 128
52　J. Basil Oldham M.A., *A History of Shrewsbury School, 1852–1952* [Oxford: Blackwell, 1952], pp. 136 & 137
53　Mrs H. W. Moss, *Moss of Shrewsbury* [London: Sheldon, 1932], pp. 136–139
54　W. D. Smith, op. cit., p. 41
55　W. F. L. Newcomb, op. cit., p. 37
56　B. Currie, op. cit., p. 12
57　*Army Cadet Story, 1860–1980*, op. cit., p. 16
58　R. A. Westlake, *A Register of Territorial Force Cadet Units, 1910–1922* [Wembley: Westlake, 1984] pp. 1 & 2
59　Army Orders No. 197 *Regulations Governing the Formation, Organisation and Administration of Cadet Units by County Associations* [London: H.M.S.O., 1910], pp. 5 & 6

60 Ibid.
61 Ibid.
62 *The Army Cadet Story, 1860–1980*, op. cit., pp. 13–16
63 H. J. Harris, op. cit., p. 150
64 *The Army Cadet Story, 1860–1980*, op. cit., p. 13–16
65 Ibid.
66 An Englishwoman, 'The Work of the Navy League' in *The Navy League* journal, January 1903, pp. 10–11
67 Ibid.
68 *The Navy League* journal, April 1910, p. 107
69 Ibid.
70 Ibid.
71 M.A.O. 8, op. cit., p. 2
72 Octavia Hill, *Our Common Land and other short essays* [London: Sydenham, 1877], p. 97
73 *The Times* 25 July 1884, in C. R. L. Fletcher, *Edmund Warre* [London: Murray, 1922], pp. 106–107
74 Baden-Powell to Churchill, holograph draft 10 May 1920, Scout Archives Vol. IV, Ref. 9, in J. Springall, op. cit., p. 123
75 *The Cadet Story, 1860-1980*, op. cit., p. 18
76 Edward Spiers, 'The Late Victorian Army 1868–1914' in *The Oxford History of the British Army* [eds.] David Chandler & Ian Beckett [Oxford: OUP, 1996], p. 20
77 Ibid., p. 205
78 Ibid., p. 190
79 John Wells, op. cit., pp. 84–85

Chapter 2 – From Boer War to the First World War

THE GROWTH IN YOUTH organisations during the Edwardian period was large in numbers but, despite the efforts of such people as Octavia Hill, was socially restricted. In the main, cadets in the 'open' units came from families whose father was a 'white collar' worker. Expansion in working-class membership was less marked. Evidence indicates that most of the army and navy cadets who were over 14 years of age, and had left school, were in skilled and semi-skilled employment.[1] There were very few unskilled labourers or unemployed youngsters amongst the post-school cadets. The price of a uniform and the rates of subscription, such as that levied on the Navy League cadets at the Paddington Brig, indicates that costs would have been beyond the means of many working-class families.[2] The army cadets, despite having some material assistance from the County Associations, had to be financially self-supporting. In order to meet costs sponsorship was sought from local firms and dignitaries. At Stockport in 1911, the mayor headed an army cadet committee that raised, from business contacts within the town, £82 for a clothing fund and £90 for other expenditure such as rent for premises and annual camp expenses. The cost of ammunition and weapon maintenance was, fortunately, the responsibility of the County Association, and transport expenses could be covered by the army authorities under the new regulations.[3] But also in that year there was a general strike on the railways, and this adversely affected hundreds of cadets who were away at their annual camp. The Cheshire Cadet Battalion, which normally relied on the railways, had no choice when their training was completed but to march the 16 miles back to their headquarters. It is reported that Reveille was at 0500 hours, and the march took four-and-a-half hours.[4] Doubtless other units were similarly inconvenienced. Despite the railway strike, there was a significant improvement in transport; the rail network was extended and there was a wider use of the bus and the tram. This meant greater mobility both for the individual and his unit, which contributed to the growth of the Cadet Movement.

Despite the reforms in the Armed Services, the image of the Army Private and the Naval Rating still gave cause for concern: hence, some parents remained unconvinced that the adult military role-model was appropriate for their sons. This may explain why enrolments in the church-connected organisations, where the emphasis on moral behaviour was more pronounced, outnumbered those in the cadets. In 1911 there were 14,399 army cadets in 251 units – excluding the public and grammar school O.T.C. contingents: the Boys' Brigade numbered 63,126 and the

31

Church Lads' Brigade 36,000.[5] There are no figures for the Navy League cadets whose number was in hundreds rather than thousands. The Boy Scouts had even larger numbers. The Church Lads' Brigade (C.L.B.) had a syllabus with a military slant and maintained a close association with the local army cadets and the Territorial Associations; in fact, they relied upon them to provide instructors. Such was this dependency that in 1911 the C.L.B. applied for full affiliation to the Territorial Cadet Force. Permission was granted and those individual units of the Brigade that chose to join abandoned the C.L.B. uniform and donned the khaki of the army cadets. Numbers in the T.C.F. increased considerably as a result, and by 1912 the total number of army cadets had doubled to 34, 474, and this increased to 41,108 the following year.[6] No doubt the adoption of a more-up-to-date army uniform aided recruiting to the Church Lads' Brigade as their number also increased. The influx of C.L.B. officers, who were men motivated by social and moral values, meant that the Army Cadets once again embraced the twin aims of promoting military service and social development. Thus the affiliation was of benefit to both organisations.

It may sound as if the whole idea of cadet training was an exercise in military and social manipulation by middle-class officers: in effect, a method of controlling the youth. To a great extent that was true. It must be remembered, however, that both the navy and army cadet organisations were voluntary – a cadet could join and leave when he chose. There were advantages to be had by being a member of a cadet organisation. Cadet training provided interesting evening activities; it gave a boy the opportunity to do things he might not otherwise do such as play in a band, shoot on a range, and take part in sport. For the Navy League cadets, training would obviously include water-based activities, for the army cadet in the Territorial Cadet Force it would be fieldcraft and basic military manoeuvres. There were weekends away from home and, most importantly, the chance to spend a week with one's friends at annual camp. Time spent under canvas, free from the grime and squalor of an urban existence, must have been a pleasure to many a cadet from an industrial location. There was always the possibility of doing something different, with the potential for adventure and excitement in a more pleasant environment. It also gave cadets the chance to gain confidence by carrying responsibility, and to attain promotion. For the unskilled youth, whose opportunity for employment was limited, a boy could, via the cadets, gain access to the Royal Navy, Merchant Navy, and Regular or Territorial Army. Outside of the military, involvement in the Cadet Movement could, writes Mackenzie, provide an 'opportunity for those seeking upward mobility', a means of acquiring a public or grammar school ethos, a 'respectability acceptable to employers'.[7]

A number of much smaller youth organisations appeared during this period; for example, a group called the Weybridge Scout Cadets appeared in the Army List under the 6th Battalion, East Surrey Regiment in 1911, but then withdrew their affiliation the following year.[8] The interesting question is: was this an attempt to carry out Baden-Powell's original idea, or was it a new group that did not know where it belonged? The Church Lads' Brigade began Scout-Brigades, and there were Sea Scouts too. It is difficult to establish which organisation some of the smaller youth bodies were actually affiliated to. It was obviously advantageous, for reasons already mentioned, to be associated with the Territorial Cadet Force. Hence units such as the Hertford Cadet Company 2nd (Watford Scouts) joined the 2nd Hertford Battery R.F.A. in 1911.[9] There were numerous others. Unrealised until now, or at least not mentioned in the Sea Cadet Corps' historical notes, is the fact that naval units were also affiliated to the army's Territorial Cadet Force. In 1912, the 1st Somerset Naval Cadet Corps joined the T.C.F.; and the Wimbledon Boys' Naval Brigade became part of the 2nd Cadet Battalion, East Surrey Regiment in 1913.[10]

In the country at large the level of housing for the majority was substandard, and medical facilities were inadequate in pre-First World War Britain, particularly in the larger conurbations. This meant that any organisation, such as the cadets, that promoted physical fitness and social responsibility was bound to interest people who were concerned with youth welfare. It is evident that in post-1910 Britain, the State and local authorities were taking greater control and responsibility in promoting activities for the young. In 1910, the Mansion House Advisory Committee of Associations for Boys was formed with the Lord Mayor of London as President. The chairman was Colonel Ford, Commandant of the London Diocesan Church Lads' Brigade, with representatives from Commerce, the Board of Trade and, amongst others, the Navy and Army Cadets. Given the predominance of representatives from the uniformed organisations, the Committee not unnaturally encouraged their respective bodies to co-ordinate and standardise their aims, procedures and training. Efforts were made to collect and collate data 'to aid Government Departments concerned with the physical and industrial wellbeing of the people'. According to some historians, this was the thin end of the wedge, as the Committee became 'quickly involved in the possibility of recruiting for the Armed Forces'.[11] Indeed, in 1912, consideration was given to forming a 'British Boys' Training Corps'. The only 'advantage' of such a Corps would be to regularise training, but any initiative on the part of different bodies would have been lost, and in the event it was not really needed as the uniformed organisations were, to varying degrees, already undertaking basic military training. *(Plate 5)* Sir Ian Hamilton, who was one of the architects of the new cadet regulations, said – and with some justification – that cadets were not just 'playing a silly game', and that what they were doing had a 'direct bearing on war and on the defence of the country'.[12] History shows that this was a prophetic announcement.

On 4 August 1914, in defiance of the Treaty of London, 1839, which guaranteed Belgian neutrality, Germany crossed her frontiers and began the invasion of Belgium. In response Britain declared war on Germany. The defence of Belgium was not the sole reason for Britain declaring war with Germany. There was a growing feeling of hostility between the two powers. The major reasons concerned a growing commercial rivalry due to Germany's increasing industrial power; Germany's desire for expansion and the resultant colonial rivalry in South-West Africa and the Pacific; the building of a powerful German navy and the threat it posed to Britain's naval supremacy; and the envisaged threat to British trade. The three crises between 1906 and 1911 – at Algeciras, in Bosnia and at Agadir – resulted in closer ties between France and Britain, and a greater distrust of Germany. Germany had, three days previously, declared war on France and Russia, and it is highly likely that Britain would have come to the aid of France even if Germany had not invaded Belgium. War was inevitable.

Following the announcement of hostilities, volunteering was brisk and the Royal Navy had little difficulty in obtaining officers. There was a large number of Royal Navy Volunteer Reserve (R.N.V.R.) officers, many of whom were trained merchant seamen. As regards the young Royal Navy Dartmouth cadets, a decision was made to send them to sea so that they could continue their training with the fleet, a lethal decision for some as it turned out. On 22 September 1914, the cruiser H.M.S. *Aboukir* was torpedoed and sunk off the Dutch coast, and the 13 teenage cadets that were on board, along with 1,500 crew members, were lost.[13] Perhaps it was partly for this reason that the Royal Navy ignored the Navy League's application for Admiralty recognition of the League's 34 Naval Brigades, coupled, no doubt, with the Admiralty's continued dislike of the Navy League's propensity for being critical. Whatever the reason, the Royal Navy had no problem in recruiting enough boys and men for the lower deck despite the increase in demand; hence the Navy League's letter asking for greater recognition through a more direct involvement 'languished at the bottom of the in-tray till World War I was concluded'.[14]

At the outbreak of the First World War on 4 August 1914, the regular British Army – excluding reservists – totalled 247,432 officers and men, many of whom were abroad in India and Africa.[15] On 6 August 1914, Parliament authorised the first army recruiting campaign: the appeal was for 100,000 men. This, as it turned out, was an immediate strategic necessity. The British Expeditionary Force (B.E.F.) along with the French armies managed to halt the German advance on Paris albeit at a cost of half a million casualties. It soon became clear to people such as Field-Marshal Lord Kitchener, the man in charge of recruiting, that the war was not, as many believed, going to be a short encounter, let alone 'be over by Christmas'. At the end of the month a further 100,000 men were needed, and another half million by the end of September.[16] Members of the Territorial Cadet Force rallied to the call as they had during the Boer War, and cadet numbers increased substantially.

The O.T.C. never met its full pre-war establishment.[17] This was despite the increase in the number of school corps due to martial enthusiasm following the South African War and the frequent deliverance of patriotic speeches by visitors from the Navy League and high-ranking army officers.[18] However, with the extremely rapid expansion of the army, coupled with the increasing casualty rates in the British Expeditionary Force the War Office decided to 'grant temporary rather than permanent commissions to suitable young men, a major source of applicant being the Officers' Training Corps'.[19] The universities, public and grammar schools supplied 20,577 subalterns between August 1914 and March 1915.[20]

Regardless of many people's cynical views of the soldiery, the young and inexperienced flocked to the recruiting office. Those who were too young – or could not persuade the recruiting officer or sergeant that they were old enough – could join a uniformed youth organisation. It may be difficult for today's reader to comprehend the sheer weight and effect of nationalistic feeling, but Britain was still the leader of the largest empire the world had ever seen, and feelings of pride and duty were strong. Traditionally the leaders of the British Empire came from the public schools and their O.T.C. corps, and, as expected, their response to the 'call to serve', either in the armed forces or in the cadets was swift. The supply of pre-war regular officers may have been below expectations, but once war looked likely things changed rapidly. By 1914 only seven of the boys at Sherborne School were not in the corps[21]; at Rugby School, within 12 months, over 90 per cent of the boys were members of the corps[22]; by November 1914 the Merchant Taylors' School magazine included a list of 550 ex-pupils currently serving in the army and navy, and by 1917 this had risen to 1,463.[23] This pattern was repeated in public schools up and down the country. At some schools ex-pupils came back to their *alma mater* in order to renew their training or to enlist. On 30 August 1914, at Newcastle-under-Lyme School 50 ex-O.T.C. members 'paraded on the Close and enlisted in the presence of their Headmaster'.[24] At Tidworth 500 cadets and ex-cadets from Sherborne School attended camp in August 1914. All the 100 public school cadet corps reacted quickly to the demands of the nation during the years 1914–18. Such was the demand for officers that even O.T.C. certificates were waived and a public school background was sufficient to obtain a commission, writes Stevenson in his account of *British Society 1914–45*. In fact, 'Marlborough, Eton and Charterhouse between them sent more than twelve hundred sixth-formers straight to France as Second Lieutenants'.[25] In the first months of the war alone, the number of commissions taken by ex-O.T.C. school members fully justified Haldane's formation of the Corps in 1908.

The rush to join the Colours was no less prolific in the 'open' units that were stationed in towns and cities scattered around the country. Before the war the number of cadets (excluding the O.T.C.) was approximately 40,000; by 1918 the total had risen to 105,121.[26] There was a phenomenal increase in the number of boys from working-class homes eager to serve the country. This does not take into account the thousands who, on reaching conscription age, left the cadets and were drafted directly into the Services. It is impossible to make a close estimate of the number of boys that received their basic military training in the Territorial Cadet Force, but there were certainly hundreds of thousands of them.

The increase was not just in terms of numbers; there was also a concomitant growth in units. In 1912, in the rural county of Shropshire there were only three army cadet units, one at Bridgnorth and Shrewsbury, and one at Whitchurch, but between July and September of 1915 another 11 companies were formed.[27] The response to the needs of the time could, conversely, have the opposite effect on a unit's existence. The Frimley and Camberley Cadet Corps disappeared as a result of the war. In 1914 every fit cadet of the 100-strong corps – some of whom, no doubt, were under age – joined up, and those deemed unfit worked in the munitions factory at Crayford. The collapse in number plus the absence of instructors owing to service at the Front meant that in 1917 parades had to be suspended until the war had ended.[28] This, although not usual, was nevertheless not unheard of in other parts of the country. It was not always the lack of recruits but rather the shortage of officers and instructors that had a devastating effect on the organisation. The loss cannot be gauged in numbers alone, there could be a distinct change in attitude as a report of the 1st Essex Cadet Battalion shows:

> To the Battalion the war came as a disaster. All its officers of military age as well as all the senior NCOs joined up in one day. It is true that the unit carried on. More elderly men came forward as officers and the war excitement tended to increase numbers, but it was not the same thing. Recruits who join in a hectic enthusiasm of war do not equal those who deliberately and calmly accept the obligation of Service in peace and all the keenness and enthusiasm of officers could not replace those lost when all the NCOs went.[29]

The lack of younger leaders and the increase in new units was almost overwhelming. In 1916 a new battalion was formed at Exeter and 'over 400 Cadets joined within four weeks'.[30] This is equivalent to the total membership of some of today's counties. Even after the war, in 1919, a company started in the Ayrshire Docks quickly attracted 80 boys.[31] Loyalty and fierce patriotism were distinctive features of most members of the military services, particularly in the first two years of the war. The loyalty was, of course, not only to the country but to the locality, witness the renowned Pals Battalions, and the cadet equivalent such as the Frimley and Camberley Cadet Corps. A sense of loyalty could go beyond enlisting with one's peers. At Shrewsbury School where, at the beginning of the war, a temporary recruiting office was set up for a day in the hall, 38 Old Salopians turned up to enlist. After spending a night at the school they marched off the next morning to the nearby barracks. Normally they would all have been commissioned into the 5th Battalion King's Shropshire Light Infantry – the county regiment – but 'one of their number was coloured and therefore ineligible for commissioned rank'. However, such was their sense of *camaraderie* that 'they all made a self-denying ordinance that they would refuse commissions, and none did accept one until, after his death, they felt released from the obligation which they had imposed upon themselves'.[32]

The Government took great interest in the cadet movement during the First World War. Those in authority were aware that the cadet units, of whatever affiliation, were providing the army with partially-trained recruits. And in an effort to assist them the Government instituted a system of capitation grants. This was for all Territorial Cadet Force units which, of course, included all army cadet detachments and affiliated Church Lads' Brigade units – in fact, all of the latter that were not otherwise attached by 1917 became affiliated to the King's Royal Rifle Corps Cadet Battalion.[33] Those sea cadet units that were affiliated to the T.C.F. also qualified for the grant. It is not known how many there were of them but in addition to those already mentioned, there were another two sea cadet units in Surrey: one that was formed at Wimbledon prior to the war, in 1913, and a second unit started at Richmond.[34] In recognition of the important work done and the role the Territorial Cadet Force had played during the war H.R.H. The Prince of Wales became its Colonel-in-Chief.

Prior to capitation grants, monetary awards came via the Territorial Force Association which, for administrative reasons, kept 25 per cent of the money. Therefore, local units had to spend time on fund raising. Uniforms were not free, unlike today, and there was a shortage of weapons. Drill Purpose (D.P.) Carbines were issued to the cadets, but there were not enough rifles for each boy to train with one. In order to make up for this deficiency the well known London store Gamages was offering a dummy rifle for sale at 1s 3d. This appears very cheap – less than 10p in decimal money – but it must be remembered that the average working-class wage was just under £1.50 a week; this had to support the average family of father, mother and three or four children.[35] Needless to say the more imaginative unit commanders and instructors would improvise, and accounts show that Shaftesbury School bought 90 feet of iron piping in order to make dummy rifles.[36] Uniforms too had to be bought. A jacket cost 11s 6d (about 60p today). By 1915 the distinctive uniforms of the various school and county units had all but disappeared, and khaki Service Dress with stand collar and four pockets was *de rigueur*.

Training during the war was strictly on military lines. National and county shooting competitions were halted owing to lack of ammunition, rifles and accessibility of ranges. Clearly the Armed Services had to have priority regarding equipment and training areas. Where possible, schools collaborated in training. In 1914 schools in the London area combined in organising 'field days on a huge scale bringing together all the various O.T.C.'s for tactical exercises in Richmond Park'.[37] A year later Eton, Harrow and Rugby had a combined field day at which the Rugby School Field Telegraph Section made its first appearance.[38] In the Midlands in 1915, Rugby had combined manoeuvres with King Edward's and the Oratory School, both from Birmingham, and field days were also held with Oundle, Uppingham and Oakham Schools. By 1918 ammunition was becoming easier to obtain, and shooting competitions were resumed, with Rugby School winning the National Public School Sniping competition. Training in telegraphy and Morse code became an increasing part of the syllabus. And, following the reformed army method of progressive training, practice and instruction throughout the O.T.C. and T.C.F. was now done first at platoon, company and then battalion level. The importance placed on cadet training varied from school to school. At Shrewsbury, in 1913, it was thought to interfere with the more important activity of games; however, come 1914 it was no longer regarded as a peripheral hobby. Boys were not now playing at soldiering, but training to be front-line troops. It is recorded that by 1915 the O.T.C. at Newcastle-under-Lyme School had become 'the most important of the School's various institutions'. As if to emphasise the point the rugby pitch was dug up to provide a 'support trench, a communication trench, and a fire trench, with traverses', and in 1917 training included grenade throwing and bayonet fighting.[39] The Certificate 'A' examination was abandoned in the schools, partly because there was neither the means to properly assess – most of the young masters who ran the cadet contingents were in the forces – nor was there time to do examinations. Besides why spend time in assessment when in perhaps a few weeks or months the cadet, by then a soldier, would be doing it for real whatever his standard? What was needed was the acquisition of basic military skills and their constant practice.

The O.T.C. school corps had advantages with regard to their training. First, they could afford to purchase, where it was available, more equipment; secondly, most of the schools were situated on large private estates, hence training areas were more readily available. Nevertheless, with a little bit of improvisation the Territorial Cadet Force commander could augment his training programme by including additional subjects that was not part of the official syllabus. One unit incorporated ambulance classes, another – no doubt with the help of the local Territorial Association – included machine gun classes. Others, presumably with the assistance of invalided veterans posted back to Blighty, included the vitally important topic of trench hygiene. There were additional first aid and Morse code classes. One unit even taught 'lesson in flight [sic]', and in 1918 the Air Ministry proposed that special platoons of army cadets should be instructed in R.A.F. duties, thus pre-empting the formation of the Air Training Corps by some thirteen years.[40] Not all units were so enlightened or capable of including new subjects as the standard of training and instruction was very varied. There was no national standard. Everything tended to be localised and the officers' commissions were valid only in the county of issue. For some units this meant an almost undiluted programme of drill. However, the Imperial Cadet Yeomanry had much more 'exotic' training. This unit was raised by the Honorable Artillery Company and was therefore mounted. It apparently caused quite 'a flutter in Cadet circles at its inception!'[41]

Cadet units had additional public duties to perform. Sometimes warwork was done on a particular occasion, as when boys from Eton celebrated Founder's Day by helping the Army Ordnance Corps with the work of dispatching munitions at Didcot, dismantling gun carriages and unloading rail wagons.[42] A more regular commitment for a unit could include the local cadet band playing at recruiting rallies or escorting departing army contingents to the local railway station. At times throughout the conflict cadets were asked to patrol vulnerable points, such as reservoirs or railway bridges, and to 'act as air-raid buglers'.[43] It was strange wrote one veteran 'to see a car going round driven by a policeman, and a diminutive Cadet bugler occupying the public's attention in this way!'.[44] In fact the Birmingham Waterworks guard was composed entirely of cadets.[45] Thus in various ways cadets could become directly involved in the war effort.

There was an apparent need for centralisation of training and control. In Northumberland, for example, the Church Lads' Brigade and the Boys' Brigade had agreed to work to a programme set and assessed by the Army Cadet Commandant's office, but not to come under his command.[46] With an increase in the number of secondary schools forming cadet corps it was decided that, as their organisational requirements differed from the local 'open' units, an additional branch of the Territorial Cadet Force should be set up to cater specifically for their needs. And in 1917 the Public and Secondary School Cadet Association was formed. This organisation catered, in the main, for grammar schools. At the same time talks were held with the Scout Commissioner with a view to forming Scout-Cadets. General Baden-Powell considered that Scouts should not become cadets until they were 16 years of age, but it was decided that a boy could belong to both organisations provided the Cadet and Scout Commandants agreed.[47] Also in 1917 the Navy League considered the question of a National Sea Training scheme for boys. The League's committee agreed that the views of the Admiralty should be sought before any progress could be made with the project, and a letter was sent to the Second Sea Lord.[48] The Navy League was ignored at first, but later, in November 1917, the 'Affiliation of the Boys' Naval Brigade with the Admiralty was again considered . . .'.[49] A few days later it was agreed to appoint an ex-Royal Navy officer to the position of Inspector of the Boys' Naval Brigade, but the Admiralty refused to release the League's first choice for the post.[50] However, by 7 February 1918, an appointment was made. Although the Admiralty had become marginally less intransigent, the Navy League and its cadets were still, in effect, *persona non grata* until 1919, as far as the Admiralty was concerned.

Such was the enthusiasm of the youth of the country to join cadet organisations that a restriction had to be imposed. In Northumberland the number of cadets within the county's Territorial Cadet Force was limited to 2,000. The restriction was for financial reasons; one of the constraining factors was the cost of kitting out such a large body of people. Throughout the country new corps were being formed, not only in towns and schools but also by the formation of works' companies.[51] By 1918 the number of cadet units nation-wide was in excess of 2,000. It is impossible to say how many of the cadets went into the armed forces each year, or indeed how many came back. Given the casualty rate in the Armed Services – nearly threequarters of a million dead – clearly many did not return home. Of those that did, many must have been part of the 1.7 million disabled.[52] There is no doubt that many of the individuals showed great courage, and most schools have kept records of those ex-pupils that gained recognition for their bravery – V.C.s, M.C.s, D.S.C.s and an array of other decorations abound. The 'open' cadet units, recruiting from a more transient and diverse population, tended not to keep records: hence it would be invidious to single out one institution for praise. Suffice to say that, as in 1900, the cadets responded to 'The Call' and rendered a great service to the country in its time of need by providing thousands of pre-trained young servicemen, although unlike in the Boer War no cadet units were allowed to fight abroad. Alas, however, the enormity of the sacrifice by the young men who did experience combat meant that there was bound to be a psychological backlash. As it turned out, this was not the only problem the cadet organisations had to face in the following two decades.

Chapter 2 References

1. 1st Cadet Battalion, *The Queen's, Royal West Surrey Regiment Enrolment Book*, May 1889 to June 1891
2. *The Navy League* journal, April 1910, p. 104
3. A.C.F.A., *The Cadet Story, 1860–1980* [London: A.C.F.A., 1982] p. 16
4. Ibid.
5. J. Springall, *Youth, Empire and Society* [London: Croom Helm, 1977] Appendix V, p. 138
6. Ibid.
7. John M. MacKenzie, *Propaganda and Empire – The manipulation of British public opinion, 1880–1960* [Manchester: MUP, 1984], p. 24
8. *The Cadet Story, 1860–1980*, op. cit., p. 16
9. R. A. Westlake, *A Register of Territorial Force Cadet Units, 1910–1922* [Wembley: Westlake, 1984], p. 28
10. Ibid., p. 71
11. J. Springall, B. Fraser & M. Hoare, *Sure and Steadfast – a history of the Boys' Brigade, 1883–1983* [London: Collins, 1983], p. 97
12. Ian Hamilton, *National Life and National Training* [London: King & Sons, 1913], pp. 19–22
13. Capt. E. W. Bush, *Bless Our Ship* [London: Allen & Unwin, 1958] in Capt. J. Wells, 'The Royal Navy – an illustrated history, 1870–1982' [Stroud: Sutton, 1994], pp. 97 & 98
14. M.A.O. 8, *History of the Sea Cadet Movement*, p. 2
15. Tim Travers, 'The Army and the Challenge of War, 1914–18,' in *The Oxford History of the British Army* [eds.] David Chandler & Ian Beckett [Oxford: OUP, 1996], pp. 211–234
16. L. J. Collins, *Theatre at War, 1914–18* [Basingstoke: Macmillan, 1998], p. 5
17. G. Best, 'Militarism and the Victorian Public School' in *The Victorian Public School* [eds.] B. Simon & I. Bradley [London: Gill & Macmillan, 1975], pp. 131-137
18. Edward Spiers, 'The Late Victorian Army 1868–1914' in *The Oxford History of the British Army* [eds.] David Chandler & Ian Beckett [Oxford: OUP, 1996], pp. 187–210
19. Peter Simkins, *The Four Armies 1914–1918*, ibid., p. 244
20. Ibid., p. 244
21. Lt.-Col. J. P. Riley M.A., 'The History of Sherborne School Cadet Force' in *Schoolboys in Uniform* [Sherborne: Shelly, 1988], pp. 44–48
22. Lt.-Col. Harris, *Rugby School Corps, 1860–1960* [London: Brown, Knight & Truscott, 1960], p. 164
23. Cdr. R. B. Hawkey, R.N.R. (C.C.F.), *History of the Corps at Merchant Taylors', 1900–1981* [Rickmansworth: George & Roberts, 1981], pp. 27 & 28

24 Col. E. R. Clowes, 'Newcastle-under-Lyme School Combined Cadet Force, a brief history' [unpublished notes: Newcastle-u-Lyme, 1994], in letter to Wing Cdr. West R.A.F., 20-8-94
25 John Stevenson, *British Society, 1914–45* [Harmondsworth: Penguin, 1984], p. 52
26 J. Springall, op. cit., p. 138
27 Author anonymous, 'A Brief History of the Shropshire A.C.F.' [Shropshire A.C.F.: Unpublished pamphlet, 1960], pp. 2 & 3
28 Col. F. W. Foley C.B.E. D.S.O., *A Short History of the Frimley and Camberley Cadet Corps, 1908–1948* [Aldershot: Gale & Polden, 1948], pp. 6 & 7
29 *The Cadet Story, 1860–1980*, op. cit., p. 20
30 Ibid.
31 Ibid.
32 J. Basil Oldham M.A., *A History of Shrewsbury School, 1852–1952* [Oxford: Blackwell, 1952], p. 208
33 R. A. Westlake, op. cit., p. 2
34 Lt.-Col. H. C. Hughes T.D. M.A., *The Army Cadets of Surrey, 1860–1960* [London: Spyer, 1960], p. 7
35 Arthur Marwick, *The Deluge – British Society and the First World War* [Basingstoke: Macmillan, 6th edition, 1986], pp. 21-24
36 *The Cadet Story, 1860–1980*, op. cit., p. 21
37 R. B. Hawkey, op. cit., p. 33
38 H. J. Harris, op. cit., p. 150
39 E. A. Clowes, op. cit.
40 *The Cadet Story, 1860–1980*, op. cit., p. 22
41 *The Cadet Journal*, Vol. V, No. 3 1943
42 Film: *Eton Boy Workers* in *Éclair Animated Journal*, No. 49, 2nd edition, 1914, British Film Institute Archives [London]
43 R. A. Westlake, op. cit., p. 2
44 *The Cadet Journal*, Vol. V, No. 3, 1943
45 Ibid.
46 *The Cadet Story, 1960–1980*, op. cit., p. 22
47 Ibid., p. 23
48 *The Navy League* journal, 7 June 1917
49 *The Navy League* journal, 15 November 1917
50 *The Navy League* journal, 29 November 1917
51 *The Cadet Story*, op. cit., p. 23
52 Ian Beckett, 'The Nation in Arms, 1914–18' in *A Nation in Arms* [eds.] Ian Beckett & Keith Simpson [London: Donovan, 2nd edition, 1990], p. 27

CHAPTER 3 – THE INTER-WAR YEARS

IN 1917, THE NAVY LEAGUE was considering the 'Question of the Organisation of a National Sea Training scheme for Boys', but before proceeding it was agreed that it would be desirable 'that the views of the Admiralty should be known to the Committee'. Hence a deputation consisting of the Duke of Somerset, the M.P. Mr Bains E. Peto, and the General Secretary arranged to 'wait upon the Second Sea Lord', and ascertain his views.[1] The Navy League had approached the Admiralty in 1913, and earlier in 1917, but was ignored. However, during 1914–18 the naval cadet units had usefully produced – as much for the army as for the navy – partially trained personnel to fight in the Great War. It may have been assumed, therefore, that this was an opportune moment to approach the Admiralty once again. This latest communiqué was not so much a request for recognition, but a seeking of approval and advice. The Navy's response was not immediate. In 1918 the Admiralty, after refusing the League's first choice of candidate, agreed to the appointment of an ex-service officer to the position of Inspector of the Boys' Naval Brigade.[2] A year later, when the war was over, the Admiralty, at long last, 'graciously' agreed to 'afford recognition of efficient units in six Central Associations'.[3] They were: The Navy League, the Marine Society, the Church Lads' Brigade, Scarborough Education Committee, the Boy Scouts Association and Watts Naval Training School.[4] The British Sailors' Society was recognised some seven years later.

It is not clear what happened to all the naval units. Two are known to have been disbanded: the Kensington and Hammersmith Navy League Boys' Brigade in 1917, and the Greenwich Naval Cadet Unit in 1919.[5] Some units changed from one organisation to another as they found where their true allegiance lay. In Wales the Newport Sea Cadet Corps [T.S. *Resolute*], formed in 1900 under the name Maindee Church Lads' Brigade, later combined with St Paul's church unit, to become the Newport Church Lads' Naval Brigade, before finally joining the Navy League Sea Cadet Corps when Admiralty recognition was granted in 1919.[6] The Portsmouth S.C.C. unit (in H.M.S. *Nelson*) began life as the R.N. Barracks Boys' Brigade in 1900, but was later designated as a Royal Naval Cadet Corps unit.[7] The historical picture is further complicated as a number of the naval units were affiliated to, or absorbed by, larger organisations; for example, during the First World War the naval section of the Folkestone Church Lads' Brigade, was absorbed into the larger 2nd Canterbury Cadet C.L.B. Battalion, and the 1st Somerset Naval Cadet Corps, after three years of affiliation, withdrew from the Territorial Cadet Force in 1915.[8] A few of the smaller units may, as happened with some of the army cadet

45

corps, have had to be closed during the First World War because all the instructors were serving in the armed forces. The 1st Royal Marine Light Infantry Company from Chatham was affiliated to the Royal West Kent Regiment in 1912, the R.M. Depot Cadet Corps to the East Kent in 1913, and the Portsmouth Division of the R.M. Light Infantry Cadets actually joined the army's Territorial Cadet Force in 1919.[9] This transference of Royal Marine badged units to the army cadets was not surprising as the Navy League did not, at that time, cater for their marine-orientated cadets. There is no evidence of Royal Marine cadet units transferring from the T.C.F. to the Navy League. The Richmond Boys' Naval Cadets affiliated to the 8th Bn. Surrey Volunteer Regiment, in 1917, before later amalgamating with the Wimbledon Naval Brigade to form the 2nd Cadet Battalion, East Surrey Regiment. The two units eventually moved to their true home, and transferred to the Navy League Sea Cadet Corps in 1919. A year later the Wandsworth Boys' Naval Brigade also came under the auspices of the Admiralty.[10] This recognition, and involvement by the Admiralty, although belated, did begin to bridge the divide between the Senior Service and the Navy League. It also helped to provide the naval cadet units with a sense of unity. This was reflected in the all-embracing new name, the Navy League Sea Cadet Corps. From now on, Royal Naval involvement and a unit's continued recognition depended on a successful annual inspection and the subsequent report by the representative of the Admiral Commanding Reserves.

At the cessation of hostilities in 1918 the Secretary of State for War issued a letter of gratitude to navy and army cadet units, commending them 'for the important role they had filled during the war'. This public recognition seems to have jolted the Sea Lords at the Admiralty into officially recognising the Navy League Boys' Naval Brigade.[11]

THE 1920s

An additional acknowledgment of the sea cadets and their adult instructors' contribution to the war effort was the granting of honorary R.N.V.R. commissions to the officers of 'recognised efficient units'.[12] However, this bestowal of privilege was too much for other R.N.V.R. officers who, it appears felt that their status was being undermined. In 1922 the R.N.V.R. Committee argued that the Navy League Sea Cadet Corps officers were not proper officers, as they did not carry out R.N. Reserve training, and were not liable for immediate mobilisation. The Admiralty upheld the Committee's objection and reversed the decision, deciding instead to appoint, rather than to commission Navy League Officers, who, from then on were known as Sea Cadet Lieutenants.[13] It is hard to tell what the officers of the day thought, but this raising and lowering of status could not have helped the morale of the Navy League Sea Cadet Officers. However, they were allowed to wear the R.N.V.R. Special Branch uniforms, 'with green stripes between their wavy stripes'. It also meant the officers were eligible for free uniforms and upkeep allowance, plus limited pay when attending courses.[14] So, at least in appearance, they could act the part.

The willingness of a large number of teenage boys to serve in the army cadets continued until 1921, when the number of cadets (excluding the public school Officer Training Corps, but including the affiliated Church Lads' Brigade and Boys' Brigade) totalled a record 119,706.[15] But then came the slump. By 1925 the numbers had fallen dramatically to 48,841. A census taken at the time (excluding the O.T.C.) shows the following strength return:

Number of units		Strength
258	Secondary School units	18,260
449	Church Lads' Brigade	18,189
41	Jewish Lads' Brigade	2,342
13	Catholic Cadet units	1,180
11	Industrial Schools	758
181	Open units	9,112
953	units	48,841 cadets[16]

The fall in numbers is partly explained by the withdrawal of the Boys' Brigade units from the Territorial Cadet Force in 1924.[17] This was due to the understandable post-war reaction against militarism. Four years of fighting and the experience of the horrors of war left an indelible mark on the men that had been at the Front. Some managed to adjust to a peacetime existence; other did not. A. B. Jefferies – wartime soldier, and master at the Merchant Taylors' School – explained how many of those returning from the Front must have felt when he said:

> Many did not live to face the future, but those of us who survived could not help but be greatly influenced by our former experiences, our enthusiasm and disillusionments. When I left the army in March 1919, I felt a sense of profound relief, a great distaste for all things military, and a determination never to be involved again.[18]

He did, however, eventually get involved by becoming an officer with the O.T.C. at the school, and was later to say that: 'Even more than the games field, the O.T.C. gave to the school a character and a driving force which otherwise would have been almost completely lacking'.[19]

The total numbers involved in the corps of the public schools did not appear to be greatly affected by the war's coming to an end; although it must be noted that service with the O.T.C. was compulsory in many, if not most, schools. The schools were, quite naturally, proud of the contribution their former pupils had made, and many a school had honoured them by displaying inscribed wall plaques or other war memorials. At the cessation of war the number of parades and the amount of training decreased.

Military and social conditions were vastly different after the war. There was a general winding-down of military forces and efforts were made politically to try to ensure a continued peace. These included the 1919 Peace Conference in Paris, followed by the Treaty of Versailles; the ending of conscription in the U.K. in 1920; and the disbandment of the women's army, navy and air force auxiliary services in 1921. In the following year Sir Eric Geddes wielded his 'Axe' and proposed cuts of £75 million in government expenditure, which meant a further diminution of the armed forces. In 1925 Britain and Italy guaranteed the Locarno Pacts of non-aggression between France, Germany and Belgium. Furthermore, in 1927 the League of Nations adopted a resolution prohibiting all wars of aggression. This resulted in the Kellogg Pact of 1928, in which 65 countries pledged themselves to the renunciation of war. No doubt the autobiographical accounts and other printed reminders of the horrors of wartime helped, at least in part, to elicit public support for the peace-initiatives. Apart from the published collections of war poems, there was a very successful play and several best-selling books. These included Edmund Blunden's book, *Undertones of War*, R. C. Sherriff's play *Journey's End*, both produced in 1928; in 1929 there was Richard Aldington's book *Death of a Hero*, E. M. Remarque's *All Quiet on the Western Front*, and *Goodbye to All That* by Robert Graves. A year later Siegfried Sassoon's *Memories of an Infantry Officer* was published. This political and literary activity may not at first appear to be relevant to the future of the cadets, but it voiced many people's reaction to the war, and their hopes for peace: hence the desire of some people in authority to distance themselves from anything military, and this included the Territorial Cadet Force.

A significant number of the Church Lads' Brigade units, and many of the Jewish Lads' Brigades, either disaffiliated themselves from the T.C.F., or disbanded altogether. The relationship between a military organisation and a religious one appeared rather incongruous. Once the war was over, and the call was for peace, it seemed reasonable that the religious-based organisations decided to go their own way, particularly as the moral and social aims of the army cadet movement had been totally subsumed by the military requirements. The military masters had ignored, forgotten or did not want to remember the nineteenth-century aims proffered by the reformer Octavia Hill and others. It was partly the militaristic-myopia of those in charge, the failure to adjust to peacetime demands, and the change in public opinion, that led to the decline of the army cadet movement. At the same time other youth movements, such as the Boy Scouts and Boys' Brigade, were going through a period of phenomenal expansion.[20] The Scouts appealed more to middle-class families, and were concentrated mainly in London and the Home Counties. The Boys' Brigade had a greater following in the north of England, and particularly in Scotland. Alas, the traditional working-class areas from which the army cadets were recruited during the war were not well served. The Territorial Cadet Force failed to consolidate its success. In fact, between 1921 and 1939 membership fell by 70 per cent[21]; or '21 per cent of all youth' according to the 1934 Carnegie Trust data.[22] In short, a great opportunity was lost, and it was as a result of lack of foresight and 'indifferent leadership'.[23]

The Governments, both Labour and Conservative, were of little help as they both, at different times, withdrew grants from the Cadet Force. The capitation grant was removed in 1923, but was fortunately restored two years later in the form of a block grant that had a fixed limit. The loss of revenue was not in itself too great a hardship as most units were self-supporting, but it was a psychological blow. The volunteer officers running the cadet units had done an efficient and useful job preparing boys for the wartime army and thus felt 'personally slighted' by the Government's financial penalty.[24] At the same time, in 1923, the War Office handed over the administration of the army cadets to the County Territorial Associations. Astonishingly, 31 County Associations decided not to continue their army cadet units.[25] In addition, the privileges of borrowing camping gear, and permission to use War Department land, were withdrawn. Given the militarily negative social climate, and the resulting practical problems, it is not surprising that the number of 'open' units slumped to 181 and their membership to just 9,112. The army cadet movement (outside the schools) was in a parlous state. Worse was to follow. In August 1930 the Labour Secretary of State for War, Mr Tom Shaw, announced that official recognition of all cadet units would be withdrawn from 31 October. This meant that there would be no grants and no rifles, and no regimental insignia – recognisable buttons or badges of affiliation – could be worn. Drill halls would in the future be available for physical training only, and not for military instruction. This caused quite a furore, and many articles appeared in the newspapers castigating the Government for its short-sighted views. An article published in the *Sunday Times* was typical of the response. It reads:

> The aim of the Cadet Force is to give mental, moral, and physical instruction to the boys who join the organisation. Instead of hindering

patriotic work of this kind, the Government ought to be encouraging it. The building up of character, on which all good citizenship must rest, should be a primary duty. There is no connection between the Cadet Force and a rabid militarism, and Mr Shaw might as well prohibit the Salvation Army from wearing uniform as penalise the Cadets because they go in for physical drill on Army lines. But Mr Shaw's pinpricks will only stimulate the friends of the of the Cadets to greater efforts. A great national movement cannot be killed by a handful of cranks.[26]

The internal voice of protest came from a co-ordinating body, the Central Council of the Territorial Associations (C.C.T.A.). The War Office no doubt dealt with the protesters reasonably politely, but their response was off-hand in manner and merely passed the buck. In effect they said, 'if that's how you feel, do it yourself'.[27] In spite of its lack of interest, the War Office did however impose certain restrictions, which turned out to be damaging.

First, in order for a unit to be recognised, it had to provide a definite military programme. Complementary character-building activities were considered superfluous if not of a strictly military nature. Military training was seen as an end in itself, but there was no set syllabus. The unit commander may have had the *Manual of Cadet Infantry Training*, but without the use of training areas and equipment the training must have consisted of little more than drill and route marches, and shooting (if a range was available). The more imaginative unit commanders may have included some first aid and sport. Given the restricted scope and aims of the training it is not surprising that numbers dwindled. The Certificate 'A' syllabus was not available to the Open units. However, any cadet who wanted an army career, and perhaps, had an ambition to become an officer, needed to undergo Certificate training before taking the Army Entrance exam. This entailed taking extra instruction at the nearest Territorial Army Centre. The cadet units, even if they had the expertise, would have been of limited help because they did not have the necessary equipment. Only the most diligent cadet from an open unit, who had a nearby TA centre willing to help him, would stand a chance of passing the stiff written and practical Army Entrance Exam.

An annual inspection for each unit was instituted, and every cadet was assessed according to his efficiency. The efficiency insignia – a four-pointed blue star – was acquired by parading on 20 drill nights. It was, in effect, a badge of attendance. Officers were granted Lord Lieutenants' Commissions, and wore a letter 'C' on their uniforms. There was much debate about the quality of the officers, but 'there was no means of training them'. And it was constantly pointed out that 'one could not discuss the status of the Cadet officer as he had none'.[28] The Central Council of Territorial Associations was a consultative and co-ordinating body, not an executive one, and therefore its powers were limited.

Although the C.C.T.A. had little effect on the military training of cadets, it was able to broaden the curriculum and encourage other non-military pursuits. The Council made a contribution, on a national basis, by organising competitions in sports and shooting.

The national sports competitions included the Lady West Memorial Shield. This required cadet teams to perform 10 group gymnastic-style exercises. Judging by the entries this was the most popular event.[29] A boxing competition was also instituted, the finals of which were held in London, the main prize being the Prince of Wales's Shield. This was an expensive venture but costs were defrayed by charging each unit an entrance fee.

The C.C.T.A. managed to obtain sponsorship for the competitions from Sir Julian Cahn and the Lucas Tooth family. A *Victor Ludorum* trophy was instituted and presented by the Lucas Tooth Foundation. The trophy was initially known as 'The County Association Championship Shield for the Lincolnshire A.C.F. for Efficiency'. Sleaford Grammar School Cadet Corps was the first unit to be presented with the trophy in 1923–24.[30] It was awarded for a variety of activities, including physical training demonstrations, sports and drill. The Foundation generously donated a Lucas Tooth Shield to each county, and they are still competed for today. The Lucas Tooth competition can be viewed as an effort to reward all-round performance. Yet it is recorded that in 1924 strong representations were made to the Foundation by some counties to limit the activities mainly to drill, and some other military-based activities. Fortunately the members of the Foundation had more foresight. They refused to alter the rules, and the matter was dropped.[31] Today the Lucas Tooth competition includes practically every aspect of Army Cadet Force activity.

The C.C.T.A. also began the practice, which is still carried on today by some counties, of organising annual tours to the First World War battlefields. However, all the good work done by the C.C.T.A. came to an abrupt end in 1930, for on 24 March 1930 the Government announced that from 1 April that year the Cadet Force would cease to exist. Army cadets, throughout Britain, had seven days in which to finalise affairs and close down.

A worsening economic situation and growing unemployment had resulted in a change of Government, and the Labour Party was elected to power. Financial constraint was a priority, but the dissolving of the army cadets was more to do with the spirit of pacifism that prevailed. In sympathy with the general anti-military feeling some education authorities banned cadets in their schools, which caused a number of secondary school units to close.[32] Once again there was a strong nation-wide reaction. There were complaints of course, from the C.C.T.A., and speeches in both the House of Commons and the House of Lords. The Headmasters' Conference complained that it had not been consulted, and the Anglican Church Leader, Dr Lang – the Archbishop of Canterbury – said that boys would be deprived of additional moral and educational training. Admiral Lord Jellicoe intervened on behalf of the army cadets. The economic saving was ridiculously small; the total grant to the Territorial Association for cadets amounted to only £11,000 per annum. The Government was adamant nevertheless. The only concession obtained was a deferment of the closing-down date. It was now to be 30 October 1930. From that day on, 51,000 army cadets from the church organisations, school and open units, along with their officers and instructors, ceased to exist, officially.[33]

THE 1930s

A degree of co-operation existed between the public and secondary schools during the difficult years of the 1920s. The C.C.T.A., for administrative and practical reasons, organised combined camps. The result of this liaison was the creation of the Public and Secondary Schools Cadet Association (P.S.S.C.A.). It so happened that in 1930 when the P.S.S.C.A. was about to hold its annual meeting, the Government unilaterally decided to disband the Cadet Force. The chairman of the P.S.S.C.A.'s Joint Committee, Field-Marshal Lord Allenby, along with other representatives – including the Church Lads' Brigade and Jewish Lads' Brigade leaders, and the ex-Territorial Cadet Force commandants – decided to form a new organisation. It was to be called the British National Cadet Association. Its aims were:

> To give mental, moral and physical training to boys, and so to form the character of each as to enable him to make a good start in life; to develop in them patriotism and good citizenship and to fit them, in the event of national emergency, to take their place in the defence of the country.[34]

The B.N.C.A. also intended to spread its influence abroad to the Dominions and Colonies. The underlying purpose was, of course, to keep the army cadet movement going until such time as Government recognition was restored. In order to do this it was imperative that the aims reflected the broader purpose of the cadet movement. The inclusion of the social, as well as the military objective, needed to be emphasised: this would ensure that the religious and educational establishments had no difficulty in supporting the cadet movement. The cynic might have called it merely window-dressing, designed only to create public support. In fact it did not need to do that as the plethora of newspaper articles in support of the Cadet Force demonstrated. More importantly, the cadet movement, by re-embracing the twin aims of patriotism and character training, was returning to its nineteenth-century roots.

The B.N.C.A., in effect, came to fulfil a similar role to that undertaken by the Navy League in the sea cadet movement. The army cadet movement was now being kept alive by private subscription. There the comparison ended, however, as the positions were reversed; at least the sea cadets had some recognition from the Admiralty, whereas the army cadets were now disowned by the War Office. But too many people of influence were interested in the plight of the army cadets movement to allow it to continue in this unsatisfactory way. Through the efforts of the Prince of Wales, who agreed to become patron of the Cadet Force, the good leadership of the B.N.C.A. chairman Lord Allenby and Lieutenant-General Sir Hugh Jeudwine who had been Director General of the Territorial Army, the support of the Association of Scottish Cadets, which became a sub-committee of the B.N.C.A., and the commendable philanthropy on the part of Colonel Sir Philip Carlebach – who provided £500 to cover the Association's expenses – with the eager efforts of various commandants and units commanders, the Army Cadet Association was saved from becoming moribund. In fact, such was the commitment and determination by the Committee, that within a year the B.N.C.A. felt confident enough to launch the first Cadet Force magazine.[35]

The units located at T.A. drill halls faced eviction in 1930, but within a short space of time the B.N.C.A. won a concession. It was agreed that the cadets could remain providing that the T.A. incurred no expense, and that no military training was undertaken – and this included map reading! Whether or not the unit commanders obeyed this order is not known. It must have also been a particularly difficult time financially for many of the T.C.F. army cadets, as a large number of those over 14 years of age were unemployed. They would therefore have had difficulty in buying boots and other pieces of kit, in addition to paying subscriptions and fees for camps.

Within a period of two years, however, the Government was persuaded to change its mind. The Cadet Force was again officially recognised, and the B.N.C.A. was made fully responsible for its management. The period of impoverishment for the army cadet movement was fortunately relatively short. In 1937 the National Government restored the grant; and five shillings was paid for each cadet who gained certain military qualifications.[36]

As more grammar schools attained independent status so their cadet affiliation changed from Territorial Cadet Force to Officer Training Corps. This was particularly true of the schools that were also part of the Public and Secondary School Cadet Association. There was, however, at least one known exception. In 1935 Reigate Grammar School, formerly an O.T.C. contingent, joined the 1st Cadet Battalion, the Queen's Royal Regiment (West Surrey). In so doing the unit was re-designated 'D' company although it was not the only school-based unit in the Battalion; 'C' company was composed of pupils from the independent Croydon High School. The latter was to become a casualty of the war, and the school, along with its cadet company, ceased to exist in 1940.[37] In 1936, a ruling came from the National Headquarters of the Church Lads' Brigade that no C.L.B. unit was 'to do Cadet training any longer'; it was stated that increasing numbers of C.L.B. officers had difficulty in reconciling their religious beliefs with military training.[38] Although the numbers had diminished considerably, there was a discernible change in the character of the army cadet movement. The new units being formed were almost exclusively 'open' units, and recruited mainly working class boys.[39]

In the meantime the O.T.C., with its specific purpose of producing potential officers, had a less arduous route. Its only real inconvenience was due to the economies of 1932, under which Territorial Army camps were cancelled. It is written in the A.C.F.A. historical accounts that the public schools had 'the good fortune to keep out of party politics' and by implication thus safeguard their future.[40] This is a rather naïve statement. The fact that they were financially independent, and therefore not reliant on Government subsidy, was the main reason for their survival. In addition they had support in high places. In 1931 the Duke and Duchess of York (the future King George VI and today's Queen Mother) made a second visit to the Merchant Taylors' School where members of the school's O.T.C. formed a Guard of Honour.[41] In 1936 the same prestigious opportunity was afforded the cadets at Haileybury School, when they provided a Guard of Honour to attend the proclamation as king of Edward VII by the High Sheriff of Hertfordshire at Hoddesdon.[42] Similar high-profile visits took place at other well-known public schools. The 'open' units in working-class areas had no such opportunities. In addition the War Office, rightly fearful of Germany and the possibility of another world-wide conflict, was concerned about a likely shortage of junior commanders. Hence staff officers visited secondary schools that had a T.C.F. affiliation unit, the object being to persuade them to transfer to the O.T.C. so that their cadets could undergo pre-officer training.[43] By the outbreak of the Second World War in August 1939, the O.T.C. had a combined strength of 30,000 cadets in 183 contingents.[44] Clearly the

O.T.C. would not produce enough potential officers and a change of officer recruitment was required. Early in 1939 the War Office, in order to counter the dearth of officers, introduced a system of commissioning from the ranks. In a concomitant change the privilege of direct commissions for those cadets passing Certificate 'A' was abolished: thus a change of title became necessary, and the O.T.C. was re-named. The university units became the Senior Training Corps and the school-based units the Junior Training Corps (J.T.C.).

At the beginning of the decade efforts were still being made to ensure peace. In 1930 there was an international disarmament conference in London, and in 1932 another was convened at Geneva. They both failed. The various countries could not agree about the reduction in size of their armed forces. For a variety of reasons the international 'police force', the League of Nations was not doing what it was intended to do. The USA, the world's most powerful country, had refused to become a member. The League of Nations' powers, and hence its effectiveness, were therefore considerably reduced. And, significantly, both Germany and Japan withdrew from the League in 1933. It was therefore no surprise that the 1934 disarmament conference in Geneva adjourned *sine die*. Germany then decided to rearm in defiance of the Versailles Treaty. The economic sanction aimed at stopping Italy's aggression in Abyssinia between 1934 and 1936 did not work, and the League of Nations continued to display its lack of power. In 1936 Hitler annexed the Rhineland. The Locarno Treaties, which were supposed to guarantee the existing frontiers between Germany and her western partners, were swept aside. The seeds of war had been sown, which would promulgate destruction throughout Europe, and then the world. Everyone would feel the effects, including the cadet organisations.

In London on 9 March 1937, at a meeting in the Mansion House, a campaign was launched to expand the Navy League Sea Cadet Corps. The meeting was presided over by the Lord Mayor, Sir George Broadbridge, and there were speeches from Sir Thomas Inskip – Minister for the Co-ordination of Defence – Sir Alan Anderson M.P., Admiral the Earl of Cork and Orrery, and Lord Lloyd – the President of the Navy League.

The Lord Mayor spoke of the need for the 'provision of a reserve of man power' for the Royal Navy, and the requirement for patriotic and trained personnel. He added:

> ... this is what the Sea Cadet Corps movement provides, and it is to inaugurate a large development and expansion of this branch of the Navy League that this meeting has been called to-day.[45]

He lamented the fact that the City itself had no Sea Cadet Corps. Lord

55

Lloyd emphasised the difference between the countries dominated by dictators, such as Germany and Italy, where the youth was trained under compulsion, and the League's reliance on voluntary service. He added that if the desired expansion were to take place, money was necessary for investment in equipment and accommodation. Fortunately a benefactor was forthcoming in the form of Lord Nuffield, who said he would give a substantial amount to the Sea Cadet Corps. However, there was a condition. Lord Nuffield offered the large sum of £50,000, providing the Navy League raised another £100,000.[46] This the League vowed to do. There were also gifts from 'The Maharaja of Patiala, from Lord Wakefield, from Morgan Grenfell and Messrs. Vickers . . . P & O, Furness Withy, Royal Mail and Lloyds Bank'.[47]

There was a steady if unspectacular growth in Navy League cadet units during the early 1930s. But in the 12-month period from June 1937 to June 1938 there was a great increase, no doubt made possible by the large injection of cash from Lord Nuffield and the other donors. Twenty more units had already started, and another 11 were in the process of being formed.[48]

The unit at Harrogate was one of those formed during this period. Commander J. Irving of the Navy League, speaking at the opening of the unit, re-emphasised the message put forward by those ex-Crimean veterans who talked of disciplining the youth. He said:

> We dress the boy in the uniform of one of his Majesty's seamen, which immediately makes the boy want to play the part of the man.[49]

Commander Irving referred to the problem of Britain's Merchant Fleet being manned largely by foreigners. He said that the League did not function as a recruiting scheme for the Royal Navy or the Merchant Fleet. In spite of his words, his audience was aware of the increasing aggressiveness of Germany and the growing possibility of war, and may have felt that a greater degree of recruitment to the navy would be one of the results of the formation of the unit. Indeed, at a meeting in October 1938, the Navy League's sub-committee (which dealt specifically with the Sea Cadet Corps) considered the matter of how the Cadet Corps could best be utilised in the event of war. The League's Secretary visited the Naval Recruiting Officer in Whitehall, and agreed with the Assistant Director of Naval Recruiting that a roster of cadets willing to serve at sea 'for hostilities only' should be compiled, and should be made available to the Admiralty in the event of war.[50] The availability and suitability of sea cadet officers was also debated. It was decided that owing to the 'variety of age, experience and qualification' it was impossible to establish a formal system and that, so long as recruitment was voluntary, the officers should be allowed to select the Service of their choice.

The parents and the boys at Harrogate were obviously not deterred by the fact that war was on the horizon, as 63 boys enrolled and the unit became the 32nd of the Navy League Sea Cadet Corps units. It was not officially affiliated to the Navy League until 27 January 1939, by which time the company had expanded to 123 members. This rate of growth was not untypical. Since the injection of cash from Lord Nuffield the League was now able to give a grant of 30 shillings (£1.50) for each new recruit. There was also an initial free issue of uniforms, flags, rifles and so on, after which the unit was expected to fund itself. The age of entry was set at 12 and boys were asked to pay a subscription of a penny a week until they reached 14, when it rose to twopence per week.[51]

In April 1939 the President of the Navy League Cadets, Lord Lloyd, had a conference with the heads of the National Cadet Association (army) and the recently formed Air Defence Cadet Corps. It was decided that a demand for increased finance should be made 'to the authorities concerned, at the same time informing them that Parliamentary backing was available to support their request'.[52] Clearly, the cadet services realised the role that would be played by the uniformed military-affiliated youth organisations should the country go to war.

The year 1938 was significant, not only for the preparation of the Navy League Sea Cadets and the Territorial Army Cadet Force for war, but also for the formation of a third cadet organisation: the Air Defence Cadet Corps.

The Air League, an avionic equivalent of the Navy League, was formed in 1909. Its main objective was to stimulate an interest in aviation, and to educate people as to the 'vital importance to the British Empire of Air supremacy . . .'.[53] In 1910 the army developed military aviation on Salisbury Plain, and a year later the Air Battalion of the Royal Engineers was formed. This became a separate corps in 1912 and was then known as the Royal Flying Corps (R.F.C.). In 1914 the Royal Navy too had its own flying branch, namely the Royal Naval Air Service (R.N.A.S.). It was as a result of lessons learnt during the First World War about the needs and specific problems of air warfare that an amalgamated and separate military service, the Royal Air Force, was formed on 1 April 1918. Since 1921 the Royal Navy had fought to regain control of its air service, then renamed the Fleet Air Arm, which was an integral part of its fleet. However, it was not until 1937 that the Navy finally re-took control of the Fleet Air Arm from the R.A.F. The expansion in flying in general, and military aviation in particular, caught the imagination of many boys, and in retrospect it seemed inevitable that a youth organisation based on flying would be formed.

In 1929 two ex-R.A.F. members founded the Bournemouth Young Airmen's League with the idea of spreading 'the gospel of "airmindedness" among the younger generation'.[54] The Air League helped them in their endeavour; but it was not until the ex-pilot and retired R.A.F. officer, Air Commodore J. A. Chamier, became Secretary General of the Air League that a national air cadet organisation became a possibility. An initiative in teaching the young about flying had already been undertaken some years earlier when the Army Cadets, acting on the proposal of the Air Ministry, formed special platoons to be instructed in R.A.F. duties.[55] Cadets from Marlborough and Radley Colleges began to receive instruction in R.A.F. training at airfields in the mid-1930s. Rugby School had already formed an Air Section in 1937 as part of a plan to interest public-school boys in the work done by the R.A.F. Rugby's air section was small – its average pre-war strength was 15. It was attached to No. 18 Squadron R.A.F. Upper Hayford, near Oxford. The R.A.F. squadron occasionally provided instructors and even donated an old Bulldog frame with a Jupiter engine, and provided flights in Hind and Blenheim bombers. It is related in the history of Rugby School that at the following two annual camps, which involved 250 cadets each year, the R.A.F. provided squadrons of Ansons – 34 aircraft in total – for a whole week. They were used to ferry cadets 'each day to see demonstrations of the work of the various R.A.F. Commands'. In 1938 the final Field Day parade was inspected and addressed by the Marshal of the Royal Air Force the Viscount Trenchard, the founder of the R.A.F.[56] The enthusiasm was obviously there, but what was needed was a person with planning skills to expand the interest shown at Rugby and other schools, on a national basis. Air Commodore Chamier, Secretary-General of the Air League, was the best person to do this.

The scan of a demographic atlas quickly indicated to the Air Commodore which towns were large enough to support an additional youth organisation. The first problem would inevitably be to do with cost. The Army and the Navy League had addressed this question, and no doubt Chamier cited the Navy League's practice when he approached the Air Ministry for funds. The Air Ministry was enthusiastic and decided to match the sea cadet funding. It gave a grant of three shillings and sixpence a head (17p) to each squadron that passed certain efficiency tests.[57] The Air Ministry also gave the units free publications, loaned them training films and, where possible, affiliated their squadron to R.A.F. stations so that cadets could gain some flying experience. The money from the Air Ministry, although crucial, would not be sufficient. A plan had to be devised whereby a squadron could be self-financing. At an Air League luncheon given by the Duke of Sutherland, President of the Air League, a plan for the setting-up and running of an air cadet organisation was formulated. The new organisation was to be called the Air Defence Cadet Corps (A.D.C.C.).

It was envisaged that the air cadets would buy their own uniforms and pay a subscription of threepence per week. This was more expensive than the sea cadets and certainly beyond the pocket of most army cadets. This meant that membership of the air cadets, whether by design or not, was in practice restricted to boys from the middle classes, and older members who had a job. Perhaps this was inevitable, as starting an organisation from scratch was a very expensive business. Money was needed to pay for a central headquarters: it was estimated that £25,000 would cover this and the cost of eight regional organisers. It was also decided to copy the Navy League and set up civilian committees, whose job it was to raise funds for the squadron. Later in 1938 a group of prominent financiers from the City was gathered together by the Lord Mayor of London. And, as with the Navy League, they were persuaded to support a military-orientated youth organisation. Again Lord Nuffield assisted by donating £10,000, providing that the Air League raised the other £15,000. When a newly formed squadron wished to register with the A.D.C.C. H.Q., it had to demonstrate that it had or could raise, at least £200 to cover the first year's costs, and could also raise a similar sum for each of the following two years.[58]

In July 1938 the first two units were established – No. 1 (City of Leicester) Squadron and No. 2 (Watford) Squadron. In September another squadron was raised in Watford, and No. 4 Squadron was formed in Ilford. By the end of 1938, 42 squadrons had been established as far afield as Glasgow, Liverpool and London. Air Commodore Chamier said that the aim was to raise 50 squadrons by the end of 1938, and 'in 1939 we want to increase this number to two hundred'.[59] The first target was reached in January 1939 when Lambeth became the fiftieth to be inaugurated. The first 50 squadrons are distinguishable today by having the letter F included after their number.

There was obviously no shortage of recruits. A squadron would normally consist of 100 cadets in four Flights with seven officers and two adult warrant officers; in addition there might be civilian instructors who were 'employed' to teach specific topics. As in the army there were both 'open' and 'closed' (school) units. The former, like the sea cadets, had the major problem of finding suitable accommodation. Many of the new Air Defence Cadet Corps officers were teachers, and no doubt it was, in part, through their influence that a number of squadrons secured the use of a school as their H.Q. The more adventurous ones, such as Nottingham Squadron, raised enough money (£1,400) to a build a new hall, and to 'acquire 8 acres of open land for playing fields, parade ground and tracks for taxying practice ...'.[60] They then raised a further £3,000 for a new hangar and workshop, and an additional £2,000 to complete the project.

Squadrons soon became organised into formations known as Wings, and these were then grouped into Regions. The Wings equated to the T.C.F. counties. And, like the army cadets, the air cadet units became affiliated to regular or voluntary service units. In the case of air cadets these would be R.A.F. stations and/or Auxiliary Air Force Squadrons. This affiliation gave the air cadets supervised access to airfields, and, at times, additional expert instruction and hands-on experience. As in the other Services, each unit had a degree of autonomy, but the Wing and Regional Headquarters kept a supervisory eye on operations, and any communication with the Air Ministry was channelled through the A.D.C.C. at the Air League H.Q. in London.

The amount of aviation instruction and flying experience a cadet received depended on the expertise of his instructors, and the nearness of a unit to a R.A.F. station. Some of the larger public schools, as already noted in the case of Rugby School, had, because of their connections in the corridors of power, a distinct advantage. They even had combined operations. Haileybury, Rugby, Harrow and Berkhamstead Schools were in the habit of 'fighting' each other in joint exercises on, for example, the Duke of Bedford's estate. And the Royal Air Force would co-operate in these manoeuvres 'by sending fighters to throw flour-bag bombs at all troops who were badly concealed'.[61] This cavalier mode of training came to an abrupt end in 1939, and as far as it is recorded, has never been repeated.

By 1939 there was no pretence that the cadet movement was only providing a disciplined environment where a boy's character could be developed, and where if he so desired, he could pursue his interest in one of the Services. Clearly, efforts to recruit boys with the specific purpose of training them for entry into the Royal Navy, the Army or the Royal Air Force had become of paramount concern. The army and navy cadets had a long affiliation with their parent Services, and the word 'Defence' in the A.D.C.C.'s title indicated the aim of that organisation. The S.C.C., T.C.F. and A.D.C.C. were increasingly being referred to in the press and official publications as pre-service organisations. The question was: could they supply sufficient numbers of motivated, disciplined and partly trained young men for the enormous struggle that lay ahead?

Chapter 3 References

1. Minutes of the Navy League Committee Meeting, 7 June 1917
2. Minutes of the Navy League Committee Meeting, 15 November 1917, 20 November 1917 and 7 February 1918
3. M.A.O.8 [S.C.C.], History of the Sea Cadet Movement, p. 2
4. Ibid., p. 2
5. R. A. Westlake, *A Register of Territorial Cadet Units, 1910–1922* [Wembley: Westlake, 1984] pp. 25 & 32
6. Newport Sea Cadet Corps, 75th Anniversary pamphlet
7. Lt. Henry D. Capper R.N. (compiler), Royal Navy *Warrant Officers' Manual* [Portsmouth: R.N., 1910], p. 139
8. Westlake, op. cit., p. 60
9. Ibid., pp. 13 & 19
10. Ibid., p. 67
11. Col. L. W. Bennet O.B.E., 'Origins of the A.C.F.', in *The Cadet Journal*, Vol. IV, No. 6, 1942
12. M.A.O.10 [S.C.C.], *Rank and Status of S.C.C. Officers*, p. 1
13. Ibid.
14. M.A.O.8, op. cit. p. 3
15. A.C.F.A., *The Army Cadet Force Handbook* [London: A.C.F.A., 1955], p. 13
16. A.C.F.A., *The Cadet Story, 1860–1980* [London: A.C.F.A., 1982], p. 30
17. J. Springall et al., *Sure and Steadfast, a history of the Boys' Brigade, 1883–1983* [London & Glasgow: Collins, 1983], p. 115
18. Cdr. R. B. Hawkey R.N.R. [C.C.F.] *History of the Corps of Merchant Taylors' School, 1900–1981* [Rickmansworth: Roberts, 1981], p. 33
19. Ibid., p. 34
20. John Stevenson, *British Society, 1914–45* [Harmondsworth: Penguin, 1984], pp. 246–247
21. J. Springall et al., op. cit., p. 128–129
22. Carnegie Trust data quoted in J. Springall et al., op. cit., pp. 128–129
23. *The Cadet Story, 1860–1980*, op. cit., p. 27
24. Ibid., p. 27
25. Ibid., p. 32
26. *Sunday Times*, 30 November 1930
27. *The Cadet Story, 1860–1980*, op. cit., p. 27
28. Ibid., p. 33
29. Ibid., p. 33
30. Maj. D. A. Larder, 'A Very Potted History', in *The Cadet Journal*, Vol. LIII, January 1991
31. *The Cadet Story, 1860–1980*, op. cit., pp. 33–34
32. A.C.F.A., *The Cadet Forces Handbook* [London: A.C.F.A., 1961], p. 20

33 *The Cadet Story, 1860–1980*, op. cit., pp. 27–39
34 Ibid., pp. 40–45
35 Ibid., p. 41
36 J. Springall, *Youth, Empire and Society* [London: Croom Helm, 1977], pp. 78–79
37 Author unknown, 'Notes on The History of the 1st Cadet Battalion, The Queen's Regiment (West Surrey) 1918–1944' [Surrey Bn: Gale & Polden, 1945], pp. 7–8
38 *The Cadet Story, 1860–1980*, op. cit., p. 8
39 Ibid., pp. 46–47
40 A.C.F.A., *The Army Cadet Force* [London: A.C.F.A., 1949], p. 19 and A.C.F.A., *The Army Cadet Force Handbook* [London: A.C.F.A., 1961], p. 20
41 Cdr. R. B. Hawkey, op. cit., p. 37
42 Imogen Thomas, *Haileybury* [Hertford: Haileybury Society, 1987], p. 81
43 *The Cadet Story, 1860–1980*, op. cit., p. 47
44 *The Army Cadet Handbook*, op. cit., p. 13
45 *The Navy* [journal of the Navy League], Vol. XLII – No. 4, April 1937, p. 102
46 Ibid., p. 92
47 Ibid., p. 102
48 *Harrogate Advertiser*, 18 June 1938
49 Ibid.
50 Minutes of Navy League sub-committee meeting, 6 October 1938
51 *Harrogate Advertiser*, 18 June 1938
52 Minutes of Navy League sub-committee meeting, 10 April 1939
53 Wing Cdr. H. W. Lamond R.A.F. (Retd), *The History of the Air Training Corps 1938–1983* [unpublished: H.Q. A.T.C., 1984], p. 1-1
54 AC/27351/PR(ed. 3), *Air Cadet Facts*, No. 1, January 1983
55 *The Cadet Story, 1860–1980*, op. cit., p. 23
56 Lt.-Col. H. J. Harris, *Rugby School Corps, 1860–1960* [London: Brown, Knight & Truscott, 1960], pp. 146–147
57 H. W. Lamond, op. cit., p. 1-5
58 Ibid.
59 Alison Crosland, 'From A.D.C.C. to A.T.C.' in *Air Pictorial*, August 1990, p. 292
60 H. W. Lamond, op. cit., p. 1-9
61 Imogen Thomas, op. cit., p. 83

Chapter 4 – Propaganda, Recruitment and Expansion

It has been demonstrated that cadet numbers invariably increase in times of conflict. There is no disputing the fact that many boys craved excitement and, at the same time, had feelings of patriotism, which resulted in their joining the uniformed cadet organisations in 1860, from 1898 to 1902 and again from 1914 to 1918. However, the interesting question is this: what other external motivating factors, or coercion, induced boys in such large numbers to join the cadets in times of war? And, would boys once again flock to the Colours, given the horrors of the First World War and the resultant attitude of the public, which was understandably anti-militaristic?

The lack of Government support, combined with the anti-war literature of the 1920s and 1930s, indicate little enthusiasm for getting the boys back into uniform. The reduction in numbers bears this out. However, general public opinion or conjecture is not the best measure of adolescent behaviour. A boy's desire to enlist in a military organisation depended on a combination of powerful factors that were to do with imperialism and psychology, underpinned by the determined efforts of military leaders and the power of the youth culture. To obtain the answers to the questions posed it is necessary to go back to the nineteenth century.

FROM 1859 TO 1929

The institutions that created the dominant youth culture in nineteenth-century Britain were the schools and the publishers of, for want of a better description, children's literature. It was the public school ethos and its Victorian ideology based on obedience, service and duty that prompted the schools to form cadet corps in order to repel the threatened French invasion of 1859. The small number of 'open' navy cadet units and the quickly expanding 'open' army cadet units of the 1880s had much to do with disciplining youth. There was also an underlying feeling of imperialism – of duty to Country and Empire. This was particularly true of the leaders of the cadet organisations, who used the public-school ethos as their ideological template.

Imperialism was central to teaching in all schools, both state and private. 'Thus,' remarked MacKenzie, 'the great voyages, episodes of exploration, scenes of colonial military activity ... came to be vital sources of cross-disciplinary material, appropriate to history, geography and English'.[1] Patriotism and militarism were positively encouraged both in the written word and in diagrammatic form, as the iconography on school walls showed. There were illustrated wall charts depicting the victories of Nelson at Trafalgar and Wellington at Waterloo. Teachers were encouraged to foster an interest in the military with 'free gifts' from educational publishers of posters depicting 'Famous Figures', 'Ships' and 'Areas of the Empire'.[2] Even today, those who were at school in the 1950s can still remember the large wall map with its predominantly red shading, which showed the vast extent of the British Empire. By maintaining her military superiority, Britain made possible the maintenance of this extensive domination of land, trade and people. The navy controlled the seas and the army policed the land. Many of the boys' heroic figures would have been military men.

The theme of Empire and military service predominated in the emerging boys' magazines of the mid-nineteenth century. In 1855 the first issue of the *Boys' Own Paper* was published. The paper specialised in historical fiction. Articles with titles such as 'How I won my Spurs' and 'A Boy's Adventure in the Barons' Wars' were the main features, and there were articles on 'manly exercises' and 'physical prowess'. Later came magazines like Edward J. Brett's *Boys of England*, and in the latter half of the century this was followed by a plethora of journals for boys, such as: *The Young Briton, The Young Englishman, Sons of Britannia* and *Boys of the Empire*. The Education Act of 1870, which made schooling compulsory until the age of 13, led to a substantial rise in adolescent literacy. Therefore more youths were able to read the jingoistic propaganda that was the staple fare of the boys' magazines. To what extent the 'heroic' military stories in such papers as *The Boys' Friend* had an effect cannot be accurately gauged. Judging by the popularity of these publications, however, it would be realistic to assume that a boy's enthusiasm for joining a cadet unit may well have been increased. The magazines, like many of the books published, acted as recruiting agents for the army during the Boer War, with their romanticised accounts of military life on the Veldt.

Many authors supplied stories and articles for the boys' 'papers' and wrote books as well. And much of what was written was based on experience. The authors, because of their own backgrounds, tended to write about a particular branch or Service. William Kingston was one of the authors who turned his love of the sea and travel into fictional success. In 1879 he wrote the very first serial story for the *Boys' Own Paper*, titled 'From Powder Monkey to Admiral'. Previously he had edited his own paper for boys, which ran for three years, and he was for a time editor of another boys' paper called the *Union Jack*. He is, however, best remembered for his 'quartet of boys' yarns': *The Three Midshipmen* (1862), *The Three Lieutenants* (1874), *The Three Commanders* (1875), and *The Three Admirals* (1877). As the titles indicate, they tell the story of three adventurous friends from their early days as midshipmen to their years as high-ranking officers. Another naval enthusiast and children's writer was Harry Collingwood (his real name was W. J. C. Lancaster). Collingwood had been an outstanding student at the Royal Naval College, Greenwich before he graduated fully into the Royal Navy, before defective eyesight compelled him to leave the navy and seek employment in hydrography and harbour work. Nevertheless he was an inveterate traveller and he used his experience to good effect in his writing. Typical titles of his books were *A Middy in Command*, *With Airship and Submarine*, *A Strange Cruise* and *Across the Spanish Maine*.

George Alfred Henty was a writer who drew initially on his Crimean War experiences. He later became a journalist, and it was during his career as a newspaperman that he undertook a succession of journeys with powerful political and military figures. He accompanied Garibaldi on his Tyrolean campaign; reported on the Franco-German war, and went to Abyssinia with Napier. He also reported on the Austro–Italian war and, amongst other journalistic 'adventure' trips, accompanied the Prince of Wales (later King Edward VII) on his tour of India in 1875. Given this sort of experience it was not surprising that he wrote about the 'military and the mighty'. A sample of his books for boys indicates the influence of his experiences and the good use he made of them. The books include tales about military leaders, such as: *Under Drake's Flag* (1883), *With Clive in India* (1884), *With Wolfe in Canada* (1887), *With Buller in Natal* (1901), *With Roberts in Pretoria* (1902) and *With Kitchener in the Sudan* (1903). Teachers' manuals from the 1870s, and for many years after, recommended his *Book of Heroes* and 'the works of Henty'.[3] It is perhaps difficult for us in this age of sound-bites and pithy tabloid headlines to appreciate the propagandist prose of the Victorian era. In the *Boys' Own Magazine* of 1862 the leader-writer addresses the cadets of the London Rifle Corps, saying:

> You who are English boys and the coming English men ... have a feeling fostered by the consciousness of physical power, that should ripen into true bravery when time and example have taught you to temper it with mercy and moral courage. It is the rising of the tide of British pluck and patriotism in your hearts of oak that shall never ebb again, should bear you undaunted and undismayed through every danger and difficulty of life, whether national or personal, until the Almighty fiat shall bid those hearts to cease to beat, and your spirits to return to Him who gave them.[4]

It may be hard to believe today that cadets read such overtly jingoistic prose, but Henty, for example, produced on average three hefty books a year. Each was around 100,000 to 150,000 words in length, and what is more, his titles usually sold 150,000 copies a year. A large proportion of British youth were therefore familiar with the exploits of British military heroes and though the books consist of what today might be termed drama-documentary, they embraced the propagandist spirit of Empire. On a more mundane but no less important level, popular fiction brought a sense of imperial adventure and military splendour to the perhaps otherwise drab existence of many boys; and, says Springall, 'possibly created a frame of mind receptive to uniformed organisations'.[5] In doing so they also introduced the youth to Service jargon, military technology and Service ranks and titles. The military adventure stories could therefore be both entertaining and informative.

The study of the military in schools was not confined to the classroom. Military drill was part of the school curriculum. It was first introduced into the pauper schools in the 1850s, and subsequent education manuals included advice on drill instruction. It was not until the end of the century that drill was superseded by physical exercises. The setting up of cadet corps in the latter half of the nineteenth century could be viewed, in some respects, as an extension of the military induction experienced in the classroom, and on the school Parade Square (playground). In the public schools the cadet corps became an integral part of school life.

It is no accident that the clergy before the First World War started many of the army cadet units. They took their lead from the ethos of Christian militarism and athleticism inherent in the public schools. The growth of Christian militarism, evident since the Crimean War, 'owed a great deal to the religious literature using the stories of evangelical generals to create the image of the Christian soldier as hero'.[6] The Church Lads' Brigade units, most of which were affiliated to the Territorial Cadet Force prior to the First World War, would have embraced this perceived relationship between Church and State – Christianity and combat. Ideas about the proper development of boys and their religious beliefs – ideas that were associated with cadet training – were handed down the social scale via penny magazines, adventure books, school textbooks, teachers and cadet youth leaders.[7] The apotheosis of this constant propagandist pressure on cadets occurred in 1900 when a contingent of volunteers from the 1st Cadet Battalion the King's Royal Rifle Corps was sent to South Africa to fight in the Boer War.

The Navy League had since its inception kept up a constant propagandist mission in schools. Until 1903 this was predominantly in the public and preparatory schools for, as a writer in the League's journal put it, 'the classes from which the quarter deck is manned are educated'.[8] The elementary schools and the lower deck were not being totally ignored. After 1897 the Bristol and Liverpool Branches of the Navy League made the teaching of 'Naval History in the Elementary Schools their principal aim'.[9] In 1897 the Central Committee sent two circulars on naval history to schools throughout the country, one addressed to the masters the other to the boys. The Bristol Branch, when distributing the circulars, also invited the students to compete for prizes for the best essays on naval history of a specific period. The local Branch seems to have been reasonably successful in their endeavour as the following table shows:

Year	Subject	Schools	Boys
1897	The Seven Years' War	7	21
1898	The War with Napoleon	9	26
1899	History of English Navy During the Elizabethan Period	32	1,774
1900	History of English Navy During Period 1652–1659	38	2,388
1901	History of English Navy During Reign of Charles II	38	2,590
1902	History of English Navy During Period 1689–1748	38	3,039[10]

As a prize for the best essay, one of the League's Vice-Presidents presented a challenge shield. And in 1903 the competition, with a separate shield, was extended to include girls' elementary schools. The Navy League also instituted essay competitions 'to stimulate the scientific study of sea power', and, says MacKenzie, to 'encourage the development of the Nelson Cult'.[11] The prizes were presented on Trafalgar Day.

In addition to the circulars, the Navy League also distributed free textbooks on naval history to schools. This propagandist 'largesse' was not, however, popular with everyone. There was a certain amount of dissension in Bristol. It was not the masters or the boys who complained but, according to the Branch's Honorary Secretary, it was the 'peace-at-any price members of the School Board', who feared that by teaching naval history the Navy League and the school were encouraging a 'warlike spirit among the boys'.[12] The Navy League complained that if it were not for the lack of support from some members of the School Board the numbers participating in the competition would have been much larger. In 1908 the Education Committee of Surrey County Council ordered 400 copies of Admiral Eardley-Wilmot's book *The British Navy Past and Present*, which was published by the Navy League. The book was specifically for use in elementary schools.[13] The local branches appear to have worked hard and enthusiastically in their efforts to win support. In some schools the effort went beyond competitive essays and included the formation of League sub-branches. In 1910, for example, a meeting was held at the Grammar School in Burton with such a purpose in mind.

Lantern lectures were held in towns throughout the country. It was reported in March 1910 that lectures were being given on the aims of the

Navy League, the importance of naval defence and the history of the Royal Navy on three or four nights a week in south Oxfordshire. The same Branch had a further 18 illustrated lectures scheduled for the following month. The venues included village halls, town halls, and grammar schools.[14] Given the extent of coverage by the Navy League, both geographical and institutionally, it seems inevitable that a Navy League Boys' Brigade would eventually be formed, as in fact it was in 1910. Indeed, patriotic propaganda seems to have been everywhere. In the 1908 issue of *The Navy League* journal the advertisers announced that four more railway companies had bought copies of the large Navy League wall map, and that a third edition was now in production.[15] The League also produced postcards and cigarette cards depicting naval scenes; the latter were avidly collected by boys of all ages. While the Navy League was encouraging boys to take an interest in the Royal Navy and the Navy League, there were other associations that were also intent on capturing the interest of British youth.

The National Service League (N.S.L.) was founded in 1902 and its aims were not dissimilar to those of the Navy League. The N.S.L. also advocated compulsory military service, and although it was predominantly army-orientated it did not confine its membership to that particular Service. 'It incorporated Lord Meath's Lads' Drill Association of 1899, school cadet corps and more than 1,000 rifle clubs,' writes MacKenzie.[16] The N.S.L. used all the techniques employed by the Navy League plus public displays by the Territorial Cadet Force and performances by the Church Lads' Brigade bands. As its leader it had the prestigious Field-Marshal Lord Roberts, veteran of the Afghan and Boer Wars. The Field-Marshal toured the country speaking on behalf of the National Service League, and between 1910 and 1913 efforts were made to increase working-class membership; to this end Lord Roberts encouraged the formation of 'open' cadet units.[17] By the outbreak of war in 1914 the League (but not the cadet force) claimed a membership of 220,000.

The Imperial Federation League, which was founded by Lord Roberts in 1884, only lasted until 1893. There was also the League of the Empire that directed its efforts towards schools, and there was the Victorian League. There was even a Boys' Empire League, the secretary of which was Sir Arthur Conan Doyle, author of the Sherlock Holmes stories, who had seen service in the Boer War. Apart from the detective stories he also wrote adventure yarns about the military, such as *The Exploits of Brigadier Gerard* (1896) and *The Adventures of Gerard* (1903). Given the shocked reaction to the struggle in South Africa and the subsequent weight of propaganda promulgated in schools, the youth organisations and society at large, it is not surprising that cadet units increased tenfold.

Feelings of patriotism and imperialism and, as it turned out, a false expectancy of a quick victory at the outbreak of the First World War in 1914 saw an added increase in volunteers for the military, and this included the cadets. By the end of the war in 1918 there were 119,000 cadets in the Territorial Cadet Force. However, the enthusiasm for military youth organisations, particularly the T.C.F., was to change considerably at the termination of the war.

The horrors of the First World War are well documented, and it was said that it was the 'war to end all wars' – nothing so horrific could happen again. As a result it was to be expected that by the end of the First World War most adults ceased to want anything to do with the military. The disintegration of the Territorial Army Cadet Force was, in part, a reaction to the anti-war sentiment. It would be fair to assume therefore that the publishing of propagandist war tracts would be curtailed. In adult literature this may have been so, but with juvenile literature the reverse was true. The war accelerated production. Publishers such as Amalgamated Press increased their production of free cigarette cards of British and Colonial regiments, war heroes and naval engagements. It was said that the boys' papers produced by the media baron Lord Northcliffe, and his Amalgamated Press did 'more to provide recruits for our Navy and Army . . . than anything else'.[18] The *Daily Telegraph* began issuing a series of war books before the war ended. They were priced one shilling and by 1915 over 20 titles had already been produced. They included books on the navy, different regiments and battles fought. The fourth edition of the children's book, *The Wonder Book of Soldiers*, published just after the war in 1919, concentrated on the glamorous and adventurous side of war. The historical interpretation was both romantic and, at times, prone to hyperbole. Trench warfare was described as 'a wonderful development'.[19] The writers did not accurately communicate the reality of war to the adolescent reader, but preferred to concentrate on the heroic exploits. The popularity of Henty after the war never waned. He continued to inform schoolchildren about British heroes, the explorers, the admirals and the generals. Indeed, in the 1950s his publisher boasted that his books had sold over 25 million copies.[20]

The boys' papers, despite the printing restrictions and paper shortage during the First World War, continued to be produced and were popular. The concentration on military action acted as a stimulus to recruiting and gave the uniformed youth organisations 'a significant part in the war effort'.[21] The stories concerned with observation, passing of military messages and spy catching could be imported into the cadets' training. Indeed, according to Springall, members of youth organisations were urged to wait around on stations to look out for deserters and to ensure that recruits joined their trains.[22]

The inculcating of a sense of duty and service was not confined to lessons and the written word. Reginald Brabazon, twelfth Earl of Meath, made the socio-psychological 'tradition' of the Empire movement and its concomitant demands for discipline, duty and defence, into a public demonstration. He did this through the Empire Day Movement. Earl Meath, a diplomat, had served in Germany in the late nineteenth century where he became concerned by that nation's imperialist ambition. He believed that British youth, to combat this, 'required a further and deeper understanding of the glory which was the British Empire in order to ensure its survival'.[23] And later, in the Edwardian period, he found the vehicles that were most suitable for demonstrating his patriotic feelings, and propagandist aims. He became Vice-President of the Navy League (1909), and a member of several patriotically-orientated organisations, namely: the Executive Council of the National Service League (1910–14), the General Council of the Legion of Frontiersmen (1911), the League of Empire and a Commissioner for the Boy Scouts Association (1910). All these bodies were involved with schools and, albeit indirectly, with the cadet movement. He was also on the Committee of the Lads' Drill Association, which was not dissimilar to the army cadets, its aims being to promote the 'systematic physical and military training of all British lads, and their instruction in the art of the rifle'.[24] The propagandist message was, writes Mangan, 'chauvinistic, severe and puritanical'. Labour and Liberal Members of Parliament alike voiced their concern. They were worried by the emergence of militarism in British education, encouraged by such individuals as Earl Meath and his associated youth organisations. The patriotic and jingoistic Earl was not alone in his views, however. The philosophy of the Empire Movement is demonstrated in a tract titled *Essays on Duty and Discipline: a Series of Papers*. Supporters of and contributors to the tract were eminent figures of the Establishment. The list includes the Earl of Cromer, Lord Curzon, Viscount Esher, Baden-Powell and Winston Churchill.[25] The churches too, from the Archbishop of Canterbury and the Roman Catholic Archbishop of Westminster (who wrote an essay titled 'The Paramount Need of Training in Youth') down to the clergy of various denominations, who were padres to the cadet units, were keen supporters of the cadet movement.

The Empire Movement, which Earl Meath set up in 1913, was not inconsequential. In 1928 the *Morning Post* claimed that five million children took part in the Empire Day Ceremonies. Empire Youth Sunday, like Remembrance Sunday, was an occasion when cadets paraded publicly. On Empire Day Sunday it was often the cadet organisations that led the procession. They provided the parade commander, the ceremonial drill, the standard-bearers and the bands. In fact the Empire Day ceremony and accompanying parade provided the cadet organisations with maximum publicity by giving the cadets the chance to be reviewed by high-ranking military and civic dignitaries. The Empire Day parades were seen throughout Britain and in those colonies that had cadet corps of their own. 'The presence of uniformed youth in these rituals,' wrote MacKenzie, 'reflected the origins and history of such movements in late Victorian and Edwardian times.'[26] The Navy League had, since 1919, distributed circulars and leaflets to all education authorities requesting that Trafalgar Day be celebrated, and that a half hour be set aside to discuss the sea services and the debt the Empire owed to the Royal and Merchant Navies. The sea cadets were to the fore in celebrating the Trafalgar tradition. Each year the Navy League had responsibility for the presentation and arrangement of the Trafalgar Day ceremonies in London's Trafalgar Square.

The stress on the importance of Empire may have become less militaristic after the Great War but it was nonetheless still powerfully patriotic, particularly with regard to the training of youth. George Orwell, writing in the midst of the Second World War, explains how youth, since 1918, had never really stopped being prepared for war:

> As the war fell back into the past, my particular generation, those who had been 'just too young', became conscious of the vastness of the experience they had missed. You felt yourself a little less than a man because you had missed it. I spent the years 1922–7 mostly among men a little older than myself who had been through the war. They talked about it unceasingly, with horror, of course, but also with a steadily growing nostalgia. You can see this nostalgia clearly in the English war-books. Besides, the pacifist reaction was only a phase, and even the 'just too young' had all been trained for war. Most of the English middle class are trained for war from the cradle onwards, not technically but morally. The earliest political slogan I can remember is 'We want eight [eight dreadnoughts] and we won't wait'. At seven years old I was a member of the Navy League and wore a sailor suit with HMS Invincible on my cap. Even before my public-school O.T.C. I had been in a private school cadet corps. On and off, I have been toting a rifle ever since I was ten . . .[27]

THE 1930s

The 1920s can be seen in antithetical light in that publicly there was a definite move away from things military, and yet tremendous efforts were made to promote the very thing which depended, in large part, on the military: namely, Britain's Empire. This dichotomy was manifested in two ways, first, the anti-war adult literature and the opposing jingoistic propaganda in children's books; secondly, the uniformed youth movements were dividing themselves into two camps: the minority affiliated to the military, and the 'civilianised' remainder, the majority. With regard to the latter, the Boys' Brigade had divorced itself from the army cadets, and the Church Lads' Brigade finally severed its relationship with the T.C.F. in 1934. The major military youth organisation, the Territorial Cadet Force, was now more isolated, some might say independent. However, the 'non-military' uniformed organisations still retained their military-style structure, training and accompanying trappings.

The 1930s saw a convergence of aims and objectives, particularly those appertaining to the military cadets, as the threat of war grew nearer. Expansion in the cadet movement, prior to the Second World War, was brought about, in the first instance, by technological advances in aviation. The sea and air cadets' development was also helped significantly by a large injection of cash from Lord Nuffield. And pressure groups led by leading military figures ensured that cadets from each of the services were as ready as could be expected for the forthcoming conflict. There was a change of public attitude towards the military, and hence towards the cadets, as the possibility of war became more evident. The interest of youth in things military was stimulated by what could be seen in the cinema, and in the writings of Captain W. E. Johns and other notable children's authors.

The greatest advance, certainly in military terms, was the growth of aviation. As aircraft technology advanced so records were being broken regularly. In June 1919 Flight Lieutenants John Alcock (pilot) and Arthur Whitton-Brown (navigator) were the first to fly the North Atlantic. They did this in a Vickers-owned Vimy bomber and won £10,000 in prize money. The first flight to Australia was undertaken in the same year. Also in 1919 the first commercial air service to the continent was started. The following year the R.A.F. held its first flying pageant at Hendon. But perhaps the greatest fillip to aviation came from Jacques Schneider, a Frenchman, who started an international airspeed competition for which he presented a trophy in 1913. In 1925 the R.A.F. set up a High Speed Flight specially designed to compete for the Schneider trophy. In 1927 the R.A.F. team won the trophy for the first time. The speed achieved was 281.7 mph. They won it again in 1929 with a speed of 328.6 mph, and repeated their success again in 1931 at a speed of 340 mph. Thus having won it on the third consecutive occasion the competition was ended. This feat was to have an important effect later on when the Spitfire was being developed. At the time the race for the trophy generated a great deal of interest in flying and the R.A.F.

The success of the R.A.F. flying team was echoed by the exploits of the civil aviators. The most notable of these was the first solo flight across the Atlantic from New York to Paris by the American pilot Charles Lindbergh, in 1928. Two years later Amy Johnson made the first solo flight by a woman from England to Australia. There were many other notable civilian aviation achievements. It was about this time, in 1930, that the R.A.F. began to take a greater interest in promoting the Service. The Air League formed by army aviators in 1910 and then taken over by the R.A.F., started Empire Day air displays in 1934. The air festival, which took place every summer, marked Queen Victoria's birthday, which was on 24 May. This became Britain's annual national aviation festival. It received tremendous public support and thereby 'stimulated recruitment to the R.A.F.'.[28] No doubt the increasing high profile of the R.A.F. also hastened plans for the formation of an air cadet corps.

When Air Commodore J. A. Chamier, the Secretary-General of the Air League, began his plans to start the Air Defence Cadet Corps (A.D.C.C.) in the mid-1930s there were already thousands of young enthusiasts just waiting to join such an organisation. As noted in the previous chapter, it was a question of raising the cash, formulating a policy, obtaining accommodation and organising training. It was not an easy undertaking, but the task was made considerably easier by the public's enthusiasm for flying and the Air Ministry's drive for recruits.

A youngster who was enthusiastic about aviation and wanted to join the A.D.C.C. may have counted one of those trans-oceanic or Schneider trophy race record breakers amongst his 'heroes'; however, the chances are that the most influential figure was neither, instead it was a fictional character. The most widely followed 'aviator' among the young, and arguably the greatest individual recruiter the Air Training Corps, the R.A.F., and the Fleet Air Arm ever had was 'Biggles', or to be more correct, his creator the author Captain W. E. Johns. William Earl Johns was born in Hertford and educated at the local grammar school. At the beginning of the First World War he enlisted in the Norfolk Yeomanry. After service in Salonica he was commissioned before being seconded to the Royal Flying Corps in 1916. He was then 23 years of age. He later saw action in France as a fighter-pilot before being shot down by the famous German air ace Ernst Udet in 1918. He was subsequently captured and sentenced to death, but managed to escape. He was recaptured and spent the remainder of the war in a punishment camp in Bavaria. It was his wartime experiences with the R.F.C. and the R.A.F. that were the basis of his many books. Johns enjoyed his time with the R.F.C. and decided to remain in the forces after the war. He served with the R.A.F. until 1930, when he transferred to the Reserves, retaining his old R.F.C. rank of Captain.

W. E. Johns began writing about aviation for youngsters when he contributed to the twopenny weekly magazine *The Modern Boy* in 1929, and soon he was writing a regular feature under the title 'Flying Officer W. E. Johns'. In 1932 Johns became a founder-editor of a new aviation magazine called *Popular Flying*, which was primarily aimed at the adult market. At the time most of the tales of aerial combat written for youngsters were in American pulp magazines, in which the aerial adventures attributed to the US airmen had been, according to Johns, performed by British pilots.[29] Therefore he wanted to 'put the record straight' and at the same time portray the realities of air combat and 'present a true picture of the kind of officer who had served in . . . the Royal Flying Corps, the Royal Naval Air Service and the Royal Air Force'.[30] Thus he included a series of short stories in *Popular Flying* about a young pilot called James Bigglesworth of No. 266 Squadron – the best Sopwith Camel pilot in the R.F.C. The first story was called 'The White Fokker'. Later he began writing books. One of the earliest was *Biggles Learns to Fly* (1935), a retrospective story that became the start of Biggles' career, in paperback. As Johns' experiences related to the First World War the opponents in his books were, more often than not, German, and with the rise of Hitler and the Nazis in the 1930s there was no reason to change the enemy's nationality. The war provided the author with a panoptic field for his writings. This is evident by a selection of his wartime titles, which include: *Biggles Goes to War* (1938), *Biggles Secret Agent* (1940), *Biggles Defies the Swastika* (1941), and *Biggles Sweeps the Desert* (1942).

W. E. Johns was not the only writer of military fiction for younger readers. Captain Charles Gibson, who served in the army in the Boer War and the navy in the First World War, began writing military adventure stories in 1908. He was still penning novels during the Second World War. They had such 'evocative' titles as *Out of the Nazi Clutch* (1940), and *Sons of the Sword* (1941). There were other writers of this genre, some of whom were more prone to jingoistic hyperbole than others. Inevitably W. E. Johns, being the best known and by far the most prolific of the writers, came in for criticism, the bulk of it retrospective. He was accused of being a warmonger, an accusation he vehemently denied. As Ellis and Williams, W. E. Johns' biographers, point out, his loathing of war is apparent in his writing. As evidence they cite a passage which is untypical of the usual 'blood and thunder' stories for boys that was produced by other authors. It comes from the 1939 Biggles book entitled *The Rescue Flight*. It concerns the thoughts of a young pilot flying over the lines of the Western Front in the First World War:

For the first time he began to perceive what war really meant: he felt the relentlessness of it – the ruthlessness, the waste, the cruelty, the incredible folly of it. It gave him a shock to realise that he did not know what everybody was fighting for. Something about Belgium . . .[31]

Nevertheless Johns believed that military strength can act as a deterrent and he therefore advocated re-armament and supported the idea of a 'balance of power'.[32]

Despite the opinion of critics, Johns was considered an asset by the military authorities. At the outbreak of war in 1939 he attempted to enlist, but was told that at 46 years of age he was too old. He was offered a post at the Air Ministry, but rejected it. Instead he offered his services to the Air Defence Cadet Corps. And so the editor of the *Air Defence Cadet Corps Gazette* was able to write in August 1940 that:

> We have been fortunate in securing the collaboration of Captain W E Johns, well-known to all of you as the editor of *Popular Flying* and author of many thrilling books of air stories. In this issue he writes an interesting article on the qualities that make up an air 'ace'.[33]

He was to become a regular contributor to the air cadet magazine. Captain Johns was also employed as a volunteer lecturer with the A.D.C.C., and continued to do this work when it became the Air Training Corps in 1941. He lectured on subjects as diverse as 'Combat Tactics in the Air' and 'Escaping from POW Camps'. By all accounts his manner was enthusiastic and, of course, his talks were enlivened by countless personal anecdotes.[34] Johns also began a regular column in the *Boys' Own Paper* called 'Skyways: Jottings from My Log-Book'. This was devoted almost exclusively to the activities of the Air Training Corps. He did the same in the *Girls' Own Paper*; in this case the subject matter was the Women's Auxiliary Air Force (W.A.A.F.). Indeed, in response to popular demand and prompting by the Air Ministry, Johns produced a Biggles counterpart, namely *Worrals of the WAAF*. The stories feature Flight Officer Joan Worralson, and her friend Section Officer Betty 'Frecks' Lovell. The girls were pilots and their main task was to fly aircraft from the manufacturing depots to the fighter stations; the stories mirrored what the women pilots were actually doing at the time. The publishers of the second Worrals book *Worrals Flies Again* (1942), Hodder & Stoughton, remarked that Captain Johns was alive to every phase of R.A.F. history and was not likely to overlook the part women were playing in that 'new historic age'.[35] The readers naturally expected Biggles to take part in the major battles, hence there had to be a book about Biggles and the Battle of Britain. However, Johns had to up-date his R.A.F. jargon otherwise Biggles would be seen to be woefully out-of-touch. In the earlier books Johns' pilots were not using r/t (radio/transmitters) which had become standard equipment by the 1940s, and pilots no longer referred to 'Archie' but used words like 'flak' and 'ack-ack'. And so, after some consultation with an R.A.F. officer, who supplied him with a list of common usage and contemporary slang, he up-dated his flying vocabulary. The result was *Spitfire Parade*.[36]

The War Office noticed the effect the Biggles books were having on A.T.C. and R.A.F. recruiting, and therefore asked Johns to produce a soldier hero. The outcome was the appearance of a commando, Captain Lorrington King, known as 'Gimlet'. Gimlet was not Biggles in khaki uniform; he was a different sort of character altogether. As the blurb on the jacket of *Gimlet Goes Again* (1944) explains:

> His methods are not always as gentlemanly as Biggles. When things get rough he's apt to get tough. Which is why, of course, he was given a bunch of wildcats to command. After all, kid gloves are about as useful to a commando on his job as roller skates would be to a steeplejack.[37]

The first of his wartime Gimlet books was *King of the Commandos* (1943). The reviews of the book were very favourable, and the *Times Educational Supplement* critic said that everything Gimlet and his three close companions do is 'made to seem plausible, possible and at the same time exciting'.[38]

Between 1931 and 1939 Capt. Johns wrote hundreds of articles, produced numerous tracts on flying and had 40 books published, 18 of which were about Biggles and his flying adventures. According to the compiler of *The Who's Who of Children Literature* 'he did more for service [and cadet] recruiting than a million posters'.[39] Alan Morris in his book about the R.A.F. says:

> I cannot express the Nation's debt to his (W E John's) 'Biggles' books, which encouraged thousands to join the Auxiliary Air Force and R.A.F. Volunteer Reserves or to acquire an A Licence in time for September 1939. These, together with his mid-thirties advocacy – often impish but always unmistakable – of an appropriate strategic bomber force can never be properly rewarded.[40]

The very large number of future R.A.F. pilots of the time, perhaps the majority, acquired their initial interest from 'Biggles' and their subsequent training from the Air Defence Cadet Corps.

The Navy, and hence the sea cadets, was not without its unofficial recruiters. The best known was Cecil Scott Forester, the creator of Horatio Hornblower R.N. The character Hornblower first made his appearance in the novel *The Happy Return* (1937). Although the stories are set in the late eighteenth and early nineteenth century they evoked feelings of pride in the sailors of the twentieth century. He wrote *Flying Colours* (1938), the award-winning *A Ship of the Line* (1939), and *The Commodore* (1944). Forester's consummate talent as a storyteller, and his ability to convey the challenge and satisfaction of life at sea, must have drawn boys to join the sea cadets, with the eventual aim of enlisting in the navy. Hornblower was not depicted as a 'gung-ho' sort of hero, he was, as Evelyn Hughes says, likeable and believable in that he was an 'unheroic hero, liable to make mistakes and face up to the consequences'.[41] And this was what made the stories so popular with the public. Forester was also a Hollywood scriptwriter in the 1930s.

Warfare contains all the ingredients – tension, conflict, romance, glamour and excitement – necessary for cinematography. The army was aware of this, and comprehended the power of film from an early date. Film had been used in a documentary and propagandist manner during the Boer War. Later, during the First World War, the War Office realised more than ever the power of film and set up an official Cinematography Committee in 1916 to make army and navy films.

In the 1920s and early 1930s public war films were popular, although films like *Tell England* and *Journey's End* (1930) could be considered as nostalgic anti-war movies. There were sentimental films such as *Mademoiselle from Armentieres* (1926) and *Blighty* (1930). In film, the 'image is the message'; the film maker is more reliant on emotion and less on reality. Reality may be historically correct, but it may not be very entertaining, and is not usually good box-office. Walter Webster reviewed *The Charge of the Light Brigade* (1936), a film dealing with the heroism of the British Army, and said inter alia:

> Of course it is not true but it does give Hollywood the chance to present to the world a magnificent picture of the splendour of British rule . . .[42]

Other entertainingly propagandist films of the 1930s included *The Lives of a Bengal Lancer* (1935), *The Drum* (1938), *Gunga Din* (1939) and *The Four Feathers* (1939). In the last, the director changed the authentic dark blue uniforms worn by the officers at the regimental ball to scarlet, remarking that 'This is Technicolor'. The effect was historically inaccurate, but according to *The New York Times* the film was 'an imperialist symphony'.[43] The films of the period reinforced the patriotic teaching in schools, and the messages conveyed in the Empire parades headed by the cadets, and they encouraged the resurgent interest in the military. As Richards points out:

It is surely more than coincidence that many of the leading soldiers of the Empire – such as Gordon, Rhodes, Kitchener, Stanley and Baden Powell – through their achievements, and known support for youth activities, became icons for the youth.[44]

The 1930s were 'pre-eminently Hollywood's imperial decade, when the ethos and rituals of British imperialism were given glamorous celluloid life'.[45] It was also a time when the average weekly cinema audience rose from 18 to 23 million – about 50 per cent of the population. The greatest number and most frequent cinema-goers came from the 'working-class urban young'. Given the interest of the cadets in the military it is safe to assume that many of them must have taken a keen interest in such films, which further stimulated their enthusiasm for military service. This use of film was to be employed to good effect during the war, when for the first time films were made specifically to encourage the recruitment of cadets.

THE ONSET OF WAR AND THE 1940s

Whenever the country goes to war there is a renewed wave of patriotism and propaganda. The shortage of paper and the resulting printing restrictions meant that publishers directed most of their output towards the patriotic war effort. Other publications, such as comics and much of the children's literature, ceased to be produced. No doubt the more literate cadets scanned the adult magazines dealing with military matters. The sea cadets, for example, could read *The Navy Today* (1939) published by Blackie, and Low and Odhams' illustrated volumes on *Britain's Merchant Fleet* (1942). Significantly, though, despite the paper restrictions, all three arms of the cadet services were permitted, and no doubt encouraged, to start producing their own journals.

The expansion of the cadet movement occurred in two distinct phases, before 1942 and after 1942. The catalyst for this development was the Government. In 1916 the Government wanted to deal with the problem of juvenile delinquency, during the 1930s the drive was for physical fitness. In the 1940s, writes Springall et al., the Government was primarily concerned with the 'all-round' development of 'Britain's nearly 3 million 14 to 20 year-olds who had left school and whose welfare had for too long been neglected by the State'.[46] A National Advisory Youth Council was established. This was the foundation of today's Youth Service. The Board of Education, in consultation with the National Advisory Youth Council produced the Government Circular 1516, *The Challenge of Youth*, in June 1940 which detailed the aims for expansion. It also contained a directive to Local Education Authorities instructing them to set up boys' clubs, youth centres, evening institutes and other clubs. Thus the local authorities were encouraged to help provide training centres for the ever-expanding youth organisations and this included the pre-service Cadet Movement.[47] A subsequent document, Circular 1577, issued in December 1941, had the greatest impact on the cadet organisations. It recommended the registration of all young people of both sexes, aged from 16 to 17, for national services. This was to be supervised via officials appointed by the local office of the Ministry of Labour. This Government involvement was as a result of tours of the manufacturing areas of the midlands and north-west in 1940 by Ernest Bevin, the Minister of Labour and National Service.

Bevin was concerned that many of the facilities previously available to the youth had been withdrawn and other activities had been curtailed. A resultant worry, as experienced in the First World War, was the increasingly disruptive and alienating behaviour of some teenagers. Many men – fathers, teachers and youth leaders – were in the Forces and more mothers were being employed in war work, hence the youth were under less parental control.[48] Another reason given for an increase in crime was the arrival of evacuees from the cities to the quieter rural areas. For example, it was reported in the *Shrewsbury Chronicle* that growth in juvenile crime in the town was due to the influx of evacuees from Liverpool.[49] Bevin felt that the youth of the country was being forgotten, and was not being properly supervised. In order to tackle these problems he sanctioned, indeed positively encouraged, the expansion of youth movements.[50] Youngsters who registered by order under the Defence Regulations were invited to attend interviews conducted by representatives from the local Youth Committee, voluntary youth organisations including the Sea, Army and Air Cadets, and the Home Guard.[51] Those interviewees who were found to be 'unattached' were advised, though not compelled, to join a suitable youth organisation or pre-service (cadet) unit. For example, in Shrewsbury in January 1943 the Higher Education Committee reported that '4,500 boys and girls (in the 16 to 17 age group) had been interviewed; of these 3,200 were advised to join a youth organisation or do community service: 1,300 had done so. Many of them joined the growing pre-service A.C.F. and A.T.C. units'.[52]

What came to light during this national youth registration was the lack of facilities for girls. They, like their male counterparts who were doing pre-service training, wanted to be involved in the war effort. As a result the Girls' Training Corps, Women's Junior Air Corps and the Girls' Naval Training Corps were formed during the war. These organisations were not affiliated to the Service Departments, but they were supported by the Ministry of Education. However, there was a close liaison between the Girls' Corps and the cadet organisations. Funding for the girls' organisations came from the Local Education Authority.[53] The girls' units did benefit by receiving instruction from officers and adult N.C.O.s serving in the cadets. The amount of assistance depended on the degree of co-operation that existed at the local level. There was also a social mix at unit dances; parties and social evenings were often combined. However, it was to be another 30 years or more before girls were finally admitted to the cadet movement proper!

'This interference' as Springall puts it 'of the State in the liberty of the adolescent has excited little comment from the historian.'[54] Accounts vary as to the amount of pressure that was exerted on an individual to join an organisation. The voluntary nature of the organisations and the Youth Service meant that, even in wartime, no one could be forced to join or serve. What the process of registration of youth did was alert the adolescent to the options available; this was a useful service, particularly as some of the organisations and their local units were very new. The author of the army cadet history made an interesting and valid point when he wrote:

> It is remarkable how the largest expansion that the Cadet movement has ever seen, and which was entirely military in nature, to meet war conditions, had its primary origin deeply rooted in a social need. It was the needs of the adolescent first, rather than the military necessity, which caused the development.[55]

PRE-SERVICE CADET ORGANISATIONS

Expansion of the sea cadets from 1939 onwards was evident, not just in the number of units, but in the sizes of the units. Those inland training ships that were located near ports which had a long naval tradition attracted large numbers of cadets. Bristol, for example, had 155 cadets in April 1939; by February 1944 there were over 300. Indeed, even inland units such as Canterbury had over 100 boys on parade for their annual inspection, and the newly formed Cheltenham unit had 75 cadets. When war broke out in the summer of 1939 there were 100 Navy League Sea Cadet Corps units with 9,000 cadets in training.[56] This, however, was not enough. The Second World War, like the one 20 years previously, was evidently going to be a long drawn-out and protracted affair. In order to sustain the effort for an indefinite period more and more trained seamen would be wanted, for both the Royal and the Merchant Navy. As a result of meetings between the Navy League Committee and the Admiralty, approval had been given for an expansion to 25,000 cadets in 250 Units.[57]

Numbers grew steadily and, compared to today's figures, units were extremely large. In 1940 the Bournemouth unit had 134 cadets, Brighton 170. To maintain the units, fund-raising became a major occupation of the

Navy League Sea Cadet Corps. Efforts to raise cash were often combined with social occasions. These could be profitable affairs as there was nearly always a full turnout of cadets. Hence, Worthing's first dance attracted over 150 cadets; there were 120 at Swansea's Christmas party despite the hazard of getting to the headquarters through the blackout. And at Halifax's first 'parents and friends night' in the summer of 1940, there were 90 cadets on parade ready for inspection. The response regarding recruitment in the first 18 months of war was gratifying, but would it be enough?

On 27 September 1939 the Prime Minister Neville Chamberlain ordered the Royal Navy's fleet to be mobilised. There was no immediate need for recruits as the British Navy was superior in size to the German and Italian navies combined.[58] But within a year the balance of naval power began to change. The invasion of Norway and Denmark by Germany in April 1940 signalled the beginning of the enemy's control of the European coast from the Arctic to the Bay of Biscay. In June 1940 the Royal Navy took part in the largest combined operation ever seen. This was the evacuation of British forces from the beaches of Dunkirk. The Royal Navy and the Merchant Fleet, along with hundreds of small private craft, evacuated 338,226 soldiers from Dunkirk's coastal battlefield. The army lost most of its equipment, and its casualty list during the months of May–June amounted to 68,111. The navy also suffered considerable losses. Six destroyers and 7,000 sailors were lost during the operation.[59] In the same year the navy incurred the loss of 26 submarines. The deficiency in manpower, particularly in experienced officers, could not be made up simply by training more ex-public schoolboys to man the ship's bridge, or drafting in additional R.N.V.R. personnel. The navy was still to some extent restricted by the harness of social tradition until Winston Churchill, ex-First Sea Lord, became Prime Minister in 1940. One of his notable 'prayers', writes Captain Wells, was to 'overturn an Interview Board decision on Dartmouth entry that failed three candidates on the grounds that one had a slight Cockney accent and the other two were sons of a chief petty officer and a merchant navy engineer'.[60] Clearly there was little point in having a competitive examination if the criterion for entry was social class; pragmatic efficiency was the new order. The navy was becoming more technically advanced and personnel required more training. This was to affect sea cadet training. The Royal Navy would experience a fourfold increase in numbers in the years from 1939 to 1945. In the Battle of the Atlantic, which was to reach its zenith between March and June 1941, much merchant shipping was lost; in April alone 700,000 tons of shipping was sunk. And the repercussions of this were felt in the cadet movement.

81

The year 1942 was a watershed in the development of the sea cadet movement. The words 'Navy League' were dropped from the Corps' title, and it was renamed the Sea Cadet Corps. At the same time the Admiralty and the Navy League became as close as they had ever been since the Admiral Commanding Reserves took over the training role. The Corps also achieved greater public recognition when HM King George VI became Admiral of the Corps. In keeping with the closer ties with the Admiralty, and perhaps in recognition of the essential war work being done, Sea Cadet officers were granted Royal Navy Volunteer Reserve status, although in the case of part-time volunteer officers, this was to be a short-lived privilege. In February 1942 the Admiralty, in order to make up for the shortfall in recruits and to cut down on training time by enrolling more partly-trained cadets, was most eager to expand the Sea Cadet Corps. The Admiralty was anxious to increase the number of units to 400 and to double the number of cadets to 50,000.

The Navy League, ever-suspicious of the Admiralty, was concerned that if the League did not undertake this expansion it would 'run the risk of having the whole administration of the Sea Cadet Corps taken out of their hands and run as a department of the Admiralty'.[60] Some, no doubt, saw this possibility as a distinctive 'plus'; finance, accommodation, administration, kitting-out, training and equipment would then be the problem of the Admiralty. It would also mean that the new-found status of the officers and, hence the Corps, could be safeguarded. The Navy League hierarchy, however, was not about to acquiesce. The S.C.C. Secretary attended a conference at the Whitehall with Admiral Sir Lionel Halsey, and made certain tentative financial proposals. In effect he proposed that the Navy League would undertake the expansion provided it was not necessary to draw upon its invested reserves, which were the ultimate guarantee of the continuance of the League. At a meeting of the League's finance committee a plan was devised, and the following resolution was agreed unanimously:

> That the Committee accepts the Admiralty suggestion to increase the Sea Cadet Corps to 50,000 Cadets in approximately 400 Units by the end of 1943, relying on the provision by the Admiralty of financial assistance on the basis proposed by the Finance Committee, namely an immediate bloc grant of £7,000; the payment by the Admiralty of the salaries of Area Officers and the payment to the Navy League on the 1st July of 50% of the annual grants estimated to be payable for the year.[61]

The Committee made it clear that 'this provision was for the year 1942 only', and the League reserved the right to 'make supplementary proposals for 1943 if necessary'.[62] The Honorary Treasurer said that even if these proposals were to be approved it would be necessary for the League to sell invested stock 'to the value of approximately £10,000 to provide a float for the current expenditure' for the next six months. At the same meeting there was a review of League Staff salaries. It was agreed that when Executive staff were travelling on duty they should receive first-class railway fares and an increase in subsistence allowance. In view of the envisaged additional administrative burden for the General Secretary it was proposed that his salary be increased by £150 per annum for the year 1942. The proposals were set before the Admiralty in March 1942.

Britain was facing an acute shortage of manpower. 'Between Dunkirk and December 1941 a series of measures were introduced culminating in the National Service Act.'[63] So, in effect, and to use a naval term, the League had the Admiralty 'over the proverbial barrel'. It was no surprise therefore that on 5 March 1942 the Admiralty accepted the League's proposals. Admiral Sir Sydney Fremantle added that 'in view of the enormously increased importance of the Sea Cadet Corps' he felt that it was essential that a Senior Naval Officer be appointed to the S.C.C. to oversee the Corps operation. The main aim of the Navy League – the promotion of the navy – did not need to be pressed in time of war, as everyone was well aware of its necessity. It was essential therefore that the Navy League somehow kept control of the S.C.C. as this was now, apart from organising Trafalgar Day, its only function. For better or worse the Navy League was successful, and the proposed expansion took place on its terms.

The apparently arbitrary limit of 50,000 set by the Royal Navy was fixed, according to Rear-Admiral J. G. P. Vivian, the Admiral Commanding Reserves, because 'the annual output will then be roughly, very roughly, related to the number which the Sea Services may be expected to absorb in peace'.[64] With the expansion came the inevitable problem of finding extra accommodation and meeting higher running costs. By September 1944, when the S.C.C. had enrolled 50,000 cadets in 430 units, an appeal was launched in the national press. A letter to the editor of *The Times* outlined the task the Navy League had set itself, that of raising £250,000, but the outcome of this is not recorded.[65]

The number of units throughout the U.K. and in Northern Ireland continued to grow – by 1943 there were 10 in the Ulster province. The Medway Towns unit was over 200 strong, and when the Hackney unit's stone frigate (brick built H.Q.) T.S. *Jervis Bay* was christened, 800 cadets from half-a-dozen units in London's East End were on parade.[66] The cost of the expansion could not be borne by the Navy League alone. The problem of finding local headquarters was the responsibility of the unit and its committee. The relatively small inland unit at Evesham in

Worcestershire, for example, formed in 1942 with 60 cadets, had raised £700 to build its own H.Q. Not far away the provincial town of Cheltenham launched an appeal in 1944 for £2,000 to build an H.Q.[67] Also in the midlands, Sutton Coldfield had launched an appeal for £1,000 to provide extra accommodation. It must be remembered that such monetary appeals were coming at a time when everyone was already being exhorted to support a variety of Government-backed causes, such as 'Warship Week', 'War Weapons Week' and 'Wings for Victory Week'. Various methods were employed to raise cash to aid expansion. As a reward for their efforts in national collections the sea cadet units were able, at times, to obtain a percentage of the proceeds. As a result of the Beckenham unit's effort in 'Navy Week' they received the sum of £263. All manner of fund raising was employed. Local businesses, such organisations as Rotary Clubs, and local dignitaries were asked to give donations. At Paisley in Scotland the Provost made a special appeal on behalf of the sea cadets at their Sea Cadets' Flag Day. The people of Paisley generously responded with the sum of £266. At the famous Hampden Park football stadium in Glasgow the sea cadets gave a display at the Scotland v. R.A.F. match in 1944. In addition to the '£1,000 for the British Sailors' Society, the proceeds of the match yielded £443 for the Sea Cadets' Fund'.[68]

It was during the Second World War that sea cadets first began to appear in public schools. It was not to be a large expansion, but it was no less significant for that, as future officers of the Royal Navy were to emerge from its ranks. Harrow School was the first public school to have a naval section, and this prompted other schools to follow suit. The headmaster of Sherborne School visited Harrow early in the war and was impressed by what he saw. On his journey home he called in at the Admiralty, and obtained permission to set up a navy section. This was formed in the autumn of 1942, and Sherborne was the second public school to have sea cadets. Thirty-eight boys were allowed to transfer from the Junior Training Corps provided that they first passed Certificate 'A'. A preliminary course was held on the Solent during the summer term prior to the actual setting-up of the naval section. Instruction was undertaken by an ex-naval officer. This training, it is recorded, was to be of 'immense value ... for those who wish to join the Navy'.[69]

Gradually the war at sea was being won, and there was a reduction in British ships sunk and tonnage lost. This was due in part to the successful introduction of the new aircraft carriers and the more efficient employment of convoys. The latter depended in no small measure on the bravery of the merchant seamen, whose losses amounted to over 30,000 during the war. Many of them would have come to the fleet via the Sea

Cadet Corps. There were notable naval victories for the Royal Navy, such as the sinking of the German battleship *Bismarck* in 1941. In 1943 the battle-cruiser *Scharnhorst* was sunk and the battleship *Tirpitz* was put out of action. There were many other notable battles and victories. There were also the landings in North Africa, Sicily and Italy. But no action was more spectacular than the greatest combined invasion in history, namely operation *Overlord*. In June 1944 the allied naval force of '125,000 officers and men, over 6,000 ships, including 6 battleships, 23 cruisers, 104 destroyers and over 4,000 landing craft' transported and supported the greatest collection of armour and troops ever assembled to cross the Channel.

Some cadet units have kept a log of the numbers going into the R.N. or the merchant fleet. In the three years from 1941 to 1944 the Bromley unit had trained 168 serving seamen.[70] At another inland base, Worcester, it was 208 entrants in two years; Kingston-upon-Thames sent 253 cadets to sea in the period 1940 to 1943, and in 1943 Southend's total amounted to 296, of whom seven had been lost at sea.[71] In 1943 over '7,000 cadets entered the Royal and Merchant Navies, and the figure for 1944 will be substantially larger'.[72] The Sea Cadet Corps had never been larger, or more needed. As the Right Honorable A. V. Alexander, First Lord of the Admiralty, said in 1943:

> The Corps is now established, and widely recognised, as an indispensable pre-entry service to the Royal Navy . . .[73]

The outbreak of war stimulated the Cadet Movement, as it had done in 1899 and 1914. However, there was a limitation on membership of the army cadet contingents run by the public schools. For the duration of the war the War Office restricted the Junior Training Corps – as the O.T.C. was now known – to 183 schools with a membership of 30,000 cadets.[74] A public school education was no longer a prerequisite for army officers. The army was prepared to offer commissions to men from other backgrounds. The new name and the new policy reflected this change.

Initially, numbers increased in the already established units. In some schools service with the cadets became compulsory, as at Chigwell School in Essex.[75] In the main, the boys did not consider this to be an imposition, but accepted it as normal practice; after all a sense of service and duty was an inherent part of public school culture. At Chard School in Somerset membership of the cadet corps was voluntary but, owing to pressure from the boys, parades were made compulsory.[76] The changes in policy regarding the J.T.C. meant that schools wishing to form an army cadet unit after 1939 had to do so under the auspices of the Army Cadet Force (A.C.F.). Hence Slough Grammar School Cadet Corps, which had 87 cadets in 1941, came under the 1st Cadet Bn. Oxfordshire and

Buckinghamshire Light Infantry. Tracing the history of a unit is not always straightforward as titles were apt to change; for example, the Latymer House (school) Cadet Corps changed its name to that of its affiliated unit and in 1941 became the 2nd Cadets, King's Royal Rifle Corps. The stimulus to expand came, at times, from the youngsters themselves. As a result of requests from boys in the Middle and Upper School at Yeovil a unit of the A.C.F. was started in February 1941. When formed it was affiliated to the 7th Bn. Somerset Light Infantry and to the 3rd (Yeovil) Company Somerset Home Guard.[77] Cadet units in 1939 experienced the same problems as their predecessors in 1914, namely the loss of younger officers and N.C.O. instructors. Often, therefore, it was the Home Guard that provided instructors for the A.C.F. This relationship between the cadets and the Home Guard became a very important consequence of the war for the cadet movement and will be looked at in more detail later.

The Government scheme instituted by Ernest Bevin for national registration of youth had an advantageous effect on all the pre-service cadet organisations. Even before government encouragement took effect, numbers were increasing as more and more boys wanted to 'do their bit' and to be a part of the war effort. An example that illustrates the rate of expansion is that which occurred at Ayr Academy Cadet Corps, which increased from 79 in 1940 to 184 by February 1941.[78] It was important for the B.N.C.A. to approach the local schools when starting a new unit; apart from the obvious reason of recruiting boys, the schools could also provide accommodation and training facilities. The great enthusiasm shown by boys to serve and the influx of recruits meant that the units could be selective. In May 1940 at the setting-up of the Doncaster Cadet Corps (affiliated to the 46th W.R. [Doncaster] Bn. Home Guard, King's Own Yorkshire Light Infantry) 80 boys presented themselves, 'but after rejecting the underage and the "too small", approximately fifty were left to start the Corps'.[79] Boys then came forward at an average of four per week, and by February 1941 the total enrolled had reached 119.

The spirit of the time and eagerness of boys to be useful was summed up in an article by an ex-wartime cadet in the *Hayes Gazette*. It reads:

> They were eager to do their bit as Hitler dropped bombs on London, but too young to enlist, and the cadets was the next best thing.[80]

The keenness of those boys who wanted to join the army cadets was tempered by the restriction placed on recruitment. Increasingly, the Government determined the priorities, and thus affected the way in which the cadets were run, but in doing so it also underlined the importance of the cadet services. However, recruitment to the Army Cadet Force was affected by the formation of the Air Training Corps. The A.T.C. was new; it therefore had a novelty value. Secondly, the A.T.C. had a distinct psychological advantage as a result of the Battle of Britain; following this victory on 'home soil' the R.A.F. was viewed as the most glamorous of the services. And thirdly, in 1941 recruitment to the army cadets was officially stopped for a period of six months to allow the Air Training Corps to expand. This hiatus in recruitment to both the S.C.C. and the A.C.F. had a latent, and at the time, unforeseen advantage for the cadets in blue and khaki. The Air Ministry was extremely enthusiastic about the formation of its own cadet service, and as it was 'a new toy they were prepared to give very generous treatment both regards uniform, equipment, financial backing and commissioning for their officers'.[81] As a result of this preferential treatment the other cadet organisations naturally pleaded for parity. This led to an Inter-Services Cadet Committee being formed and the existing pre-service organisations eventually received equal treatment.

It was not until 1942, when the recruiting restriction was lifted, that the A.C.F. experienced its period of greatest growth. The year 1942 was important not only for the fact that the Government took greater control of the pre-service cadet organisations, but because the War Office took over the administration. The army cadets, unlike the sea cadets, had no compunction about being directly aligned with their parent service. The A.C.F. was aware of the benefits likely to accrue from a closer liaison. The immediate improvements were substantial. There was an increase in the *per capita* grant to 8/6d, and in 1943 it rose again to 17/6d per qualified cadet. In addition there was a bonus of five shillings for each part of the Certificate 'A' passed during the year.[82] Uniforms were now issued free to all cadets between the ages of 14 and 17. The old First World War dress with its knee breeches and puttees was out, being replaced by battledress and gaiters. The organisation was re-named the Army Cadet Force and cadets wore shoulder titles with the words CADET FORCE below the title of the regiment of affiliation. Boots had to be purchased, but clothing coupons for these were made available at the rate of seven coupons per pair.[83] The cadets could now dress and feel as if they were a part of the modern army. It was in February 1942, as a result of the formation of Sea and Air Cadets, that it was felt necessary to have the distinguishing adjective 'Army' added to the title to avoid confusion.

Expansion could now be measured not just in numbers but in detachments and companies formed. The City of Sheffield Battalion expanded to 11 companies with 1,200 cadets in 1942. In the same year, the Marquess of Bath inspected 600 cadets from 15 units in the rural

Somerset Mendip area. A year later the numbers had risen to 1,000. Such was the demand that in 1943 Somerset County A.C.F. had a waiting list for enrolment.[84] In the sparsely-populated rural county of Shropshire there were two battalions totalling 1,239 army cadets. In Hertfordshire there were eight battalions.[85] In Surrey, by October, some eight months after the lifting of recruiting restrictions, there were 50 companies with a total establishment of 6,600 cadets in ten battalions.[86] The establishment of new units was not confined to England.

In the other 'home countries' expansion was no less prolific. Prior to the war Canton High School in South Wales formed a cadet corps in 1936, despite local opposition, but it was not until 1939 that a second unit appeared. The first Cardiff non-school cadet corps unit was formed in July 1940 and two more non-school units were formed in 1941. The impression given may be that, like today's membership, most of the wartime cadets were still at school. This was not the case. The school-leaving age was 14; hence most of the cadets had left school to go to work. In the 3rd Cardiff Non-school Cadet Corps, 80 per cent of the cadets were in employment (50 per cent in manual employment, 15 per cent in agricultural, and 15 per cent in clerical jobs).[87] By 1943 the total number of units in the counties of Glamorgan and Monmouth had risen to 14.[88]

In Scotland, where many regiments have a long and proud history, the number of cadets in 1942 amounted to 2,300. This may not appear to be a large number, but as the Secretary of the Scottish NCA Sub-Committee pointed out, the country had only a tenth of Britain's population. The Scottish cadets, particularly in Glasgow, had a formidable rival, namely the Boys' Brigade. It was in Glasgow that the Boys' Brigade was founded. The organisation was therefore strong in that area, and, of course, the Boys' Brigade was no longer affiliated to the army cadet organisation; as many as 10,000 Boys' Brigade members would attend a parade in Scotland's second city. Interestingly some of the Scottish army cadet units were formed in the workplace; the Ardeer Factory had a unit of 70 cadets and the Burntisland Shipbuilding Company, in Fife, a unit of 40 cadets.[89]

A decision was taken to establish the A.C.F. in Northern Ireland and on 21 January 1943 it came into being under the command of Colonel Gibbon, the retired headmaster of Campbell College. It was organised into three battalions with an envisaged establishment of 3,000 cadets. As the A.C.F. in Ulster was formed during the war, when enthusiasm for service and uniform was at its height, numbers grew quickly. The 3rd Cadet Bn. The Royal Ulster Rifles, which served the North Down area, had 'open' units in Killyleagh, Ballynahinch, Holywood, Newtonards, and a 'closed' unit at Regent House School. Within three months this totalled

212 cadets and 11 officers. The 1st Cadet Bn. The Royal Irish Fusiliers, despite not having a Battalion Commander to co-ordinate recruitment and training in the early stages, raised a battalion of 400 cadets; by the beginning of 1944 the total had reached 505. The 2nd Cadet Bn. encompassed units in the three counties of Tyrone, Fermanagh and Antrim. Those in Tyrone and Fermanagh were affiliated to The Royal Inniskilling Fusiliers, and the units in Antrim to The Royal Ulster Rifles.[90]

The Army Cadet Force increased by 80 per cent, between 1942 and 1943 and the combined number of cadets in khaki totalled 220,000. Of these 190,000 were in the A.C.F. and about 30,000 in the J.T.C. It is said that:

> By 1944 '40,000 ex-cadets, a high proportion of whom held Certificate 'A', were passing annually into the Army'. The cumulative effect of this training was evident, and by the time that the British Army took the offensive in N. W. Europe, in the final phases of the European War, the ex-A.C.F. men must have totalled several divisions.[91]

It is impossible to name all the units that were formed during the Second World War; suffice to say that 1942 was the time when the greatest expansion took place. Major-General Lord Bridgeman, the Director General of the Home Guard and Chairman of the B.N.C.A., outlined the first aim of the A.C.F. in 1942 when he said:

> The object of the Cadet Force is to create a body of boys in the country, fit in body, mind and heart, and anxious to serve the King in arms and in the Army.[92]

The second aim, training for citizenship, had not been forgotten, and the A.C.F. was linked to the Government's policy for youth training. The lessons learnt in the 1920s, following the First World War, were put into practice. Despite being a pre-service organisation, training would not be solely concerned with the acquisition of military skills. Membership of the cadets was seen as training for a boy's future, both military and civilian. Before the end of the war the B.N.C.A. were to appoint a committee with the purpose of planning for the post-war years. The immediate problem, though, was to do with finding sufficient leaders and accommodation to cope with the vast influx of recruits. In recognition of the work done by the A.C.F. so far, and as an encouragement for the future, the King became Colonel-in-Chief in 1942.

The impetus for expansion due to the Government's registration of youth schemes, as laid down in Circular 1577, assisted the third cadet service, the Air Defence Cadet Corps, to grow in numbers. And if local enthusiasts and dignitaries supported the Government's initiative then the chances for expansion were doubled. In Shrewsbury, for example, the mayor was extremely enthusiastic and was very helpful when it came to looking for suitable accommodation.

In June 1940 the R.A.F. asked the A.D.C.C. to accept and train deferred servicemen – that is men who had been attested but were waiting to be called up. The A.D.C.C. undertook this task and very soon 4,000 men were attending squadron parades. During the Battle of Britain in 1940 the need for a continuous supply of suitably-educated candidates to be trained as aircrew was emphasised. There was a shortage of pilots, navigators, observers, wireless operators and air gunners. The demand was beyond the capability of the A.D.C.C. The Government wanted to set up a new organisation under the control of the R.A.F. The R.A.F. wanted to promote training, but did not want the tasks of administration and welfare. It is fair to say that the R.A.F. had its hands rather full at the time!

At the end of 1940 the Yorkshire A.D.C.C. County Civilian Committee, which was also dissatisfied with the present set-up, after canvassing other committees, sent a Memorandum to the Government in which it said:

> The Yorkshire County Association, Air Defence Cadet Corps, comprising 22 member and affiliated Cadet squadrons, begs to voice its profound anxiety and dissatisfaction at the present policy of the Air Council which fails to give adequate encouragement to the development of the Air Defence Cadet Corps, a movement that has proved to be of inestimable value in the preliminary air training of the youth of the country.[93]

The committee outlined in detail the difficulties facing the A.D.C.C. The existing levels of finance, equipment and training were said to be totally inadequate. The moral support and subsequent granting of commission status for officers, as promulgated by the Air Ministry Order (No. A484 dated 18/7/40) was appreciated. However, the committee was later upset when the Air Ministry stated that:

> ... the wearing of uniform by Cadets and Cadet Officers should be immediately discontinued in the event of the commencement of hostilities on land in the United Kingdom, inasmuch as the Corps is not part of the armed forces of the Crown, and the wearing of uniform similar to the uniform of the Royal Air Force might expose the wearers to the danger of attack as combatants.[94]

Clearly, the officers of the A.T.C. felt they were part of the R.A.F. – after all they now held the King's Commission – and therefore did not want to 'revert' to being regarded as civilians should the country be invaded.

Members of the A.D.C.C. felt that they were doing a responsible job both for the country and for the R.A.F. They were aware of the need for change, but they did not want to be sidelined. The Yorkshire Committee advocated that the Air Ministry, via the R.A.F., should provide the following: uniform for cadets; a supply of training equipment, particularly for subjects 'desired by the Air Ministry'; an annual grant towards the maintenance of squadrons. They also wanted the Corps 'to enjoy the status of a junior branch of the Royal Air Force'. It was suggested that the Government should take over the training activities and that the welfare and administration of squadrons be left to civilian committees headed by a central civilian advisory committee at Government level. The Memorandum was signed by the President, The Right Honourable The Earl of Harewood, the Committee, the Chairmen of the 22 Yorkshire A.D.C.C. squadrons, and was supported by a further 107 squadrons.[95]

The Government liked the suggestions and, using the Yorkshire Committee's ideas as a blueprint, The Air Training Corps (A.T.C.) was formed on 1 February 1941. The A.T.C. comprised the three pre-service military air-training organisations, namely the Air Defence Cadet Corps Squadrons – by far the largest – the University Air Squadrons, and the Air Squadrons of the J.T.C. The expansion in 'open' units was echoed to a lesser extent in the public schools.

This series of events can best be summarised by saying that the Government's decision to take charge of the pre-service air training was a response to the increased demand for personnel for the R.A.F. The timing of the change, and the way in which it was implemented, reflected the arguments put forward by the doughty A.D.C.C. Committee in Yorkshire.

The A.T.C. could not be fully integrated into the R.A.F., despite the fact that from then on the officers were commissioned in the Training Branch of the R.A.F.V.R., as much of its business was run by civilians. Nevertheless, according to Springall, the A.T.C. became the first ever State-directed, voluntary, uniformed pre-entry training scheme.[96] In a broadcast on the BBC's Home Service in 1941, Mr Wolfenden, Director of Pre-Entry Training, emphasised that the boys would receive more than military training, and that the aims of the A.T.C. were – as they were in the S.C.C. and A.C.F. – both social and military when he said:

> We want to see our boys looking forward beyond the clouds of War to a world where there will be a fuller and more generous measure of social equality.... We shall have ... the boy who is earning his living, the boy at the secondary school, the boy at the boarding school, and the undergraduate at the University ... and all of them will be wearing the same uniform of the Royal Air Force blue.[97]

Initially, though, the priority was the search for technically-minded personnel and so the A.T.C. was selective from the outset. The age for joining was set at 16. This left a gap between the school-leaving age of 14 and entry into the A.T.C. In order to bridge that gap the A.T.C. entered into an agreement with the Air Scouts, whereby the latter could obtain instructional assistance from the A.T.C. The Air Scouts became in effect a recruiting ground for the A.T.C., that is until the A.T.C. reduced the age of entry to 15 years three months in 1942, and then to 13 years nine months in 1944.[98] An aspiring cadet could not just walk into a unit and enrol. He had first to attend an interview and then pass a medical assessment. Despite the rigours of selection many boys wanted to join this new Service. An example of the keenness can be judged by what happened in Shrewsbury: No. 1119 Squadron was officially recognised in March 1941, and within 18 months had expanded to include 170 cadets in five Flights.[99] In south Somerset, a month after the formation of the A.T.C., three Flights were formed at Ilminster, Axminster and Chard.[100] In Essex, 19 of the present 24 units can trace their history back to the A.T.C.'s founding year of 1941. Other places experienced equally rapid growth.

The accommodation and training of such a rapidly-expanding organisation caused problems but these were sometimes overcome by combining units. An A.T.C. squadron based at the Newcastle-under-Lyme schools comprised cadets from Newcastle and Kidsgrove in three Flights. They paraded with the J.T.C., and so the latter was able to provide instruction in drill and musketry.[101] The rate of expansion of the A.T.C., although aided by the limit put on the Sea Cadet Corps and the temporary suspension in recruiting for the Army Cadet Force, was nonetheless quite spectacular. From a total of 18,489 in the A.D.C.C. in September 1940 there was a tenfold increase to 200,000 in the A.T.C. by the end of 1942. The number of units formed were as follows: 1,043 'open' units (843 in England, 116 in Scotland, 77 in Wales and seven in Northern Ireland), plus 366 'closed' school units throughout the United Kingdom.[102] By 1944 the total number of units was 1,700. This included the University Air Squadrons, which formed part of the A.T.C. In the first three years after the formation of the A.T.C., 100,000 members were accepted by the Armed Services.[103]

The reasons for the rapid rise in popularity and numbers of the Air Training Corps, as compared with the other pre-service cadet organisations, were multifarious. First, there was the novelty value. Flying was still in its infancy, and so there was the added element of glamour and excitement. Secondly, the inauguration of the A.T.C. was the Government's idea and therefore priority was given to it, even to the extent that recruiting in the other Cadet Services was officially limited. Thirdly, the A.T.C. had a good supply of instructors. For the necessary academic instruction, much of which was in mathematics, members of the teaching profession could be used. For shooting and drill, instructors were redirected from the A.C.F. to the A.T.C. Fourthly, the R.A.F., unlike the Navy and the Army, could be seen in action. Those boys living in the south and eastern counties of England could literally watch the Battle of Britain in progress – all they had to do was look skywards. The R.A.F.'s value was obvious: hence the public's admiration and gratitude was immediate. The Navy's exploits were, for the most part, miles away in the North Atlantic, the Mediterranean Sea and the Pacific. The Army's successes were to come later on the European mainland, in the jungles of Burma and the deserts of North Africa. The Navy's and the Army's contributions were therefore confined to newspaper reports or subsequent news film.

During the Battle of Britain the newspapers covered the aerial conflict with all the energy and enthusiasm usually reserved for a cup final or test match. The headlines reported the scores: 'It's 65 for 12' was one typical headline, which informed the reader that the British had made 53 more kills than the Germans. The flyers, and fighter pilots in particular, became known as the modern-day 'Knights of the Air', with the 'flying ACE' acquiring the status of a sports star. The R.A.F. was very aware of this. In the *Air Cadet Gazette*, publicity photos of R.A.F. heroes regularly appeared, complete with names and lists of decorations (*Plate 7*). As one boy said to his father, 'But if it [the bombing] stopped, Dad . . . what would Ginger Lacey and Al Deere and Johnnie Johnson do? They wouldn't have any more Nazi bombers to shoot down!'[104] The R.A.F. was the more 'glamorous' Service, and not surprisingly, R.A.F. servicemen were sometimes grudgingly known by their less publicised comrades as 'The Brylcreem Boys'. All this of course was advantageous to the A.T.C. and helped in the drive for recruits.

Inducement to serve came, as demonstrated, from a number of different quarters. The most public and popular method of propaganda was films. Each of the Services was well catered for in this respect, and the black-and-white feature films made during the war years are still extremely popular today. There can be little doubt that many young would-be sailors watching films about the Royal Navy such as *In Which We Serve* and *We Dive at Dawn*, felt inclined to enlist. Army films like *Went the Day Well?* and *The Way Ahead* aided A.C.F. recruitment; for the R.A.F. and the A.T.C. there was *Target for Tonight* and *The First of the Few*. All these films were made between 1941 and 1944.

The films mentioned were for public consumption and were primarily 'morale boosters'. Conscription for men over 18 was in force and so there was no need to mention recruitment overtly. The cadet organisations, on the other hand, were reliant on volunteers. The Government therefore thought it necessary to produce, via the Ministry of Information or private cinematic companies, films specifically for the purpose of encouraging cadet recruitment. The Government's determination to foster the growth of the A.T.C. is evident by the number of films commissioned for this purpose. In 1941 three films showing life in the A.T.C. were distributed. *Cavalcade of the A.T.C.* was shown at Odeon cinemas, and the Ministry of Information produced another two short films titled *Venture Adventure* and *Won't You Join Us?* The first of the A.T.C. films was part of a double-bill, the other film being *Wings of the Navy*. The Ministry of Information also produced an S.C.C. film called *Sea Cadets* or *Nursery of the Navy*, in which the well-known actor Bernard Miles – playing a sailor – explained to two 17 year old boys the advantages of joining the S.C.C. and the benefits of the Bounty Scheme, which was a means of training Signallers. In 1943 J. Arthur Rank produced a film called *Sons of the Air* to encourage would-be pilots. In 1944 the War Office produced *Prelude to Service*, a nine-minute film outlining activities in the Army Cadets. A tri-service film, *Three Cadets* was released in 1944.

Despite the paper shortage all of the Cadet Services produced their own journals. Captain W. E. Johns wrote short stories about flying for the A.T.C., whilst the Sea and Army Cadet magazines related stories of past naval triumphs and included potted histories of Regiments of the Line. *The Sea Cadet* magazine also included commentaries on the Royal and Merchant fleets, and the tasks they were performing in the war.

The rate at which the A.T.C. expanded was phenomenal, and by 1943 the supply of recruits had outstripped the demand. In July 1944, following D-Day and the invasion of Europe, the Allies had gained ascendancy in the air and as a result the need for airmen was much reduced. In November 1944 the University Short Courses were cancelled and recruitment for the R.A.F. ceased. This naturally affected the numbers volunteering for the A.T.C. The emphasis was now mainly on the army. The allies had established a bridgehead on the European mainland, but much territory still had to be fought over. It was in the main the army's job to win further ground. This meant that cadets leaving the A.T.C. were now very likely to be drafted into the army rather than into the airforce. In Somerset the County Inter-services Cadet Committee was concerned that 'the training and officers may become redundant', and reiterated their recommendation formulated some two years previously, namely the 'fusion of the separate cadet corps' into one United Service Training Corps.[105] The A.C.F., A.T.C., and the Ministry of Labour and County Youth Committee supported this resolution. Thus the Somerset Committee, possibly without realising it, was advocating what Viscount Haldane had proposed in 1908 when reorganising the Volunteers. This amalgamation did not happen, as most people were less pessimistic and, besides, they wanted independence, so the idea was dismissed. Up to this time, a youth who had been in the sea cadets would in most cases naturally progress to the Navy, and similarly with the air cadets. The leaving of one military Service to join another, given the circumstances, was accepted, perhaps a little reluctantly, by ex-cadets. In addition, given the similarities within the cadet services – understanding of rank structure, discipline, leadership training and team work – meant there was a transference of values and training. However, what must have been less easy to take was the call-up for the mines. The Bevin Boys' Scheme, as National Service down the coal mines was called, was not particularly popular. It did not affect every ex-A.T.C. cadet. Selection for service in the coalfields was a lottery. If an individual's registration number matched one drawn that week he went down the pits. In total only 21,800 boys went into coal mining via the scheme: not many, but to those who wanted to go into the forces it must have been a great disappointment.

Cadet life was subject to the vagaries of wartime Britain: rationing of food and clothes, transport difficulties, the blackout, lack of equipment and training areas and the Blitz. The last of those meant the evacuation of youngsters from the cities to the country, and transference from one unit to another. Half of the S.C.C. unit's company at Merthyr Tydfil in Wales consisted of evacuees from the sea cadet unit at Folkestone. This movement of evacuated cadets could be an asset, but it could also have posed problems. Some rural cadet Training Ships became more viable by the increase in numbers, but it could put a strain on resources. There could also have been unforeseen problems.

According to one account, when the ex-evacuees, particularly the grammar school boys, returned from Wales to their re-opened Folkestone T.S. they were not welcomed. The nature of the southeast unit had changed. It had been re-opened with a supply of cadets from the local secondary school who resented those returning. They particularly resented those cadets attending the grammar school. Secondly, the returnees were not given the recognition, and hence the promotion that they thought they deserved and cadets began to leave.[106] However, despite local difficulties and the dangers of living through a war, the Cadet Movement flourished. A National Fire Service officer, speaking of the local army cadets said:

> I feel that the carry-on spirit of the local Cadets should be known. Every officer and every senior NCO instructor has been fly-bombed and about 90 per cent of the Cadets, too, yet the batteries have kept up their parades, even to the extent of the annual inspection in their severely blitzed headquarters.[107]

What was said applied equally to cadets from all Services. The effects of enemy bombing could be absolutely devastating. The army cadet centre at Haileybury House at Stepney in the East End of London in 1944 was seriously damaged, and the only thing left for the cadets to do was to try to salvage some equipment from the debris (*Plate 8*).

In spite of the difficulties the Cadet Movement contributed to its own survival by remaining in operation, and by supplying enthusiastic and partly-trained manpower for the Armed Services. At any one time there were nearly half-a-million boys in uniform and under training. The contribution in terms of numbers of young men going into the Armed Forces was 80,000 a year from 1940 to 1944.

CHAPTER 4 REFERENCES

1. John M. MacKenzie, *Propaganda and Empire – The manipulation of British public opinion, 1880–1960* [Manchester: MUP, 1984], p. 174
2. Ibid., p. 183
3. Ibid., p. 181
4. *The Boys' Own Magazine*, Vol. 1, 1862
5. J. Springall, B. Fraser and M. Hoare, *Sure and Steadfast: A history of the Boys' Brigade, 1883–1983* [London & Glasgow: Collins] 1983, p. 21
6. Ibid., p. 25
7. J. A. Mangan, *Athleticism in the Victorian and Edwardian Public Schools* [Cambridge: CUP, 1982], p. 25
8. *The Navy League* journal, March 1903
9. Ibid.
10. Ibid.
11. MacKenzie, op. cit., p. 183
12. *The Navy League* journal, March 1903
13. *The Navy League* journal, April 1908
14. *The Navy League* journal, April 1910
15. *The Navy League* journal, April 1908
16. MacKenzie, op. cit., p. 154
17. A.C.F.A., *The Cadet Story, 1860–1980*, p. 13
18. E. S. Turner, *Boys Will Be Boys* [London: Michael Joseph, 1957], p. 115
19. Harry Golding [Ed.], *Wonder Book of Soldiers* [London, 1919], pp. 83, 142–143
20. Agnes C. Blackie, *Blackie & Son: a short History of the Firm, 1809–1959* [London & Glasgow: Blackie, 1959]
21. MacKenzie, op. cit., p. 217
22. J. O. Springall, *Youth, Empire and Society* [London: Croom Helm, 1977], p. 62
23. J. A. Mangan, 'The Grit of our Forefathers' in J. M. MacKenzie, *Imperialism and Culture* [Manchester: MUP, 1986], p. 127
24. Ibid., p. 128
25. Ibid., p. 128
26. Mackenzie, op. cit., p. 240
27. George Orwell, 'My Country Right or Left' in MacKenzie, ibid., p. 255
28. Wing Cdr H. W. Lamond, *History of the A.T.C., 1938–1983* [unpublished: A.T.C. H.Q. RAD Cranwell], p. 1-4.
29. *Radio Times*, 24th August 1949
30. Peter Beresford Ellis & Piers Williams, *By Jove, Biggles! The life of W. E. Johns* [London: W. H. Allen, 1981], p. 131
31. W. E. Johns, *The Rescue Flight* [Oxford: OUP, 1938], p. 4

32 *Popular Flying*, July 1934 and *Popular Flying*, May 1936
33 *Air Defence Cadet Corps Gazette*, August 1940
34 P. Beresford Ellis & P. Williams, op. cit., p. 177
35 W. E. Johns, *Worrals Flies Again* [London: Hodder & Stoughton, 1942]
36 W. E. Johns, *Spitfire Parade* [Oxford: OUP, 1942]
37 W. E. Johns, *Gimlet Goes Again* [Oxford: OUP, 1944]
38 *Times Educational Supplement*, October 1943
39 Boyle, Brian [Ed.], *The Who's Who of Children's Literature* [London: Evelyn Hughes, 1968], p. 159
40 Alan Morris, *First of the Many – the story of the independent force, R.A.F.* [London: Jarrods, 1968], pp. 3–4
41 Evelyn Hughes, op. cit., p. 101
42 *Sunday Pictorial*, 27 December 1936
43 *The New York Times*, 4 May 1939
44 Jeffrey Richards, 'Boys' Own Empire', in J. M. MacKenzie [Ed.] *Imperialism and Popular Culture* [Manchester: MUP, 1986], p. 148
45 Ibid., p. 156
46 Springall, et al., op. cit., p. 176
47 Alicia Percival, *Youth Will Be Led – the story of the youth organisations* [London: Collins, 1957], p. 10.
48 Capt. L. J. Collins, M.A., Ph.D., *Army Cadet* journal, Vol. LVIII, January 1996, pp. 12–14
49 *Shropshire Chronicle*, 10 January 1941
50 A.C.F.A., *The Cadet Story, 1860–1980* [London: A.C.F.A., 1982], p. 67
51 Springall, et al., op. cit., p. 176
52 *Shropshire Chronicle*, 8 January 1943
53 *Shropshire Chronicle*, 18 October 1942
54 Springall, et al., op. cit., p. 176
55 A.C.F.A., *The Cadet Story*, op. cit., p. 67
56 *The Sea Cadet* journal, September 1943
57 Minutes of the Navy League Committee meeting, 27 February 1942
58 A. J. P. Taylor, *English History, 1914–45* [London: OUP, 1965], p. 432
59 Capt. John Wells, *The Royal Navy – an illustrated social history, 1870–1982* [Stroud: Allen Sutton, 1994], p. 178
60 Minutes of the Navy League Committee meeting, 27 February 1942
61 Ibid.
62 Minutes of the Sea Cadet Corps sub-committee (Navy League), 5 March 1942
63 Brian Bond, *War and Society in Europe, 1870–1970* [London: Fontana, 1984], p. 175
64 *The Sea Cadet* journal, April 1943, p. 98
65 *The Times*, 22 July 1944

66 *The Sea Cadet* journal, Vol. 1, No. 11, 1944
67 *The Sea Cadet* journal, Vol. 1, No. 9, 1944
68 *The Sea Cadet* journal, January 1944
69 Lt.-Col. J. P. Riley M.A., 'The History of Sherborne School Cadet Force', in *Schoolboys in Uniform* [Sherborne: Shelly, 1988], p. 68
70 *The Sea Cadet* journal, August 1944
71 *The Sea Cadet* journal, December 1943
72 *The Sea Cadet* journal, February 1944
73 *The Sea Cadet* journal, October 1943
74 *The Cadet Review*, January 1945
75 David Howell, 'The Public School Boy', in Jonathan Croall, *Don't You Know There's a War On?* [London: Hutchinson, 1988], pp. 104–105
76 *The Chard & Ilminster News*, 23 May 1942
77 *The Yeovillian*, The Yeovil School magazine, 1941–1942
78 *The Cadet Journal*, Vol. IV, No. 2, 1941
79 Ibid.
80 *Hayes Gazette*, 7 May 1997
81 *The Cadet Story, 1860–1980*, op. cit., p. 69
82 Lt.-Col. H. C. Hughes T.D., M.A., *The Army Cadets of Surrey, 1860–1960* [London: Owen Spyer, 1960], pp. 9 & 16.
83 Ibid., p. 15
84 Capt. L. J. Collins, op. cit., pp. 12–14
85 Lt.-Col. J. D. Sainsbury T.D., *The Hertfordshire Yeomanry – an illustrated history, 1794–1920* [Welwyn: Hart Books, 1994], p. 141
86 H. C. Hughes, op. cit., p. 16
87 *The Cadet Journal*, Vol. IV, No. 3, 1942
88 Ibid.
89 Ibid.
90 Hon. Col. F. E. Nagle, *A Record of the A.C.F. in Counties Armagh and Down, 1943–1974* [unpublished: 1980], C.T.C. Frimley Park library
91 A.C.F.A., *The Army Cadet Force Handbook* [London: A.C.F.A., 1962], p. 22
92 *Shropshire Chronicle*, 17 April 1942
93 'Memorandum for presentation to His Majesty's Secretary for Air The Right Honorable Sir Archibald Sinclair PC C.M.G. M.P., in Wing Cdr. H. W. Lamond, op. cit., p. 18-2
94 *Air Ministry Order No. A484*, 1940
95 Wing Cdr. H. W. Lamond, op. cit., p. 18-5
96 Springall et al., op. cit., p. 175
97 *Air Ministry Bulletin No. 2850*, 23/1/41 No. 13, Air Training Corps (used February 1941)
98 *Air Training Corps Gazette*, Vol. 1, No. 9, November 1941
99 *Shropshire Chronicle*, 8 January 1943

100 *Chard & Ilminster News*, 23 May 1942
101 Notes collected from *The Firefly* school magazine by Wendy Butler (librarian) at Newcastle-under-Lyme School, 1994
102 *Air Cadet Facts* [unpublished: H.Q. Air Cadets R.A.F. Newton], No. 1, January 1983
103 Douglas Cooke, M.C. M.A., *Youth Organisations of Great Britain, 1944–45* [London: Jordan, 1944], pp. 188–191
104 Leonard Moseley, *Backs to the Wall* [London: Weidenfeld & Nicolson, 1971], p. 75
105 *Western Gazette*, November 1944
106 Interview with Mr Derek Forbes, ex-Sea Cadet 1943–1945
107 *The Cadet Story, 1860–1980*, op. cit., p. 80

1. A member of the Shrewsbury School Drill Company 1860. *(Courtesy Shrewsbury School)*

4. The Ellesmere College Cadet Corps of 1902. *(Courtesy Ellesmere College)*

2. *Above:* The intrepid cadets perched precariously on the Reading Brig c.1909. *(Courtesy National Maritime Museum. Ref. G3231).*

3. *Below:* The cadets and their instructors at the Reading Brig c.1909. *(Courtesy National Maritime Museum. Ref. G3232).*

5. 2nd (Civil Service) Cadet Battalion 1913.
(Courtesy Cadet Publications)

6. Cyclist Company 1st Cadet Battalion King's Royal Rifle Corps 1907. Cycling was popular at this time and the army thought it would be of use in war. *(Courtesy Cadet Publications)*

MORE OF THE BEST
1. F/S Eric Moore, R.A.F.V.R., D.F.M.
2. F/O Granville Wilson, D.S.O., D.F.C., D.F.M.
3. W/O N.F. Williams, C.G.M., D.F.M. and bar.
4. W/C R.H. Harries, D.S.O., D.F.C. and two bars.
5. W/C D.E. Gilliam, D.S.O., D.F.C. and bar, A.F.C.
6. G/C J.A. Searby, D.S.O., D.F.C.
7. F/Lt. J.A. Broadley, D.S.O., D.F.C., D.F.M.
8. S/L W.C.E. Craig, D.F.C. and bar.
9. S/L Lewis David Leicester, D.F.C.
10. F/O A.F. Bircher, D.F.M.

7. Royal Air Force flying aces of 1944. *(Courtesy Air Cadet Gazette)*

8. Stepney ACF HQ in London after a bombing raid in 1944. *(Courtesy City of London & N.E. Sector ACF)*

10. The Bounty Signal Schools 1943. *(Courtesy The Sea Cadet)*

9. Training in Morse code for T.S. *Laforey* (Northampton) sea cadets c.1943. *(Courtesy C.P.O. S. Tilley)*

11. HMS Implacable and *HMS Foudroyant* in 1943. *Implacable* was formerly the French 74-gun *Duguay Trouin* which was captured soon after Trafalgar by Sir Richard Strachan and, regrettably, was scuttled after World War 2. *(Courtesy Imperial War Museum Ref. A19881).*

12. HMS Foudroyant signals 'England expects…' in 1943. The 120-year-old corvette provided extra accommodation for the navy trainees. *(Imperial War Museum. Ref. A19875).*

13. *Above:* Dismantling a Lewis machine-gun in 1942. *(Imperial War Museum. Ref. H9757).*
15. *Below:* A.C.F. Cadets training in Motor Mechanics in 1942. *(Imp. War Museum. Ref. H9755).*

14. Leicester ACF cadets undergoing field Signals Training c.1944. (*Courtesy Leicestershire and Northants A.C.F.*)

16. Air Commodore Chamier, Commandant A.T.C., visits Stowe School c.1943. *(Imperial War Museum. Ref. CH4125.)*

17. A.T.C. cadets clambering onto a Spitfire for closer inspection of its cockpit c.1943. *(Imperial War Museum. Ref. CH5032.)*

18. A.T.C. cadets receiving flying instruction from an R.A.F. Sergeant Pilot c.1943. *(Courtesy Imperial War Museum. Ref. CH5029.)*

19. A.T.C. cadet aboard a Skeletal Dagling glider c.1943. *(Courtesy RAF Museum, Hendon. Ref. 5835-3.)*

20. His Majesty King George VI returns the salute during a visit to an A.T.C. camp at R.A.F. Halton in 1941. *(Courtesy Imperial War Museum. Ref. CH3063.)*

21. Inspection of sea cadets at Horley, Surrey in 1945 by Rear Admiral Dickson, D.S.O., Chief of Naval Information. *(Courtesy Imperial War Museum. Ref. A28983.)*

22. A member of 285 Squadron's 'flying display team' in 1942. (R.A.F. Museum, Hendon. Ref. AL000211.)

23. 285 Squadron's 'display team' attacks the enemy in formation during a display for the benefit of King Haakon of Norway at Purley, Surrey in 1942. (Courtesy R.A.F. Museum., Hendon. Ref. AL000211.)

24. A public display with Sten guns by A.C.F. cadets at Hitchin, Hertfordshire in aid of 'Salute the Soldiers Week' in 1944. *(Courtesy Hertfordshire Pictorial.)*

25. Assault course competition for A.C.F. cadets during the same public display with Sten guns by A.C.F. cadets at Hitchin, Hertfordshire in 1944. *(Courtesy Hertfordshire Pictorial.)*

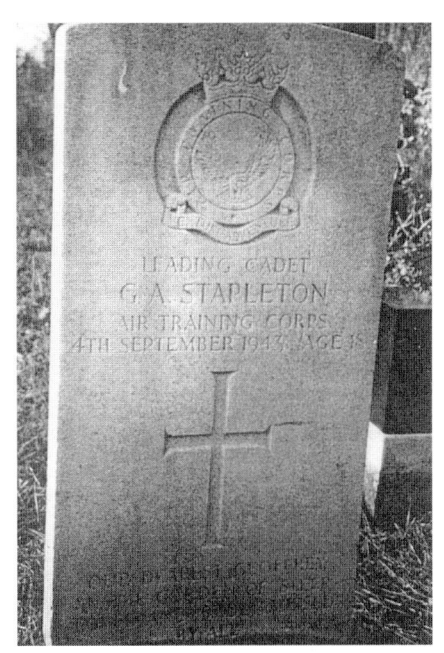

28. The headstone of Cadet Geoffrey Stapleton 271 Squadron (Colwyn Bay) A.T.C.. He died, along with Cadet Foulkes and the crew, in an Avro Anson which disintegrated over Caernarfon in 1943. Cadet Stapleton was an evacuee and the coffin was transported for burial in East Ham, his home town. *(Courtesy Air Cadet Review)*

26. A.C.F. cadets at bayonet practice during 1941. *(Courtesy Imperial War Museum. Ref. H9760.)*

27. Members of the Cotswold Sea Cadet Corps assisting the Home Guard on river patrol c.1942. *(Courtesy The Sea Cadet)*

Chapter 5 – Pre-Service Training

THE PHENOMENAL INCREASE in cadet numbers and the demands of war put a great strain on resources. The immediate problem was one of cost and accommodation. It would have seemed logical to share facilities and efforts were made to do this; there was co-operation to a limited degree but where the training emphasis became more and more geared to the needs of the parent Service more specialist facilities and instruction became essential. It is necessary, therefore, to examine the ways in which each cadet organisation coped with its particular challenges before considering inter-service training.

THE SEA CADETS

In a speech to the London Rotarians in 1943 the Admiral Commanding Reserves, Rear-Admiral J. G. P. Vivian outlined the problems regarding equipment and facilities when he said:

> Equipment has been difficult . . . boats are hard to come by these days but I appeal to yachtsmen to lend me dinghies in which . . . boys can be taught watermanship.
>
> Suitable premises as headquarters have been a great difficulty. I look forward to the time in the near future when every unit will have its own headquarters, its ship, or stone frigate . . . [1]

The problems relating to finance were a continuous concern for the Navy League; exacerbated by the League's insistence – except in the case of the training policy – on independence from the Admiralty. The 1941 audit shows the dilemma that faced the League. Expenditure was three times greater than income, and the difference amounted to £10,000. The League had to become adept at raising funds in a variety of ways. Miss Gracie Fields, one of the country's most popular singers was co-opted to the cause and raised £10,000 for the Sea Cadet Corps, whilst on a tour of Canada. The Navy League held the money in a separate General Fund account, and some economic juggling in the form of bridging loans from this fund had to take place so as to cover the annual deficit.[2]

Practically every unit within the fast-expanding Sea Cadet Corps was submitting an application for grants. Many grants were given for equipment, most of which were in the £20 to £100 range. A look at the major grants for the acquisition of headquarters indicates the financial burden facing the Navy League. The following list of loans granted in 1944, from the Navy League's funds, illustrates the problem:

> *Birmingham* 'Sherborne'- £1,000 for purchase of H.Q. building and £250 gift for equipment.
> *Gateshead and Winchester* were also granted a loan of £1,000 each

for purchase of an H.Q. building. *Whitstable* obtained a loan of £1,500.
Farnham – £700 loan for purchase of old oast house as H.Q. Wimbledon received a similar sum.
Littlehampton – had a particular problem. The sum of £765 was sanctioned for the purchase of an H.Q., but the Army then requisitioned the building. Efforts had to be made to de-requisition it.
Wisbech – obtained an original loan of £400 plus a further £400 interest-free loan. However, repayment was to be at not less than £100 per annum.[3]

These payments may not appear to be much compared to today's prices – although some of today's units would still be stretched to find such amounts of money. The raising of funds was a substantial undertaking, especially during a war. Suffice to say that without adequate accommodation proper training could not take place.

To turn a building into a naval training 'vessel' takes a considerable amount of effort and ingenuity. In 1937 a unit was formed in the rural town of Stroud in Gloucestershire – not the most likely of places to have a sea cadet unit. Nevertheless in 1939 an old stable had been acquired and the unit thus had its own headquarters.

Lighting, heating and water were installed, along with a canteen, instructional room and a 25-yard rifle range. This was achieved largely by the cadets' own efforts. Not satisfied with this, the unit launched an appeal for funds and the cadets raised £1,200.

This allowed for additional improvements and the 75-strong company had the benefit of a signals room, space for PT and drill, a wardroom and three more rooms for instruction (*Fig. 1*).

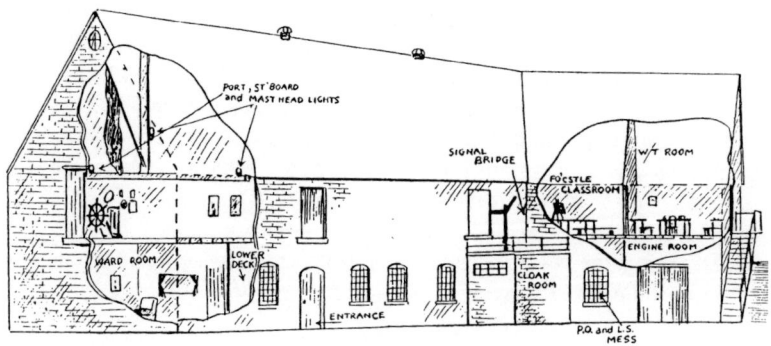

Fig. 1 – T.S. *Severn* 1944 [*The Sea Cadet*]

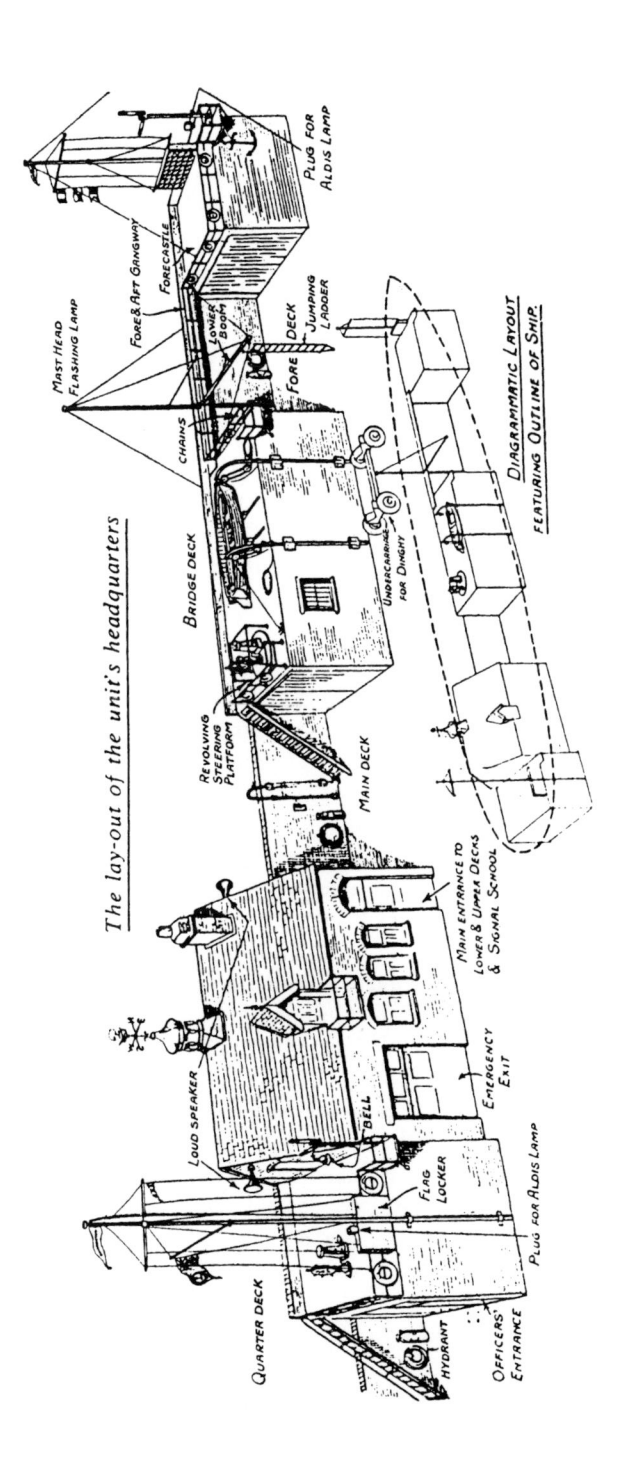

Fig. 2 – T.S. Undaunted 1944 [The Sea Cadet]

The new 'stone frigate' was 'launched' by the Admiral Commanding Reserves and named T.S. *Severn*.[4]

The aim was to make dry-land establishments as much like ships as possible. Another and more elaborate example of a conversion was T.S. *Undaunted* at Bromley (*Fig. 2*). It had both upper and lower decks. Adjoining the hall under the quarterdeck was the ship's office, library, bosun's and clothing stores, plus the armoury. The lower deck was used mainly for seamanship and navigation classes. The upper deck was the signal school. On the quarterdeck stood the ship's wheel, steering platform, binnacle and ship's bell. Also located on the quarterdeck was a lofty mast and yard (with four halyards), a flag locker together with a semaphore. Two hundred and thirty feet for'ard was another mast, yard, flag locker and semaphore. Electrical cables connected both signal stations, so communication by Aldis lamp was possible. Orthodox ship's rails and lifeboats were also fitted. The bridge deck was fitted with a revolving steering platform and binnacle 'with an ingenious device for deflecting the compass needle so that the helmsman has to turn his wheel continually to keep on course'. On the starboard side there was fitted a 15-foot dinghy which could be swung out for lowering on to its undercarriage on the parade ground and then wheeled to the lower boom 'where it can be made fast, the crew coming in-board by means of the jumping ladder'.[5] The Bromley unit was probably the exception rather than the rule, but it demonstrates what could and was done by an imaginative unit to make training as realistic as possible.

The purchase and conversion of buildings was essential. Equally important for sea cadets was the acquisition, or at least the use, of waterborne craft. Appeals from such as the Admiral Commanding Reserves no doubt helped but it was, in the main, up to the units themselves to obtain the equipment needed. In Streatham the unit's Commanding Officer launched a fund by appealing to the audiences from the stage of a local cinema. In the process he presented three cadets who were about to join the Merchant Navy. This was a profitable exercise as the collection realised £110. The unit later received a 24-foot lifeboat that was moored on the Thames.[6]

The cadets from the unit at Evesham in Worcestershire, which was started in July 1942, raised £700 towards building their own H.Q. and secured the use of a 30-foot Service Gig and the use of local rowing club facilities on the River Avon.[7] It was not always a matter of purchasing or borrowing equipment; kit sometimes had to be rescued from dereliction. The Croydon (West) unit acquired an old teak-built 18-foot lifeboat with subsidiary equipment comprising oars and crutches together with a standing mainsail and jib foresail. The boat was moored on a river but with reinforcement work on brick piers and the erection of davits, and a specially constructed wooden cradle, the boat was hoisted alongside the H.Q. The boat was mounted on castors and could when lowered be 'run away'.[8] There are numerous examples of sea cadet units profitably liaising with local sailing clubs. The 2,000 cadets of the Home Counties in Hertfordshire, Bedfordshire and Essex had the use of a small fleet moored at Heybridge. The fleet comprised an ex-Admiralty 60-ton, two-masted, petrol driven ketch-rigged vessel, which could sleep 35 officers and ratings; attached to the training ship was a flotilla of 12 smaller sailing craft. Weekend courses were implemented along with an annual inter-unit regatta.[9] At Falkirk they had the use of a steam yacht until its boilers gave out, but the Commanding Officer was fortunate in acquiring the use of another steam yacht, and the older vessel was then used as a depot ship, the latter for sailing instruction.[10] At Colwyn Bay the unit had a 26-ton auxiliary cutter and cadets were able to go to sea every weekend (weather permitting).[11] In Northampton the unit bought a 71-foot Butty barge which was fitted with upper and lower decks so as to accommodate weekend parties of cadets.[12] It is impossible to mention all the waterborne initiatives of the sea cadet units. Suffice to say that the enthusiasm and inventiveness of officers and cadets was commendable given the difficulties of wartime.

At a more mundane level basic equipment, especially for the land units, was hard to come by and each month in *The Sea Cadet* journal there were articles on how to build or adapt unlikely sources of material. The following example comes from a 1944 issue and was titled 'Seamanship on the playing field'. The diagram (*Fig. 3*) is self-explanatory. The skills to be practised and learnt included:

1. Heaving a line ashore, and catching it.
2. Flaking down hawsers, and reeving them for passing ashore.
3. Bending a heaving line to a hawser at the right place with the right hitch.
4. Passing hawsers ashore and slipping them over the far line of bollards.
5. Taking up the slack by windlass.
6. Passing a stopper to hold the hawser taut while -
7. – the hawser is removed from the windlass and belayed round bollards.
8. Securing the turns round the bollards with racking seizing.
9. Casting off, and fleeting the hawsers to the nearer line of bollards.
10. Securing alongside with headrope, sternrope, breastropes and springs.

105

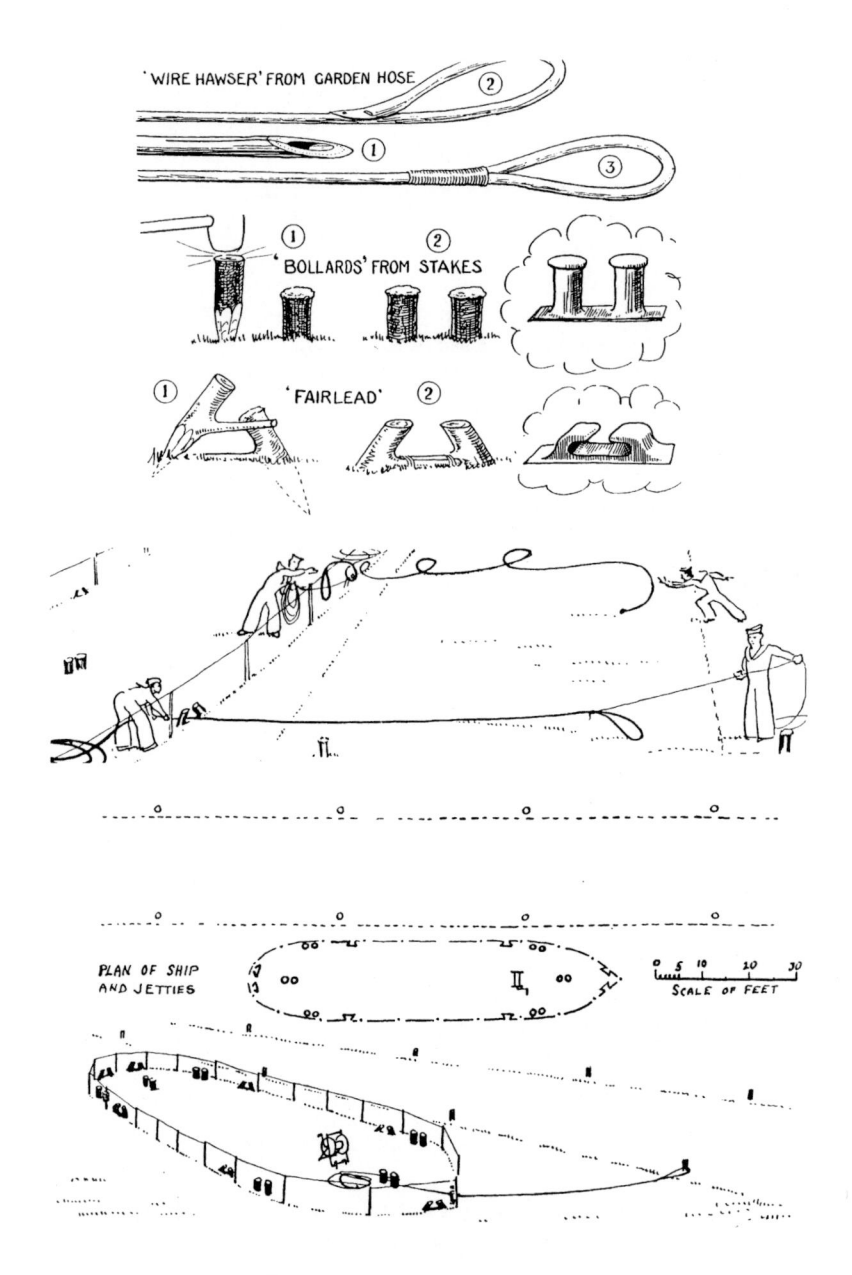

Fig. 3 – Seamanship on the Playing-field [*The Sea Cadet*]

11. Singling up.
12. Coming away with a backspring.
13. Coming away with a spring rove on a ship.[13]

This sort of training could, of course, be made more realistic if practised in a high wind and driving rain. Other articles described how to make a 'Table-top Fleet' or a 'Tufnel Box' for a few pence. *The Sea Cadet* journal was not just a purveyor of administrative information but also, in part, a training manual.

The training for a sea cadet at his twice-weekly parades consisted of five basic components: discipline, fitness, citizenship, seamanship, signals and flags. A cadet's educational standard, although not part of S.C.C. training, was noted. It was an important consideration for those seeking commissions in the future. In addition the cadet's progress, along with attendance at parades, was dutifully logged on a register. Each of the 'core' subjects was further divided into sub-sections. The list below is copied from a 1942 Attendance Register:

Discipline	*Seamanship*	*Citizenship*	*Signals & Flags*
SD	Bends, Hitches	Lectures	Semaphore
SD (rifle)	Knots, Splices	History	Morse
Hist. & Trag.	Rules of Road	Hygiene	Flashing
Salutes	Soundings	First Aid	Ship Recognition
Badges	Compass	Gas	Naval Code
Flags	Blocks, etc	Fire Prevention	
	Rigging	Meteorology	
	Boats & Gear	Gen. Knowledge	*Education*
Fitness	Anchors		
P.T. & R.T.	Navigation		*Other*
Swimming	Charts		*Subjects.*[14]

It is worth noting that although the training was regarded primarily as part of an apprenticeship for both the Royal and Merchant Navies, the subjects listed under the heading 'citizenship' were an integral part of the training syllabus. It was a balanced programme but it was inadequate for the demands of the time. Technology was advancing and the Royal Navy was demanding higher standards. As a result a new curriculum was introduced in 1943. The syllabus was widened and more specialist subjects were included such as gunnery, naval aviation, mechanical and electrical training and wireless telegraphy. There was also a greater emphasis on Leadership Training with more classes in instructional technique. The Petty Officer examination now required the candidate to pass first a new test for Cadet Leading Seaman and then complete at least

20 instructional parades where his ability to teach would be assessed. The PO examination was part oral, part written and, judging by the results, much harder. More than half of the candidates in the first batch of assessments scored less than 50 per cent.[15] The emphasis shifted from length to quality of service, as in future all good conduct badges would be 'awarded for advancement to higher rating and not for length of service'.[16] Holders were given five to six months to earn them by examination; if they failed to do this then the badges were to be removed.

Since before the war there had been competitions between units in Seamanship and Signalling. This no doubt helped to raise standards. At such a competition held on the Thames on H.M.S. *President* in 1939, units came from as far afield as Cardiff, Norwich, Canterbury, Elham Valley, East Cowes and Whitstable.[17] Alas, wartime restrictions put a stop to such activity, at least on this scale. Indeed, for some cadets travelling to their own unit was hazardous enough; travelling to other units was often impossible. In 1940 the Dundee unit, which was only a year old and had 105 cadets and a waiting list, had to reduce training to Saturday and Sunday afternoons 'so that the cadets may get home before the blackout. Some, being evacuated, have to come from a distance'.[18] The problem was even greater in cities such as London and Coventry, and the naval ports such as Plymouth and Portsmouth.

It was in 1942 that the Admiralty took complete control of naval training in the S.C.C. The Admiralty from then on made decisions about the syllabus. This included the standards of instruction, the number of cadets between the ages of 14 and 17, the strength and maximum number of units, the hours of attendance required from cadets, the ranks conferred on officers, and the numbers allowed to each unit.[19]

The initial discernible advantage following Admiralty involvement was the issue of uniforms. Each cadet aged 14 to 17 got a free issue of a 'Cap, Jumper, Trousers, Collar, Flannel and Jersey, Silk and Lanyard, Great Coat or Oilskin'. And, as mentioned previously, there was an injection of cash via grants. These were graduated according to the cadet's age, physical fitness, type of training and record of attendance. The grant for those aged under 14 amounted to 3/6d per annum. For those over 14 and 'subject to a minimum parade attendance of 75 hours each year and to the Admiralty being satisfied as to the efficiency of the unit', the annual grant was 12/- per head. There was no grant aid to those over 17 that were not contracted to go into the Royal Navy.[20] In 1944 the Admiralty further raised the training grant to 17/6d, payable for each qualified Sea Cadet.[21]

The need for pre-service specialist training became more pressing as demands on the Royal Navy training establishments increased. It was in the interests both of the Admiralty and the Sea Cadet Corps that more cadets should receive specialist training (*Plate 9*). The cadet, on joining the Senior Service, already had a sense of discipline, was conversant with the language and rank structure and knew how to drill and perform basic seamanship skills. The Royal Navy thus saved time and money as the ex-cadet could by-pass much of the basic training. The S.C.C. was delighted to know that the training being done with the cadets was both appreciated and, more importantly, was relevant and worthwhile: it gave the Corps and its members a sense of being a part of the greater war effort. In 1941 the officers of H.M.S. *Chrysanthemum II*, a moored naval training ship already involved in instructing cadet signallers, made the suggestion that cadets of 16 or over should receive gunnery instruction. As a result the 'unrivalled facilities of a gunnery training ship were placed at the disposal of the Sea Cadet Corps in London'.[22] Such was the progress that in October 1941 a demonstration was given to the Second Sea Lord, Admiral Sir William Whitworth, by three Sea Cadet gun crews manning a 12-pounder HA, a 4-inch BL and a 4-inch QF gun. They had received, on average, 16 hours of instruction. The Admiral was both impressed and satisfied with the result.[23] H.M.S. *Chrysanthemum II* along with H.M.S. *President*, was however, primarily involved in signal instruction, and it was with the training of signallers and telegraphists, via the Bounty Scheme, that the Sea Cadet Corps was to make its most telling contribution to the Royal Navy.

THE BOUNTY SCHEME

In the mid-nineteenth century the ship *Stroud Packet* had plied her trade delivering tobacco from Bristol around the West Country ports. On retirement she was used as a houseboat on the River Severn. The ship was, in fact, the home of Lieutenant Olney, the Worcester Sea Cadet unit's commanding officer. In 1940 the vessel was offered for sale to the Navy League. The League readily accepted the offer, and the newly renamed T.S. *Bounty* was 're-employed' as a training base for visual and wireless signallers. She was fitted-out to accommodate 40 cadets. On the first course 30 out of the 50 boys (some had to be billeted on land) passed the three-week course and were given their instructors' badges. The demand for such training was not great at that time and the courses ended temporarily in September 1940.

As the war gathered momentum it became apparent that the navy was experiencing an acute shortage of visual and wireless ratings. The answer to this problem was the Sea Cadet Corps. The S.C.C. was the only naval youth organisation that was providing intensive training in both semaphore and telegraphy. The Navy League, following negotiations with the Admiralty, re-opened T.S. *Bounty* in January 1941 and re-started the signalling course (*Plate 10*). The course was extended to four weeks. On completion a cadet, assuming he had reached the requisite standard and was 17 years of age, could join the Royal Navy as an ordinary signalman, or as an ordinary telegraphist at seventeen-and-a-half – the latter required more training. The normal age of entry to the navy in times of hostilities was 18, but was lowered to 17 for adequately-trained Sea Cadets.[24] The S.C.C. undertook the task of producing a group of 24 cadets every four weeks, trained to a specific standard, for drafting into the Royal Navy.[25] The demand increased when, in July 1941, the Admiralty asked for additional numbers of partially trained personnel. Accommodation was limited on board T.S. *Bounty* and so the S.C.C. headquarters at Grenville Hall, Slough was converted into a Signals School.

The opening of the Slough Training Centre meant added cost for the Navy League. Apart from anything else the Slough centre needed heating. In order for the centre to be opened in October a decision from the Treasury 'with regard to Admiralty payment for the cadets entered under the 'Bounty' scheme was necessary'.[26] The Admiralty appeared to 'drag its feet' when it came to decisions regarding finance for the Navy League. In contrast the other cadet organisations did not have these problems. The A.C.F. and A.T.C. were recognised as integral parts of their respective parent services. On the other hand, the S.C.C. was an independent organisation. As mentioned earlier, the needs of the navy were great at this time, and with the added Admiralty requirement – the expansion of the S.C.C. to 50,000 cadets – the Navy League got what it demanded in the way of finance. However, feelings between the Navy League and the Admiralty were still suspiciously frosty, despite the needs of war. The League was concerned 'as to the extent to which the Admiralty might consider taking control of . . . the training establishments'. In the Minutes of the League's meeting in March 1942, it is stated that a representative from the Navy League's H.Q. should be present at any Admiralty inspection.[27] At an earlier meeting the League's Committee had assured the Navy's representative that 'no part of the capitation grant previously allowed by the Admiralty was kept by the Navy League for administrative purposes'.[28]

Despite the distrust between the authorities the Bounty Scheme was a success. The increase in convoys meant there was a greater demand for visual signalmen in both the Royal Navy and in the Merchant fleets. At a meeting in October 1942 the Navy League agreed to comply with the suggestions of the Admiralty and the called-for increase. The number of cadets graduating from the Bounty Scheme trebled from 900 to 2,700 cadets per annum.[29] At the same meeting Rear-Admiral Attwood informed the Committee that 'now . . . the Sea Cadet movement was firmly established, it was proposed to concentrate on a higher standard of efficiency among cadets', and for this purpose the Admiralty increased the capitation grants payable to units.[30]

To get cadets up to the standard whereby they warranted training via the Bounty Scheme and then passed into the Navy was a feather in any unit's cap. In the pages of *The Sea Cadet* journal of July 1943, Birmingham (T.S. *Queen*) was congratulated on having the most candidates (23 cadets) accepted into the Communications Branch of the Royal Navy during the first six months of 1943. In fact, up to that date it had 75 cadets accepted for the branch – more than any other unit hitherto.[31] The wireless and telegraph (W/T) training remained at Worcester until 1944 when, owing to expansion, it had to be moved to Windermere, and T.S. *Bounty* was then used for other sorts of training. The visual and semaphore (V/S) side moved first to Slough and finally, in June 1943, to H.M.S. *Foudroyant* in Portsmouth Harbour. From January 1945 all V/S and W/T training was carried out at Portsmouth. The training base consisted of two old wooden sailing ships moored alongside each other, H.M.S. *Foudroyant* and H.M.S. *Implacable* (formerly the *Duguay Trouin*). This became the Headquarters afloat of the Sea Cadet Corps (*Plates 11 and 12*). During the first half of 1943 a total of 543 candidates for the Communication Branch passed into the Royal Navy to complete their signalling training. With the opening of new battlefronts in Europe the demand for V/S signallers, to man the numerous small craft needed for amphibious operations, was growing and becoming more urgent. The training that the Sea Cadet Corps was doing via the Bounty Scheme was therefore directly connected to the military war effort.

MECHANICAL TRAINING

The advantage of pre-entry training as evidenced by the success of the Bounty Scheme was obvious, and so in 1944 it was decided to widen the sea cadet syllabus even further and include mechanical training. Courses described as Petty Officer Training (Mechanical Branch) were instituted for cadet Able Seamen. The new training syllabus covered: 'mensuration and mechanical drawing; a fitting course, tools and their uses, practical work and test pieces; theoretical and practical instruction on engines, including final stages of fault finding on various types of running engines, and a detailed electrical course, both theoretical and practical, again including fault finding'.[32]

The syllabus was designed to be progressive and to occupy five consecutive courses over a period of 18 months. Progress depended on success in examinations. At the end of the first two courses a successful cadet had earned the right to wear the Cadet Mechanic's Badge. The

Entry for Sea Cadets into Royal and Merchant Navy (AS AT NOVEMBER, 1943)

Age	Branch	Continuous Service (12 years from age of 18) or Hostilities only	QUALIFICATIONS Educational	QUALIFICATIONS Medical	QUALIFICATIONS Special	Method of Entry
15–16	Artificer Apprentices: Engineroom, Electrical, Ordnance and Air.	C.S.	By Competitive Exam. held in Spring and Autumn.	Sound constitution. Normal colour vision. Distant vision standard – Snellen 6/9. (Preliminary medical exam. recommd. See paragraph 6 of pamphlet.	Limited number of nominations reserved for sons of Naval and Dockyard personnel.	Application to Civil Service Commissioners or Secretary of the Admiralty.
15.6–16.6	Seaman Class Boys, 2nd Class.	C.S.	Good Elementary School standard.	Good physique and vision standard.	Six months in S.C.C. and recommended by C.O. for accelerated entry.	Recruiting Staff Officer, R.N. and R.M. Headquarters Recruiting Office.
16–19	Engineering Cadetships for Technical Commissions in all the Services.	C.S.	School Certificate with credit in Maths. or Science or Physics.	Medical Examination after Selection Board.	Selection by interview.	Application through Min. of Labour and National Service.
16.3–16.6	Buglers in Shore Establishments.	H.O.	S.C.C. Entry standard.	S.C.C. Entry standard.	Entry as vacancies occur.	Application to Combined Recruiting Centre through C.O.
16.6.*	'Y' Scheme for leaders and potential officers in R.N., F.A.A. and R.M.	H.O.	School Certificate or C.O.'s certificate of good education and personality.	Medical Grade I. Good standard of vision, particularly for F.A.A. and Seaman.	Powers of leadership.	Application through C.O. to Combined Recruiting Centre followed by interview at Naval Centre.
From 16.9	Merchant Navy – Deck Ratings.	—	—	S.C.C. Entry standard (Exam. within previous six months.)	Up to Cadet Leading Seaman standard. Recommended by C.O.	Entry form signed by Cadet and C.O. to Registrar-General of Shipping and Seaman.
17.0–17.10	Communications Branch, *Bounty* and *Foudroyant* Scheme (W.T. and V/S).	H.O.	Good writing and spelling (Dictation Test).	V/S – Vision Standard I. Colour Vision – Grade II. W/T – Vision Standard II and III. Hearing Standard minimum II.	Prescribed Tests for Semaphore, Flashing and Buzzer.	Application to Combined Recruiting Centre through C.O.
17.0–18.0	Provisional Mechanic. Group I – General Service and Fleet Air Arm. Group II – Electrical Engineroom, Ordnance and Motor Mechanics, Air Fitters.	H.O.	School Certificate standard in Maths. and Physical Science. Above Elementary School standard.	Medical Grade I. Vision Standard III. Hearing Standard II. do.	By selection, as vacancies limited.	Naval Recruiter at Combined Recruiting Centre.
From 17	Ordinary Seaman.	H.O.	Average Elementary School standard.	Medical Grade I. Vision Standard II. Hearing Standard II.	—	Naval Recruiter at C.R.C. (Entries between 17 and 17½ are rated Seaman Boys.
From 17½	Stoker.	H.O.	do.	Medical Grade I. Vision Standard II. Hearing Standard III.	—	Naval Recruiter at Combined Recruiting Centre.
From 17½	Coder, Writer, Supply, Steward, Photographer, Air Mechanic, S.B.A.	H.O.	do.	As for Seaman, but lower visual standards.	—	do.
17.6	University Short Course.	H.O.	At least School Certificate standard.	As for 'Y' Scheme.	Powers of leadership.	Nomination by Head Master to Naval Centre, followed by interview and medical exam.
From 18	Cook.	H.O.	Average Elementary School standard.	As for Seaman, but lower visual	—	Naval Recruiter at Combined Recruiting Centre.

NOTE – As the conditions of entry into all Branches are liable to alteration, this chart may quickly become out of date and should be read as a guide only.

*Age of enrolment in unpaid reserve pending call-up.

Fig. 4 – Entry requirements for Royal & Merchant Navies 1944 [Issued as a supplement to *The Sea Cadet*, January 1944]

Admiralty stated that 'this specialist qualification ranks high in merit, and therefore takes longer to acquire'. At the end of the full course a successful cadet qualified as a Provisional Mechanic and was well on his way to a career in the Royal Navy. The branches he could enter were categorised under two groups:

>Group II: Electrical Mechanic, Engine-Room Mechanic,
>Ordnance Mechanic, Motor Mechanic, Air Fitter
>Group III: Air Mechanic

The Admiralty considered that mechanical proficiency alone was not enough for anyone who wanted to join the Royal Navy. At a later stage in the training, educational standards were set for the Group, that had to be attained. Cadets who wanted to join the navy in Group II, for example, needed to be of School Certificate standard in maths and physical science: an elementary education was not enough (see *Fig. 4*).

The Admiralty was impressed by the enthusiasm of the cadets, the majority of whom came straight from work to a unit parade, despite the blackouts and air raids. The main problem was finding suitable training facilities. The average S.C.C. unit did not possess either the instructional expertise or the facilities. Local colleges were made use of but the Admiralty hoped that local firms might provide assistance, particularly in areas where shipbuilding and marine engineering were established occupations. Some units, such as Wallsend and Lowestoft, provided their own engineering classes for the older cadets. In late 1943 the first mechanical training unit for the London area was begun. The 100 cadets attending classes in London came from the Richmond, Hayes, Twickenham, Acton, Feltham and Kingston units.[33]

The navy was also in need of artificer apprentices. Entry for the artificer was by a competitive exam set by the Civil Service Commission twice a year. The successful candidates would follow a four-year engineering course in the Royal Navy. The trade vacancies for the Royal and Merchant Navies were periodically published in *The Sea Cadet* journal under 'Continuous service' or for 'Hostilities only'.[34]

THE MERCHANT NAVY

In September 1943 units were informed of the shortened course instituted by the Ministry of War at Wallasey, near Liverpool. The plan was to provide 50 trained volunteers per month. In the first six months in which the scheme operated 732 cadets from 250 units undertook the shortened course. Of these 'no fewer than 619 obtained 1st Class passes which entitled them to be rated as junior ordinary seaman; the remaining 113 qualified as deck boys'.[35] No cadet failed, although a few were unable to complete the course for medical reasons.

A report from the Registrar-General of Shipping and Seamen demonstrated that the Sea Cadet Corps had more than fulfilled its commitment. He said in his report that, 'it is not only a major contribution to the war effort, but a guarantee that the Merchant Navy of the future will look to the Corps for much of its finest material and that in the days of peace the openings for cadets to a career at sea will not be confined to a necessarily restricted entry for the Royal Navy'.[36] Over half of the S.C.C. units sent cadets to the Merchant Navy training establishment at Wallasey. According to a report in the journal the following were worthy of mention:

> Ballyholme (14 cadets), Belfast – from all units (12), Falkirk (16), Glasgow – from all units (12), Halifax (11), Hoylake (9), Liverpool – from all units (21), Sunderland (10), Southend (9), Stoke Newington (9).[37]

Boys who had no previous sea training required a 10-week course before they could take the tests. The ex-S.C.C. cadets were able to take and pass the tests at the end of four weeks of training. So pleased were the Merchant Navy authorities with the standard of the ex-S.C.C. entrants that entry qualifications were changed. No longer did a sea cadet have to reach the rank of Cadet Petty Officer or Leading Seaman before entering the Service, instead the rank of AB would suffice. The minimum age of entry was sixteen-and-a-half. The pass rate for ex-S.C.C. cadets was 100 per cent.[38]

The maintenance of a constant output of trained ratings was important to the national war effort, especially when the loss of life is considered. In the winter months of 1942 the strain on the British fleet was immense, especially in the North Sea and the convoys to Russia. A dreadful tragedy came in June 1942 on convoy P.Q.17. A false alarm led to the dispersal of the convoy and 23 of its 24 ships were sunk. In March 1943, the worst month of the war, 477,000 tons of shipping was sunk and only 12 U-boats were destroyed in the North Atlantic. During the last quarter of the year the tables were turned – 37 U-boats were sunk with the comparatively low loss of 146,000 tons of shipping. The reversal in fortunes was due to a number of factors. These included: the provision of American destroyers as escorts; the diversion of R.A.F. bombers to escort duties; the putting out of action of the German battleship *Tirpitz* by two Royal Navy midget submarines; the sinking of the battle cruiser *Scharnhorst* by H.M.S. *Duke of York*. And, at long last, Portugal allowed the Allies to use the Azores as an air base and so reduce the gap in mid-Atlantic.[39]

Cadets were eligible to go to sea when they had reached the age of 17. The cadets who obtained a first-class pass at the end of their month's course entered the Merchant Navy as Junior Ordinary Seamen on a basic wage of £8 10s a month, plus £10 a month war-risk money. Those who got a second-class pass entered as Deck Boys at £4 10s a month, and, most extraordinary of all, with a reduced war-risk payment of £5 per month. Presumably the life of a Deck Boy was worth half as much as that of a Junior Seaman! Unlike the R.N. seaman, a merchant sailor had a disadvantage in that he had to pay for his uniform. The cost to the cadet was between £6 and £9 and included the kit worn at the training school. Should they survive a year at sea they were eligible, if they were 18 years or older, to take the Ministry's Efficient Deck Hand examination and receive the same pay as an AB, which was £14 a month and £10 a month war-risk money.[40]

SUMMER CAMPS

In 1943 the aim was to send 10,000 cadets away for a week's training in seamanship and to introduce them to a disciplined way of life in a service environment. It was hoped that this would instil in them a sense of unity and pride in the Services. Given the difficulties of wartime the statistics are impressive. In the summer of 1943, 15,300 cadets and 550 officers attended Admiralty camps; this represented 40 per cent of establishment.

Of this total, 3,400 cadets went to R.N. air stations and flew with the Fleet Air Arm. The air stations included H.M.S. *Nightjar*, at Inskip near Preston, which is now a Royal Naval wireless station and a Sea Cadet Training Centre. This was the first time sea cadets had this opportunity. Air Training Corps cadets had started attending similar camps in 1942. As the air cadets were older and had spent more time on aeronautical training, they were more advanced, but presumably the sea cadets came into their own when they provided the ship's company, duty boat's crew, mechanics, stokers and working parties for the Fleet Air Arm's yacht *Zaza*.

Sixteen of the 26 camps were at or close to naval establishments, and cadets were therefore able to gain valuable hands-on experience. Specialist training in seamanship and navigation was available for 700 cadet petty officers and leading seamen at Pangbourne Nautical College or at the Department of Navigation, Southampton University. At the camps in naval bases, cadets had the opportunity to sample some aspects of naval life. They spent time working in dockyards and gunnery schools and went on board all manner of craft including corvettes, minesweepers, MTBs, patrol boats and landing craft. In all, 7,000 cadets visited naval barracks and training establishments.[41]

Port Eynon, near Worms Head in the Bristol Channel, catered for 2,500 cadets during the summer months. Each cadet unit stayed a week. They followed the usual activities included in a tented summer camp: map reading, hill walking, climbing, team games, plus sailing and rowing.

There were separate camps for cadets in Northern Ireland and in Scotland.[42] Towards the latter half of the war training facilities were expanded. In 1944 the Marine Society generously agreed to make a grant to enable cadets to attend a four-week course at the Outward Bound School at Aberdovey each month. The objective was to 'give cadets a sea sense through practical experience afloat and at the same time to enable them to achieve a high standard of physical fitness before embarking on a sea-going career'. The courses were therefore limited to cadets who had passed their Petty Officer exam and were near the age of call-up into the Royal or Merchant Navy. The School possessed a 60-ton auxiliary schooner and an 80-ton auxiliary ketch, and so every cadet was able to go on a seven-day cruise in the open waters of Cardigan Bay. The school had smaller craft as well. Advantage was also taken of the natural mountainous terrain to do camping and map reading.[43]

TRAINING OF SEA CADET OFFICERS

In 1940 the unit in Poole, Dorset had 150 cadets and there was a waiting list of potential recruits.[44] The expansion in cadet numbers was not matched by a corresponding recruitment to the adult ranks – indeed, the reverse was true. The problem became acute when five officers were called up for active service and a further two joined the R.N.V.R. There was one Warrant Officer left, plus one Sergeant Major who took drill. The situation was by no means unique. The loss of adult leaders was a continual problem throughout the war.[45]

It was essential, indeed inevitable, that the Royal Navy, having taken over control of cadet training, should also do the same for adult training. And so, in November 1942 the Royal Naval College, Greenwich, staged the first course for the training of officers. The course lasted a fortnight and included lectures on the following topics:

> Traditions and Customs in the Royal Navy
> The Outline of Leadership, Discipline, Morale, *Esprit de Corps*, etc
> Naval History
> King's Regulations and Admiralty Instructions
> Ship and Fleet Organisation, Seamanship and Navigation, etc
> Messing and Victualling

There was also practical instruction on 'Seamanship, Field Training, Rifle and Pistol Firing, Physical Training, Signals, Wireless Telegraphy and A.R.P. Work'.[46] The course was concluded in the usual Service fashion with a formal dinner. This finale also, no doubt, served to familiarise those without Wardroom experience with the way a naval officer conducts himself on formal occasions. A total of 22 officers attended the course, all of whom had experience in commanding sea cadets, and over half had previous naval service.

Periodic courses at Greenwich were not enough. Increasingly, with officers leaving for active service and the calling up of younger adults into the Services, the onus of instruction fell on the shoulders of inexperienced officers. Some other officers were well beyond retirement age. In 1941 the Secretary of the Sea Cadet Corps put forward the idea that the Navy League's S.C.C. Committee should 'lay down a retiring age for Sea Cadet Corps Officers'. He cited as examples the Commanding Officers of Dulwich and East Cowes units, who were both well over 70 years of age.[47] However, it was better that the administrative helm should be held by an enthusiastic old 'sea-dog' than that a unit should close for want of leadership.

In order to cater for the demand, courses for officers were subsequently held on the Corps' flagship, the 120 year-old corvette H.M.S. *Foudroyant*, and the 150 year-old Trafalgar veteran H.M.S. *Implacable* (*Plates 11 and 12*). Many officers could not attend for the full two weeks and the duration of the course was accordingly reduced to one week. The shortage of experienced young officers was an inevitable consequence of the war. It was no surprise, therefore, to find that the Chief of Instructional Staff H.M.S. *Foudroyant* was a 64 year-old R.N.V.R. Lieutenant, namely Harold Wyllie, the son of the famous artist William Wyllie RA.

One of the more interesting training courses was held on a 72-foot Brixham trawler. This vessel, named T.S. *Gold Seal*, was loaned in 1943 to the Newport unit for the duration. It was used to instruct officers and senior cadets in the art of navigation and sailing. In May 1943 T.S. *Gold Seal* docked at Newport after a round trip of 200 miles at an average speed of seven knots.

The trawler was used regularly at weekends for training and for other purposes. The latter involved delivering Sunday newspapers to a lightship. Occasionally it was called out for more serious missions. In the summer of 1943, the local Admiralty H.Q. instructed its crew to investigate a report 'received of an obstruction sighted in the Channel by a merchant ship'. By all accounts the crew felt a part of the Navy on these types of trips. In this instance it was nothing more serious than a small tree with a branch sticking up; to the merchant ship's skipper it could have appeared as something more sinister! Following the investigation a signal was sent back from the lightship to the Admiralty. The ship's log shows that between May and September 1943 the vessel had been in commission for 360 hours, in addition to working parties and instructional lectures being held aboard.[48]

Specific training that was directly related to wartime necessity, such as signalling and engineering, was undertaken with great enthusiasm. The reason was obvious; it gave the Sea Cadet Corps a direct role in the war effort, and the opportunity to get afloat and engage in waterborne activities.

THE 'Y' SCHEME

The object of the 'Y' Scheme was to select, in advance, young men who were considered to be potential candidates for a commission. It was also intended to ensure that they received the most suitable form of pre-entry training. It was open to future leaders of the Royal Navy, Fleet Air Arm, Royal Marines and the Royal Air Force. Young men could volunteer for the 'Y' Scheme on reaching the age of 17. A boy who wanted to join the Fleet Air Arm but who was not already a cadet was expected to join either the Sea Cadet Corps or the Air Training Corps. He could transfer from the S.C.C. to the A.T.C. or vice versa so that he would receive the appropriate training, but once he had moved from one Corps to the other, he could not transfer back, and during the meantime he was placed on unpaid Reserve service.[49]

Candidates had to be medically Grade I and be able to produce one of the following:

1. A School Certificate, or
2. A certificate stating that the candidate had attained School Certificate standard and the reason why the actual certificate was not obtained. The certificate had to be signed by the Headmaster of the school attended, or
3. A recommendation and a certificate from his Commanding Officer stating that the candidate was of outstanding personality and of good education and had been, for at least a year, an efficient member of the S.C.C. or A.T.C.[50]

This meant that any young man not in possession of the School Certificate needed to join either the S.C.C. or the A.T.C. before reaching the age of 17. All candidates, with permission from their Commanding Officer, had to apply in person to a Combined Recruiting Centre. Provided they passed the medical examination and were considered suitable they attended a further interview at a Selection Board at the Naval Recruiting Centre.

Those applying for short courses at university had to have at least the School Certificate. The reference and nomination would, in this case, come from a headmaster rather than a unit Commanding Officer. The medical assessment and interview procedure was the same as for the 'Y' scheme candidates.

There is no doubt that those cadets who were undergoing training on the 'Bounty' and 'Y' schemes felt a part of the navy and that they were participating in the war effort. All boys were proud to be part of the Senior Service, although, in response to a questionnaire completed by ex-wartime sea cadets, this pride was diminished by the inclusion of very young cadets in the unit. A teenage cadet was aware that his training was a preparation for the 'real thing' and the older he got the more he felt this; but the presence of young 11 or 12 year-old boys in a unit dented the image. Later, in 1942, the age of entry to the S.C.C. was set at 14 years – the same as for the other pre-service cadet organisations. Indeed so keen were some cadets to appear part of the navy that they would unpick the letters NL from 'N.L.S.C.C.' on their cap ribbons, believing that the three remaining letters looked more navy-like.

THE ARMY CADETS

In 1938 General Lord Bridgeman – ex-regular soldier and in charge of the Officer Training Corps in schools and universities – joined the British National Cadet Association Committee. A year later he was to become its chairman. This was, for a number of reasons, a decisive appointment in the history of the A.C.F. First, Lord Bridgeman had taken heed of the lessons learnt after the First World War. He realised that cadets could no longer be regarded as 'toy soldiers', a mere imitation of the 'real thing'. He felt that the A.C.F. was a pre-service organisation, with stress on the '*pre*'. The emphasis was to be on the development of the social as well as the military side of training. Hence in December 1940, the B.N.C.A. stated that:

> This Association wishes to offer its full support to the efforts of those who are urging the Government to put forward a scheme for the general welfare of the youth of Britain that will cater not only for their physical wellbeing but train them in leadership and citizenship, as opposed to schemes based almost entirely on physical training.[51]

Lord Bridgeman was mindful of what was happening in Germany with the Hitler Jungend, where the wholesale military politicisation of youth was the main objective. The development of the individual was to be the A.C.F.'s main aim. Some people did think that the Cadet Movement was a British version of the Hitler Youth. However, no one could deny that Britain was facing a crisis, and that sooner or later most boys would be required to don a uniform and help defend the country and democracy. It was therefore sensible, logical and advantageous both to the individual and the Services to prepare boys for the task ahead. And the newly-formed Cadet War Emergency Committee under Lord Bridgeman, with Sir Philip Carlebach representing non-schools units and Colonel J. Huck the school units, undertook the task of re-assessing the training needs.

Secondly, in May 1941, Lord Bridgeman became Director General of the Home Guard, which was to the advantage of the Army Cadets; particularly as a month earlier a decision had been taken to transfer the responsibility for Cadets from the T.A. to the Home Guard Directorate. Although the A.C.F. formed only a small part of the Director's responsibility the effects were felt immediately. In May 1941 authority was given for a free issue of basic uniform and equipment to the A.C.F. In addition there was an increase in the grant paid to the B.N.C.A. and the *per capita* grant for qualified cadets was also increased.

THE TRAINING SYLLABUS

The overall aim was to produce a 'rounded cadet', but the needs of the moment meant that it had to be done within a war setting and this necessitated an overhaul of the training standards. The British National Cadet Association's old Green Efficiency Star became obsolete. The B.N.C.A. had been asking the War Office for advice on training. There was a call to standardise procedure, and make it more workable. As a result Certificate 'A', which had been in operation for the Junior Training Corps in schools only, was extended and was now applied to the A.C.F.

The Certificate 'A' syllabus was not appropriate for all cadets. Although under-age enrolment was strictly discouraged in the A.C.F., where the minimum age of entry was fixed at 14, some schools and a few A.C.F. units allowed 12 year-old boys to join the ranks of cadets, and for them the programme was too advanced. How prevalent this 'early' entry was in schools is not known, but there is reference to it in the *Army Cadet Journal*; for example, in a 1942 report about the St Albans School J.T.C. it is stated that:

> Boys are enrolled at 14+, having already had one or two years preliminary training in an independent 'Junior Corps'.[52]

Despite discouragement from the B.N.C.A. the training of the under-14s must have been carried out in sufficient numbers to justify the production of a separate training pamphlet for this age group. In 1942 the War Office published a training manual titled *The Training of the Younger Cadet*. It is stated in the forward that the 'book has been designed primarily to cover training of the 12 to 14-year-old cadet'. The core subjects covered are listed as drill, fieldcraft and observation, regimental history, map reading, weapon training (with .22 rifle) and verbal messages. The latter could entail acting as a 'runner' for the unit's officer, or be incorporated into observation exercises and the relaying of messages. Interestingly the observation exercises included identifying British military vehicle tracks; pictures in the manual show tracks of a 30-cwt lorry, Mark II Valentine tank, Universal troop carrier and other modes of British Army transport.[53]

CERTIFICATE 'A'

The majority of cadets were over 14 and were engaged in training for the Certificate 'A'. The onset of war and the resultant military needs gave Certificate 'A' training an added importance and both the J.T.C. and A.C.F. naturally wanted to prepare their cadets properly for service in the Armed Forces.

Examinations were now to be purely practical. This would make them more realistic, would encourage the cadets to participate, and would cut down on paper work. To help motivate individual cadets and their units to gain good results, and to produce more trained personnel, the B.N.C.A. changed the conditions governing the award of the General National Trophy – a prize awarded to the top unit. The Rifle Brigade Association Club agreed to loan the Association a trophy for the duration of hostilities. This made it possible to hold separate competitions for school units and for open cadet units. The General National Trophy was henceforth awarded to the open Cadet unit that obtained the highest percentage of War Certificates 'A' during the Cadet year ending on 31 October. The Rifle Brigade Trophy was awarded to the top 'closed' school unit on the same basis. It was stipulated that no unit would be allowed to hold the trophy more than once in four years, thereby giving all units the opportunity to be successful. It was felt that if a contingent was allowed to dominate, this would de-motivate the remainder and would be counter-productive.[54]

In early 1943 a revised Certificate 'A' syllabus came into effect and the title 'War' Certificate 'A' was adopted. The usual subjects of foot drill and arms drill, map reading, fieldcraft and signalling were maintained, and in some cases extended. The map-reading pamphlet now included sections on Intervisibility and Resection, and fieldcraft training had chapters on the Use of Sandtables and Outdoor Exercises. The most radically re-written chapter was the one that dealt with weapons training. The main full-bore weapon fired by cadets was the Lee Enfield .303 rifle, although some units had Bren guns. One result of the evacuation of Dunkirk and the abandonment of vast quantities of weaponry, including the soldiers' personal arms on the beaches of Normandy, was that many cadet units had to give their Bren guns and rifles to the Home Guard, who, presumably, had to forego their weapons for the frontline forces. The Bren Light Machine Gun was to disappear from the cadet armouries, eventually being replaced by the smaller, lighter and much cheaper Sten Machine-Carbine. In some cases training with automatic weapons was done with the Thompson Sub-Machine Carbine or, occasionally, with the Lewis Machine-gun (*Plate 13*).

Towards the latter part of the war the Bren gun became more available. The training pamphlet reflected the needs of the time, hence there were lectures on 'anti-aircraft action, [with] Bren and rifle'.[55] In the pamphlet on *Section Training Exercises* by Major Ward of Sedbergh School J.T.C. there were chapters on exercises for 'Anti-Tank Protection' and 'House and Street Fighting'.[56] This form of training was for the more senior cadets and was to be used only during the war. Once the war was over these lessons were removed from the training syllabus.

Interestingly, signalling was taken out of the basic syllabus, semaphore no longer being used. Where morse-keys and an instructor were available the Morse code was taught, but it was no longer part of the basic certificate. Later in the war more radios and field telephones became available for courses in signalling, such as those held in Leicestershire (see *Plate 14*). Training in signalling was regarded as post-certificate training. The use of the Signal Message Form AFC2136 as employed by the Royal Corps of Signals was not taught, unless it was part of a post-certificate course in Wireless and Telegraph operating. A special pamphlet was devised for training cadets in the taking and passing of written and verbal messages, and subsequently became an integral part of the Certificate 'A' syllabus. In the training manual *Message Writing for Cadets*, it is stated that:

> Within platoons and sections, with which cadet training usually deals, messages will be written on ordinary paper, or passed verbally.
>
> Every cadet must be able to write a message clearly, and pass a verbal message accurately. No cadet can do either unless he has clear handwriting, an accurate memory, and understands what the message is about. Exercising the memory and practising handwriting must, if necessary, be included as part of training in messages.[57]

Cadets had to learn the correct procedure for writing messages. That is, how to properly describe positions, the use of capital letters, description of roads and areas, the recording of bearings, and the use of abbreviations. They would also need to be familiar with the 24-hour clock and the phonetic alphabet. In short they had to learn how to accurately compose and deliver a military message. This part of the cadet's training became increasingly important later on if he had the opportunity to work as a messenger for the Home Guard, as many of them did.

The necessity for learning First Aid was abundantly apparent especially for those living in areas under blitz from the German airforce. Strangely, first aid was not part of the official syllabus but it was greatly encouraged. Physical Training or 'Physical Efficiency Preparation for Service Cadets' as the War Office termed such training, was a part of the Certificate 'A' assessment. The PT tests remained obligatory until the end of the war. They were designed to appraise four physical qualities under the headings of: agility, endurance, strength and swimming – although swimming was voluntary as participation depended on the availability of a swimming pool. The PT syllabus applied to all three cadet services.

It was assumed that a cadet required at least six months' training before taking the Certificate 'A' Part I (Individual) Examination. In fact no cadet under the age of 15 was allowed to participate in the exam. Major-General J. A. C. Whitaker, Director of Military Training at the War Office, stated that the 1943 revised training scheme's main objective was 'the production of leaders and technicians for the Army of the near future'. He added:

> The training given to Army Cadets covers the basic subjects of soldiering, which must be mastered by all soldiers before they can be efficient and certainly before they can aspire to leadership as NCOs. or as officers.[58]

In order to find and then to partly train future leaders, Part II (Section Leaders) Certificate 'A' was devised. The main objective was to 'test cadets in their knowledge of basic infantry training, particularly in individual fieldcraft and, in addition, to discover the ability of the cadet as a potential leader'.[59] The age requirement for the Part II (Section Leaders) exam was 16. The Part II syllabus was divided into four parts: drill, weapon training, map reading and section leading.

In Certificate 'A' Part I, the cadet was expected to perform certain drill movements; in Part II he had to take 'command of and drill a squad (not of the recruit stage) and to detect and correct faults of individuals . . .'. The weapon training involved passing a skill-at-arms test on the Bren LMG as well as with the rifle. Map reading was a practical test in navigation. The one section that was most important for identifying future army N.C.O.s and officers concerned section leading. The cadet N.C.O. was tested on his knowledge of fieldcraft and his ability to lead a section of eight cadets. He would have to be able to show competence, and evidence of the following:

> The organisation and equipment of the platoon
> Section formations
> Advanced observation training
> Selection of fire positions
> Battle drill for section in the attack
> Section in defence
> Giving fire control orders

Cadets would be expected to have a detailed knowledge of 'parade ground battle drill' and to have sufficient knowledge to 'apply the principles and methods tactically'. If open ground was not available the examination could take place using models on a sand table. Twenty per cent of the marks were allotted for drill, 25 per cent each for weapon training and map reading and 30 per cent for section leading. Thus, the importance of leadership was emphasised. In order to qualify, candidates had to obtain at least 50 per cent under each heading, and at least 60 per cent of the total mark.[60]

The extent to which the cadets could apply the military tactics they had learnt depended on the equipment and facilities, and on the imagination of the platoon commander. During the first two years of war equipment was in short supply. Rifle drill and fieldcraft had to be done with wooden replica rifles; and, as mentioned, the Sten gun was substituted for the Bren gun. Nevertheless enthusiasm was high and training in stalking and camouflage was not halted. Cadets always enjoy challenging exercises. At Chard in Somerset, for example, 'great interest was accordingly aroused when ... half of the Cadets tried but failed to storm and retake the boiler house at the High Street school'. Imaginary Nazis defended it in the blackout. The report stated that 'the Chard boys showed decided skill in stealthily approaching and entering the premises but their coming was heralded by a grazing horse and by bombs – or, in other words, tin lids on strings'.[61] Regardless of the outcome such exercises proved popular and, more importantly, they gave all the cadets an opportunity to try out infantry skills and gave the N.C.O.s a chance to practise leadership.

TECHNICAL TRAINING FOR ARMY CADETS

The main objective of the A.C.F. as far as the War Office was concerned was to turn out a constant flow of trained recruits for the Army. This did not mean just producing cadets who were physically fit, could shoot, read a map and go on foot patrols. It also meant giving basic training to those who would be looking after lorries, tanks, maintaining guns, operating signals equipment. For every infantryman and gunner there were another eight people working in communications, supply and maintenance. To meet this demand a Technical Training Scheme was introduced in the autumn of 1942.

Different systems of training were adopted, the variance depending upon the initiative, facilities and co-operation both of the local A.C.F. unit and the Education Authority. In the War Office pamphlet technical training is referred to under two headings, Type 'A' and Type 'B'. However, before a boy could undertake technical training he had first to pass his Certificate 'A' Part I (infantry training). This normally took place in the summer months; in the winter months preference was given to technical training.

The local Education Authorities at their technical colleges ran the type 'A' course. In Hampshire, for example, the following three types of courses were organised:

1. *Technical* – Mathematics; Workshop Drawing; I.C. Engine; or Science or Metalwork or Woodwork.
2. *Building* – Mathematics; Building Geometry; Building Construction; Practical Woodwork or Carpentry.
3. *Commercial* – English; Commercial Arithmetic; Shorthand; Typewriting or Bookkeeping.[62]

It was agreed that a cadet who was successful in any of the courses would be awarded his A.C.F. Certificate 'T'. In order that cadets should realise that technical training was just as much 'a part of national service as any other form of Cadet activity, they are usually expected to parade for these classes in uniform' (*Plate 15*). The War Office refunded the fees of all cadets who showed a satisfactory record of attendance.[63]

Type 'B' courses were run by the A.C.F. and usually consisted of classes on the Internal Combustion Engine and Motor Mechanics. This was the approach taken in Warwickshire A.C.F. where a Technical Training Sub-Committee was set up under the chairmanship of a R.E.M.E. Colonel, with technical representatives from Birmingham, Coventry and Stratford-upon-Avon Technical Colleges. Often, one of the major problems was finding instructors and facilities, but in the industrial West Midlands with its preponderance of engineering firms this was not too much of a difficulty. Some tools were available from War Office stock, but much equipment had to be scrounged.[64] The construction of a workroom with a bench and toolboxes was good training in itself. The R.A.F., which also had a great demand for tradesmen, realised the value of this branch of the A.C.F.'s work, and arrangements were made for Army Cadets who had undertaken the technical training to receive credit for it if they later joined the A.T.C. Thus there was a degree of co-operation between the cadet services.

TRAINING OF OFFICERS AND INSTRUCTORS

As the demands of the army for trained personnel increased, the cadets in certain areas began to receive more and more help from the War Office and from particular regiments. Cadets from the London Irish Rifles, along with some from the Middlesex Regiment, attended an organised intensive course on 'musketry, gas and fieldcraft' run by the 70th Bn. The London Irish Rifles. The latter also arranged for a week-long course taken by N.C.O.s of the Battalion.[65] The Westminster Scottish Cadets obtained, via the 1st A.A. Divisional Signals Regiment, the services of an Army N.C.O. for signals instruction on Saturday afternoons.[66] There were also courses specifically for J.T.C. cadets. King's School at Bruton sent cadets to the Southern Command training camp at Devizes, and received visits to the school from R.E.M.E. Repair Units, and lectures from army officers about the German Army and Operations in France. In 1941 the school formed a Commando Platoon, 'which acted as an opposition force for exercises and Field Days'.[67] Clearly, where possible the units became more military in the way they operated. However, not every school was able to continue with the Field Days, and sometimes the personality of the individual in charge was less than helpful. An ex-wartime cadet from Shrewsbury School remembers the OC conducting his task of umpiring an exercise on a large grey horse. This resulted in concealed positions being revealed to the enemy.[68] The King's School at Bruton appeared to be more fortunate than most as Regular Units from the army joined in their Field Days in 1942 and 1943, with two troops of Scout cars and a 6-pounder A/T gun.[69] At Latymer Upper School Cadet Corps, the Welsh Guards provided a practical course on automatic weapons, including the 2-inch mortar.[70] In August 1945, when the war in Europe was drawing to a close, the army could afford to be more expansive with its assistance. At the 1st and 2nd Bn. King's Shropshire Light Infantry Cadets' camp at Dryffyn-on-Sea, for example, there were demonstrations both by the Army and the Royal Marines. The Royal Signals set up a signal station; the R.E.M.E. gave a demonstration of vehicle recovery; there was also a troop of light and heavy fighting vehicles, and the Royal Marines showed how to destroy a supposed Japanese command post.[71] This sort of demonstration and any instruction by Regular Army officers and N.C.O.s was dependent upon the availability of personnel, and presumably the nearness of a unit to a training camp. Such demonstrations were therefore held as and when it was possible.

From mid-1943 to the beginning of 1945, more than 4,000 officers and cadets had attended courses and been on detachment with the Regular Army throughout the U.K. At first this seems a lot, given the constraints of war, but it must be remembered that there were over 200,000 army cadets.[72] There was increasingly more skill-at-arms training. The increase in signals training was limited by equipment and by a paucity of instructors. One interesting experiment was carried out in 1944 when 30 J.T.C. and A.C.F. cadets attended an airborne training course at the London District P.T. School, Hendon. The aim was to find out how such training could be developed as a post-Certificate 'A' subject. Although the course was a great success, the idea went no further once the war had ended.[73]

The loss of trained adult personnel, particularly in the first two years of war, was considerable. In the 1st Cadet Bn. The Royal Fusiliers (City of London Regt.) 20 of the 28 officers on the strength had gained commissions in the Army.[74] War Office assistance with training did not start happening officially until 1942. Prior to this the Army, particularly since Dunkirk, had neither men nor equipment to spare. The fact that recruitment for the army cadets was restricted for the first two-and-a-half years of war can be seen in retrospect as a blessing; despite the fact that a number of instructors and officers were 'poached' by the newly-formed A.T.C. The existing A.C.F. personnel could not have coped with an 80 per cent increase in units, such as happened in 1942. The pressure to get cadets trained and ready for the armed forces was immense, and could even prove fatal. In October 1941 Captain George Groves, a teacher at Ilminster Grammar School and O.C. of the School's A.C.F. unit, collapsed and died while on a route march with cadets. He appeared to be in his usual good health until after a mile-and-a-half he was seen to clutch at the railings at the side of the road and sink to the ground. He had had a heart attack. Capt. Groves was a keen sportsman and veteran of the First World War. He was thought to be in his 60s, but it was discovered that he was, in fact, 76 years of age.[75] The unfortunate officer may be judged as being foolhardy for undertaking such an arduous task, but as nearly all the young staff had been called-up, he may have felt that there was no choice.[76] Even if the remaining schoolmasters were not enlisted the chances are they would have had additional wartime roles as A.R.P. Wardens, firewatchers or as members of the Home Guard. Indeed it was the Home Guard that provided the greatest help to the Army Cadet Force during the war.

The extent of cadet involvement with the Home Guard will be examined more closely in the following chapter. It was with mutual interest that the Home Guard and the A.C.F. worked together. The latter often acted as enemy when on exercise with the Home Guard, and the A.C.F. provided the officers and assistant instructors when there were large numbers of people to teach. In return the cadets got the instructors they so badly needed and the opportunity to use more advanced equipment. The cadets could, if the relationship between the two organisations was strong in the area, obtain training in other subjects such as anti-tank warfare, even unarmed combat. The H.G. had a vested interest in training army cadets – as declared in *The Cadet Journal* in October 1941, which reads:

> All Cadets are expected to join the Home Guard on reaching the age of 17, since young men of that age should be prepared actively to take up arms in the defence of their country should invasion occur, and this applies to members of the Cadet Force even more than to others, since they have already been trained in the use of arms. A Cadet unit is a training establishment with no operational role; the Home Guard has an operational role and therefore that is the unit in which the young man should fight between the age of 17 years and the time of his calling up for service in the Army.[77]

Thus the H.G. by assisting the cadets was, in effect, training its future members. The intention of the War Office was not that the cadet should leave the A.C.F. once he joined the Home Guard. The idea was that he should remain with the Cadet Force until he reached the age of 18 'in order to pull his weight as a leader of the younger Cadets'.[78] Thus a senior cadet could be in both organisations. It was intended that a cadet who joined the Home Guard should first satisfy the Commanding Officer that he was sufficiently trained to carry out an operational role. If the cadet had already passed Cert. 'A' Part I, for example, he would be excused much of the elementary Home Guard training. And, of course, any knowledge gained from advanced training he received as a member of the H.G. could, in turn, be imparted to cadets.

Unfortunately a proportion of the serving A.C.F. adults not drafted into the Armed Services were not, for one reason or another, the best people for the job. As a result, and to overcome the dearth of officers, training courses for adults were organised.[79] Week-long courses were started in 1941 at Pirbright, Malvern and Oxford. The course held at Malvern was run by the Regular Army and was attended by 176 officers, the youngest of whom had never been on parade before, and the oldest, who had never 'missed a parade or fell out, admitted to being 76 years of age'. It was certainly an intensive course as the list of subjects demonstrates. There were classes in:

> Drill, Weapon Training, Fieldcraft, Field Engineering, Attack and Defence Problems, Map Reading, Message and Report Writing, Lectures, Organisation of Infantry Battalions, Tanks and Supporting Arms, Gas, Man Management, Hygiene, and Umpiring.[80]

The syllabus went way beyond the Certificate 'A'. The working hours were extended to cater for the workload; classes began at 0845 and went on to 2130 hours. On the Wednesday there was a night compass march which lasted until 2330 hrs, and went on to 0230 hrs on the Thursday for those who had lost their way. The Coldstream Guards' R.S.M. was impressed by the improvement in the squad drill. The officer cadets were up early, but whether this was out of sheer enthusiasm to do drill, fear of the R.S.M. or, as was suggested, to work off the stiffness caused by sleeping on straw palliasses on wire beds will not be known. The course culminated with a farewell dance at the Winter Gardens.[81] The setting up of Officer Cadet Training Units (O.C.T.U.) for the A.C.F. was a significant step forward in both the training, and the recognition of its importance. Many of these new officers were, or could be, serving in both the A.C.F. and the H.G., and the depth and breadth of training appears to cater for this dual purpose. Nowhere is this mentioned but it seems a logical conclusion. In addition to the basic officers' and instructors' courses, there were more specialised courses in P.T. and there was even a 10-day Officers Toughening Course held in Snowdonia in January, 1945. The Ulster cadet battalions appeared to be better provided for as they each had a Permanent Staff Instructor who was a serving senior N.C.O. seconded from an affiliated regiment.[82]

Greater public recognition of the importance of training the youth came in 1942 when the status of officers changed. They were granted Commissions in the Territorial Army Reserve to the rank of Lieutenant, thereafter it was Acting rank. In a foreword in *The Cadet Journal* of November 1943 the Director of Military Training, War Office, Major-General J.A.C. Whitaker, thanked the officers and instructors who had devoted so much of their time to the Cadet Movement saying:

> You will require no greater reward than the knowledge that your aid is furthering a national service of the highest importance both for war and for peace.[83]

Despite all this effort to recruit and train officers and instructors there still remained the problem of there not being enough adults, plus the fact that some of them were physically unsuited to training young teenage boys or young men of 17 and 18. Making use of the Junior Training Corps from the public and grammar schools solved the problem in part.

The more senior cadet N.C.O.s in the J.T.C. and any Cadet Under-Officers were used to assist the A.C.F. units. Most of the J.T.C. units, because they were school-based, paraded during the afternoon, which meant that it was possible for their instructor to be available for the A.C.F. So it was that Under-Officer Paul Webber, who attended a grammar school in Birmingham and was a part of the J.T.C., was able in the evenings to instruct A.C.F. cadets.[84] And at Ilminster in Somerset two cadet Sergeants from the grammar school were co-opted to instruct at the newly-formed Chard A.C.F. unit in 1942.[85] It was not uncommon for the A.C.F. to approach the long-established J.T.C. unit commanders and ask for their help in providing instructors and demonstrators. In 1942 Shropshire A.C.F. asked Shrewsbury School to send a demonstration platoon to the county A.C.F. camp.[86] The school acceded to the request some two years later having once formed and trained a Demonstration Platoon. They first provided a demonstration of a 'Night Patrol' for the benefit of the junior cadets and the local Home Guard.[87] Although the local A.C.F. unit had long been using the school's facilities it was not until 1944 that the Demonstration Platoon went to an A.C.F. annual camp at Kinmel Park in North Wales. This was, in fact, the first time that Shrewsbury School had made official contact with the A.C.F. The Kinmel

Park camp experiment was, according to a report in *The Salopian*, a great success. It gave the J.T.C. cadets confidence and, perhaps more important than that, it was the first time that many members of the public school from Shrewsbury had met 'on more or less equal terms, boys coming from homes that were widely different from their own'. At a subsequent camp near Holyhead the J.T.C. cadets were dined out by the A.C.F. officers.[88] Sadly, there are no reports on what either the J.T.C. or A.C.F. cadets thought of these social encounters. Summer camps on training areas in the countryside, whilst being beneficial for all types of cadet organisations, were crucial for the training of army cadets.

ANNUAL CAMPS

The camp was, indeed still is, the most important operation undertaken by cadet units. It is the largest logistical exercise organised by the A.C.F. Wartime conditions posed additional problems. Rations, equipment and transport were hard to come by and there were regulations regarding camouflage, the blackout and the construction of emergency slit-trenches. The Army occupied all the recognised training campsites and so the A.C.F. had to find its own grounds. Fortunately records show that landowners were very co-operative, particularly if the A.C.F. contingent offered to help the landowner or farmer by providing free labour. It became increasingly difficult to provide mass camps, particularly bearing in mind the vast increase in units and numbers. Today camps are organised on a county basis. In 1941 the County of London Cadets had to hold two major camps, one at Whitsun, and one in the summer 'and in 1942 the same county had to split into no less than 12 sites for the annual camp'.[89]

The Public and Secondary Schools Cadet Association (P.S.S.C.A.) was not able to hold a camp until 1942. When it did, 800 cadets were accommodated, although three times that number applied to go.[90] Some of the Certificate 'A' senior N.C.O. cadets from the P.S.S.C.A. and the J.T.C. did, individually, go to camps with the A.C.F. and acted as instructors. One of the objectives of camp was 'To allow for central demonstrations by Army units', and this included the J.T.C. and the Home Guard.[91] Occasionally it meant taking the cadets to the demonstration. This happened in November 1941 when the Frimley and Camberley Corps visited the Free French Forces. They saw a display of tanks on exercise and were driven over rough terrain in armoured track vehicles. At the conclusion of the visit the Commandant presented 40 carbines for the use of the cadets; the weapons had been used in Norway by the Free French.[92]

Occasionally camps were a mixture of 'open' and 'closed' units. Such was the case in Northern Ireland in June 1943. This camp was for the 3rd

Cadet Bn. Royal Ulster Rifles and the 1st Cadet Bn. Royal Irish Fusiliers, and for school units from Campbell College and Armagh Royal School. This was the Province's first wartime camp.[93] There was another camp for the remaining 'closed' school units in the following month. In Leicestershire the summer camps were held at Bitteswell Park, where 1,000 cadets would spend a week under canvas in bell tents. They were joined by the Oundle School J.T.C. contingent from Rutland. At the Northamptonshire wartime camps held at Overstone the facilities were very basic. One ex-cadet remembers that there were no kit bags and so cadets were issued with hessian sandbags. One ex-cadet recalls his father cutting a wooden disc for the bottom to make it into a kit bag. Accommodation was eight to a bell tent, and the bed was a straw-filled palliasse.[94]

Evacuation meant that units otherwise unknown to each other had to share camp accommodation. In 1944 J.T.C. cadets from the South of England based at Lancing College shared a camp with the King's Shropshire Light Infantry A.C.F. at Church Stretton. It was a typical A.C.F. camp. Reveille was at 0700, and because of the minimal facilities washing had to be done in relays. Breakfast was at 0800. The morning consisted of lessons in skill-at-arms with rifles, Bren and Lewis machine guns, mortars and grenades. The afternoon sessions included tactical exercises and inspections, and there were visits to the local cinema to see instructional films. Concerts at the Y.M.C.A. and sports, including swimming, were held in the evenings. In the first week the camp was inspected by General Lord Bridgeman, and in the second week the cadets paraded before Lord Croft, the Under Secretary of State for War.[95] It was not always easy for a boy to go to camp as the majority started work at 14 years of age. Time off for camp was therefore dependent upon the benevolence of a cadet's employer. However, in this case, it was noted in the local paper that almost without exception employers willingly released boys for camp. The size of a camp differed enormously, and in the more rural counties they could be quite large. In 1943 the Marquess of Bath inspected 1,200 Somerset cadets at their Dunstan Beach camp.[96]

To run a camp needed not only the ability to organise but also required a degree of initiative and adaptability. Most obstacle courses were temporary erections, and in today's safety-conscious regime would be unacceptable, but part of 'the fun' was erecting such a training facility. It is recorded that at a 1943 A.C.F. camp in Western Command the cadets designed and rigged-up the obstacles course, which entailed:

> Traversing a long narrow plank carrying an ammunition box before crawling under a tarpaulin, then cross a stream by rope and wire, climb up a vertical ladder and down the other side before going through a suspended tyre, then climb an inclined and horizontal rope,

run round a field and cross a stream 8' wide by hanging rope and climb a smooth 10' wall, and finally swim 5 yards clothed across a river carrying a rifle.[97]

One of the big advantages of going away to camp was the food. The cadets had the same rations as soldiers under training, which meant that they got much larger helpings than they would be allowed at home; food rationing did not apply at camp. If a cadet was lucky enough to visit an American base then 'the perks' could be even greater, not to say 'exotic'. One wartime cadet remembers visiting the U.S.A.F. base at Barrington where the pilots flew B-17 Fortress and B-24 Liberators. Cadets were allowed onto the aircraft, but the real treat was being fed steaks at lunch with ice cream for dessert. They also received tinned peaches, chewing gum and chocolate Hershey Bars: unheard of luxuries for the wartime British.[98]

An army cadet, in order to do applied and realistic training needs to exercise on a training area in the countryside. Therefore, annual camps, particularly for the urban-based cadet units are essential. And, perhaps the biggest achievement of the expanded A.C.F., 80 per cent of whose units were new, was the large-scale camping. Despite the restrictions and vagaries of war, and even in 1942 when the threat of invasion was still very real, 'over 100,000 cadets went to camp for a week in the summer'.[99]

THE AIR CADETS

Captain H. H. Balfour – Under Secretary of State for Air – writing in the *A.D.C.C. Gazette* in December 1940, outlined the immediate needs of the R.A.F. The R.A.F. was going through a rapid expansion, and concluded Capt. Balfour, 'an ever-increasing number of candidates for aircrew duties will be required. It is hoped that the A.D.C.C. will provide more and more pilots, observers, wireless operators and air gunners'.[100] The A.D.C.C., which provided an essential starting point for a boy's life in the R.A.F., was found to be in need of a total 're-fit' if the Under Secretary's aims were to be met. This led to the formation of the Air Training Corps, which came into being on 1 February 1941.

On 23 February 1941 Mr J. F. Wolfenden, Director of Pre-Entry Training for the A.T.C., spoke on the B.B.C. Home Service. In the evening postscript to the 9 o'clock news the Director publicly outlined the aims of the A.T.C. saying:

> ... The plain fact is this. To man and look after our ever increasing number of aircraft in the next two years we want more men. The best way of producing them is to raise to Royal Air Force standards ... as many young men as we possibly can. In this way we shall keep up our quality and at the same time increase the quantity of men available.[101]

With the formation of the A.T.C. the number of air cadets under training expanded tenfold. The raising of standards did not just depend on an increase in numbers; it necessitated a total re-organisation of training and an improvement in facilities, which required a concomitant change in finance policy.

In 1940 the Secretary of State for Air appointed two standing committees to monitor the training and finance policies of the new corps. The committees saw the demise of the A.D.C.C. and the emergence of the A.T.C., which included the incorporation of the University Air Squadrons into the A.T.C., although the latter would come under the policy direction of the Air Ministry. Control at the Air Ministry was transferred from Manning to Training and a new office headed by a Director of Pre-Entry Training was instituted.

The new Director of Pre-Entry Training, Mr J. F. Wolfenden, was the Headmaster of Uppingham School. His background in teaching in schools and in higher education meant that he was ably suited to organising the training for boys and young men between 13 and 21. It was Mr Wolfenden and the Commandant of the Air Training Corps – Air Commodore J. A. Chamier – who were the architects of the new organisation. The Commandant, in an open letter in *The A.T.C. Gazette*, spelt out the priorities of training when he wrote:

> The most important part of our training is the training of air crews; and we want every young man of fitting character . . . suitable physique and education sufficient to enable him to profit by the course, to be given the opportunity of joining an air crew . . .
>
> Not all can fly, because there will be some who by reason of health or other causes cannot pass the necessary standards. These are also required in the technical ranks of the Royal Air Force, and these may also in time win distinction, and possibly a commission and honours.[102]

The Commandant made an interesting distinction between the pilot and the non-flyer. It is quite clear from what he wrote where the status lay and a cadet could be forgiven for thinking that the attitude towards the engineer officer, traffic controller or administrator seemed a trifle patronising. The assumption is that everyone wanted to fly and those with a technical-based expertise were of secondary importance. This attitude was natural enough in the aftermath of the bravery of the Battle of Britain pilots. The heroic view of pilots was expressed by the Under Secretary of State when he referred to the pilots as 'the knights of the air'.[103]

At first, membership of the A.T.C. was for 'young men' between the ages of 16 to 18. Provision was made for those under 16 provided the squadron had room and the training could be undertaken 'without detriment to the training of older cadets', but they could not qualify for grants or be issued with a uniform. The Air Scouts partly filled the gap for the young teenagers of 13 or 14 who were waiting to join the A.T.C. In some units cadet N.C.O.s could 'get valuable experience of "command" in drilling Scout patrols'. Arrangements could be made for Scouts to use the A.T.C. Morse code equipment, and some squadrons allowed them to join their parades and take part in physical training.[104] At Chard in Somerset the overwhelming demand for Air Scouting warranted the re-formation of the local troop to include an Air Scout Flight. It was called Stringfellow Flight after the local hero and father of powered flight. It was stated that the Scouts could concentrate on subjects 'which will be useful when boys are old enough to join the A.T.C.'.[105] These subjects included basic training in air navigation, air mechanics, air spotting, signalling, basic electricity and first aid.

The A.T.C. had reached its peak by 1942, but so many were leaving to join the Services that the organisation was shrinking in number. It was therefore necessary to lower the age of entry in order to make up the numbers, and in September 1942 the age of entry was lowered to 15 years. That is, a boy could join at 15 and on the completion of three months' probation he could be officially enrolled.[106] Although this may have led to a decline in the co-operation that existed between the Boy Scouts Association and the A.T.C., the relationship did not cease. In 1943 the training agreement that existed was made official, and following talks between the Air Ministry and the Boy Scouts Association the underlying principles of operation – which pertained to wartime only – were agreed. The attachment of a Scout Troop was subject to four principles, which were:

> (i) Attached Scout troops may for the purpose of training in air subjects be granted such free use of A.T.C. accommodation and equipment as may be mutually convenient, provided that no expenditure is incurred on the provision of additional accommodation or equipment in consequence.
> (ii) Attachment does not entitle Scouts to any other privileges authorised for A.T.C. cadets.
> (iii) Scout troops will at all times retain their own separate identity and control.
> (iv) The mutual co-operation and assistance afforded by virtue of this agreement will involve no alteration to the basis on which grants are now made to the Boy Scouts Association from public funds.[107]

It was realised that an A.T.C. officer who had previous scouting experience could hold a dual appointment, which meant he could be both a scoutmaster and an officer with the A.T.C. There are no statistics available, but it seems likely that this reciprocal arrangement whereby A.T.C. instructors taught Scouts may have been of particular benefit to the Air Training Corps, in that the Scouts provided a quantity of ready-trained A.T.C. recruits.

THE TRAINING SYLLABUS

The A.D.C.C.'s syllabus was in radical need of modernisation, for, as Group Captain Jordan, explains in his autobiography, the training had little to do with flying. It appears that the staple diet consisted of drill and lectures on the Lee Enfield .303 rifle, and with luck, on the Thompson submachine gun. Apparently the most exciting practical training consisted of an evening's instruction on motor cycling 'which really had my adrenaline pumping'.[108] Other than that the training was uninspiring for the aspiring pilot. Some units did have a more aeronautically-based syllabus, but what was taught depended largely on the interests and expertise of the OC and his instructors. Training of cadets and staff was clearly in need of re-thinking and re-structuring.

The practical aeronautical subjects taught under the former A.D.C.C. syllabus were retained, but there was a re-classification of Proficiency Certificates. The First Class and Leading Air Cadet classifications were dropped and in their place a system of Star Badges was instituted. To be adjudged proficient, cadets would have to pass a written examination, set and marked by the R.A.F.'s Central Trade Board on three examination dates a year in each of the specialist subjects as follows:

a. Aircrew Candidates, a pass in at least 3 subjects one of which must be navigation.

b. Technical Candidates, 40% of the marks in the papers for the 'course' in which he offers himself for examination.[109]

To be eligible to sit the proficiency examination cadets would first have to serve for six months, and pass tests at squadron level in each of the 'Initial Subjects'. The A.T.C. syllabus was thus divided into two levels. First there were the Initial Subjects that every cadet undertook, and secondly, there were the 'specialisation' subjects for potential aircrew or technicians. The A.T.C. syllabus therefore consisted of:

a. Initial Subjects – Drill, Physical Training, and Elementary Maths, and Morse (up to 4 words per minute).

b. Specialisation:

Either   (1) Aircrew Candidates – Mathematics, Navigation, Morse code, Armament, Anti-gas, Aircraft Identification, Administration.

135

or   (2) Technical Candidates, one of the courses in: Wireless Operator; Wireless Mechanic; Radio Mechanic; Flight Mechanic; Instrument Repairer; Electrician and MT Mechanic.[110]

For those cadets who wished to go to university and join the R.A.F. as pilots or observers, the Director of Training implemented the Air Council's arrangement of special six-month courses. Cadets between the ages of 17 and 18, who had passed the School Certificate, could join a University Air Squadron for six months and learn to fly. At the same time they studied mathematics, mechanics and physics, and did a course in one of four subjects – magnetism and electricity, engineering, meteorology or navigation. The Air Ministry provided an added incentive for doing the courses by bearing the entire cost of board and lodging, and tuition.[111] Month-long courses were also started at institutes of higher education, such as those at Loughborough College, which included everything from drill instruction to wireless operation and air navigation.

Motivating cadets, of whatever Service, to learn, was not too difficult. They all had a definite and realisable objective: they knew where they were heading and how to get there. The syllabuses written by H.Q. Training Command for the cadets in schools and 'open' units therefore had two simple aims: first, to teach the subject-matter that the R.A.F. required; and secondly, to re-write the technical texts in language easily understood by 16 year-old boys.

Technical knowledge and information was disseminated from H.Q. Training Command in loose-leaf book form in three categories. First, there was the 'Blue Book' issued to squadrons. This contained the syllabus and information on Methods of Instruction and R.A.F. training practices. Secondly, there was the 'Yellow Book' for instructors which included subject details and lecture notes. The third category was the 'Buff Book' for cadets. The system, particularly regarding the Buff Book, had the advantage of providing material for the cadets to study in their own time, and they could catch up on any classes they had missed. The A.T.C. Headquarters printed an initial batch of 100,000 of the 'Buff Book' and thereafter churned out subject material at a rate of 5,000 copies a week. The Proficiency Examinations were set from the issued texts, and thus there was a common standard throughout the A.T.C.[112]

After an initial period of adjustment and practice the system was extended to include a second level, Proficiency Part 2. This entailed the study and examination of the same subjects but at a more advanced level. However, the latter was dropped in the A.T.C. 'open' units as it was found that most squadrons had neither the equipment nor the instructors to carry out advanced training. It was retained in the School and University Air

Squadrons. Initiative and leadership training, called Post-Proficiency training, was put in the place of the Proficiency Certificate Part 2. It consisted of what is now termed Command Tasks or Initiative Exercises. There was also a greater emphasis on physical fitness. Lectures on great leaders of the past were included, as was air/sea rescue training (set up in 1943). Senior cadets had the opportunity to instruct the junior cadets. The changes in content were not universally popular as many felt that the emphasis had moved away from aeronautical training to physical based activities. Wing Commander Lamond commented that the Proficiency Certificate was not easy, 'in 1944 . . . only 14,000 cadets out of the then strength of around 156,000 passed the examination'.[113] The primary aim for the majority was the attainment of the educational qualifications for entry into the R.A.F.

A.T.C. cadets could also take advantage of the Royal Navy's and Fleet Air Arm's 'Y' Scheme, which was for potential officers. The details of the scheme have been described in the section on the Sea Cadet Corps.

Articles in the *Air Training Corps Gazette* augmented the technical information contained in the training pamphlets. In the first issue there was an article on the magnetic effects of an electrical current and notes on the use of a compass in aircraft navigation, as well as a section on aircraft recognition. Later issues contained articles that explained to cadets what life was like in the R.A.F. And stories about the exciting adventures of W. E. Johns' fictional characters stimulated the interests of cadets.

Once interest had been aroused then the appetite had to be satisfied. This required equipment. It was not uncommon to see 'cadging letters' in the local press, such as the one in the *Chard and Ilminster News* which said that the A.T.C. was on the scrounge for 'wireless sets, headphones, condensers, loud speakers, soldering irons, spanners, drills and other tools'.[114] Stowe School was able to obtain aircraft, albeit obsolete ones, to train with (*Plate 16*). Some units were more fortunate. The 414 (Epping) Squadron was based at R.A.F. North Weald and thus had access to proper equipment, and ample opportunity to examine the latest fighter aircraft (*Plate 17*). Other units, however, had to make do with what they could get their hands on. The A.T.C. had to rely, as did the other Cadet Services, upon the philanthropy of other organisations and individuals.

In 1943 another new syllabus was introduced which included air/sea rescue training. Provision was made to equip 66 centres throughout the U.K. and Northern Ireland. Swimming and life-saving was included. In order to carry out this training the A.T.C. became affiliated to the Amateur Swimming Association and the Royal Life-Saving Society. The two bodies rendered great assistance to the Corps through instruction given voluntarily by their members.[115] In some cases the air/sea rescue centres were set up at local swimming baths. In Scotland, 109 (Port Glasgow, Greenock and Kilmalcolm) Squadron specialised in this sort of training and devised an apparatus at their camping ground for dropping cadets into a deep pond in parachute harness thus requiring them to practise 'releasing the parachute and setting up and climbing into a dinghy'.[116]

GLIDING AND FLYING

The *raison d'être* for the R.A.F. and the A.T.C. is flying, and what most of the cadets wanted to do was get airborne. Whenever possible an A.T.C. officer would get his cadets on air experience flights. What sort of aircraft a cadet went up in depended on what was available and suitable for carrying passengers. An ex-cadet, Arthur Pearcy, in an article in *Aviation News*, tells of his wartime visits to R.A.F. Driffield where he flew in Halifax and Wellington bombers, a Dakota and a Stirling Mk. V transporter.[117] An ex-A.D.C.C. and A.T.C. cadet from Leeds remembers, at the latter end of the war, members of his squadron accompanying Wellington bomber crews on Coastal Command patrols. He said he missed out on this but was compensated with a flight in a Fairey Battle. He was given a parachute that clipped onto the side of the cockpit, although, apparently, he was never told how to use it![118] Other wartime cadets remember air experience flights in Oxford trainers and two-seater Avro Ansons. Some of the flying training was done in aircraft of older vintage (*Plate 18*).

The air experience flights served two useful purposes. First, they gave cadets some insight into the workings of aircraft and the R.A.F. Visits to airfields and R.A.F. stations and going flying were the highlight of most boys' training. Secondly, and equally important, they provided a cadet with the chance to find out if he actually liked flying and wanted to serve with the R.A.F. – most did, but those who didn't at least had the opportunity to make an informed choice.

An ex-A.T.C. bandsman recalled visits to R.A.F. Church Fenton in Yorkshire, where he spent 'a considerable amount of time, marching to and from the local cemetery burying dead air crew, most of whom seemed to be air gunners': a disconcerting experience. He was equally unimpressed with the ground staff, although for different reasons. Seeing men working on lathes, milling machines and other workshop activities did not fit 'the glamorous image we had [of the R.A.F.] in those days at the age of 17', he said.[119] There were, however, more satisfactory ways of experiencing R.A.F. training.

Another and cheaper method of flying was gliding. The value of gliding – to teach airmanship – had been realised before the war, and the A.D.C.C. had summer gliding camps. The first A.T.C. Gliding School was founded at Kirkbymoorside, Yorkshire in 1942. In 1943 there were 29 elementary gliding schools and two special schools for teaching instructors. The ultimate aim was to have 100 gliding schools. The increase in gliding was fairly prodigious considering the handicap of war – lack of instructors, equipment and airfields. By September 1944 the number of schools had increased further to 77 and the number of instructors had trebled to 292. By the end of April 1944 there had been 200,000 glider launchings with '1,300 cadets gaining proficiency in various stages'.[120] The number of gliding schools finally totalled 83 by the end of the war in August 1945.

A cadet's first experience at 'flying' was often on the Kronfield ground-trainer. The Kronfield was a powered Lowe-Wilde glider that looked something like a Dagling, but without the full wing surface. The idea was to manoeuvre along the ground using the controls without becoming airborne. The Air Ministry did not approve of such trainers because the control movements were 'too coarse to simulate actual aircraft taxying', but several squadrons took no notice and built their own. The advantage of such trainers was the fact that cadets could actually carry out pre-flight checks, engine starting checks and ground airmanship drills.

A more sophisticated version of the trainer was designed and built at No. 1440 (Shoreham) Squadron. It was called the Hoppity, and its fuselage was mounted on a gimballed joint on a three-wheeled undercarriage. Cadets could progress from stationary balancing with the engine running to taxying down a runway, turning into wind, and simulating a take-off by 'flying' down the makeshift runway. No. 315 (Didsbury) Squadron made a similar version using a Douglas motorcycle and scraps of junk metal. Such home-made but effective training aids meant cadets could more easily progress from the classroom to the practicality of the airfield without having to travel miles to an aerodrome.

The cadets who went to No. 49 Gliding School at Burnaston went through a solo gliding programme that started with ground slides in the Skeletal Dagling trainer before, as they did at Dunstable, turning the glider into wind and then using cadet-power to get it launched (*Plate 19*). Other gliding schools had the winch-launched Slingsby Kirby Cadet Glider.[121]

One of the major problems of getting flying time had nothing to do with the availability of aircraft but more to do with the vagaries of wartime travel. In 1942 the visits made by 1476 (Rayleigh) Squadron to Rochford Airfield depended on whether or not cadets had bicycles, as petrol shortage and an inconvenient transport system made travel difficult. Some units, because of the close proximity of airfields, had a choice. The 1096 (Bishop Stortford) Squadron, for example, could alternate between flying in Ansons at R.A.F. Debden and flying in Marauders at the United States

Air Base at Stansted.[122] The squadron from Chard, Somerset was more fortunate than most in that it was attached to an aerodrome that had an aircraft solely for the use of the A.T.C. The training that the cadets received was comprehensive and challenging. Each cadet was supplied with a question paper and expected to answer questions on flying and map reading during his airborne trip. As the aircraft used by Chard squadron was dual-controlled and for the sole use of the A.T.C. it meant that those cadets selected as potential aircrew had the opportunity to receive a certain amount of actual flying instruction. This, it was recorded at the time, was a further step in the pre-entry training programme.[123]

TRAINING OF OFFICERS AND USE OF CIVILIAN PERSONNEL
In order that the Secretary of State for Air's aims might be accomplished, recruitment and training of officers had to be a priority.[124] In the A.T.C. magazine it was suggested that squadron commanders and their civilian committee chairman should approach 'the local Masonic lodge, Rotary club, Round-Table club, sports club, schools, aircraft works and all other organisations which might help'.[125] As it turned out it was the schools that were to prove the most helpful.

The appointment of Wolfenden, the headmaster, as Director of Pre-Entry Training was an inspired decision. He understood and 'spoke the same language' as the county education officers. He wasted no time in soliciting the assistance of the local education authorities, via the Board of Education in England & Wales and the Education Department in Scotland. The result of this was that teachers in local colleges and schools gave extra classes in the evenings for cadets, chiefly in English and Mathematics. At a meeting in Chard at the formation of 1078 Squadron in 1941, of the 20 people who offered their services as instructors, five were qualified teachers and seven more were ex-servicemen. Three of the latter were Home Guard and they would have also been involved with A.C.F. training.[126] However, it was reported in a 1943 issue of *The A.T.C. Gazette* that schools under the control of the Glasgow Corporation were 'forbidden to form units of the A.T.C.', although they actively assisted in the formation of open units. The same applied in one other unspecified Scottish city. This was considered rather odd, as 50 per cent of the A.T.C. officers were teachers. The Secretary of State for Scotland was asked to look into the matter, but said that he had no power to do anything about the situation.[127]

Those schools that did form A.T.C. squadrons had ready-made instructors among their staff. Mathematics and English was, of course, part of their everyday curriculum and subjects such as meteorology, navigation, the use of electricity and basic engineering had obvious connections with aviation which must have provided interest for learners and teachers alike. Educational institutions were ideal headquarters for A.T.C. squadrons. The Technical College in Colchester was the H.Q. for 308 Squadron, and the College's Principal, Squadron Leader Enoch, was the squadron commander. In this environment it was no surprise that the squadron had 220 members, indeed it was found necessary to start another unit – 1904 Squadron – in Colchester with a Detached Flight in the town itself, and another two, one at Clacton, the other at Brightlingsea. The first CO of another Essex unit, 1474 (Wickford) Squadron, was a headmaster.[128] This collaboration between the A.T.C. and schools and colleges was repeated throughout the country.

In 1942 Mr Wolfenden returned to the job of being headmaster. He was superseded by Mr (later Sir) W. W. Wakefield. Mr Wakefield was an ex-serviceman and a flyer, and was Parliamentary Private Secretary to the Under-Secretary of State for Air, Captain H. H. Balfour. William Wavell Wakefield understood the world of flying, the service environment and had connections in Parliament; he had, as they say 'military clout'. Mr Wolfenden had, in the meantime, been awarded a C.B.E. for successfully discharging his duties during the inaugural year of the A.T.C. and was to remain as an educational advisor.

The training of adult officers, warrant officers and civilian instructors in the ways of the R.A.F. was a necessity. All adults were encouraged to attend R.A.F. courses. In 1942, courses of one-week's duration were set up in Scotland and England for the training of R.A.F.V.R. (T) officers. The course content included drill instruction, with lectures on R.A.F. and A.T.C. administration. There were also talks and discussions on the problems of maintaining discipline, and about the leadership of young people. There were voluntary sessions of P.T. and swimming. Obtaining a commission or being granted a warrant in H.M. Forces is very much like joining a particular type of club with its own rules, etiquette, behaviour, standards and subtle nuances. One of the aims of such a course – known humorously in the Navy as the 'knife and fork course' – was to introduce new officer to the Forces' mode of behaviour. The aspiring cadet could obtain advance information by reading Capt. W. E. Johns' articles dealing with the officers' mess in *The A.T.C. Gazette*.[129]

Special courses were started at several educational institutions such as the Loughborough Summer School. Here officers and instructors could undertake short week-long courses in elementary and advanced aeronautics. Other courses included navigation, drill, armaments, aircraft recognition, wireless, and there was a separate course for model aeroplane-making. The cost was £1 10s for a week-long course, or £3 10s for the four-week course.[130] Adults could obtain further specialist knowledge in other subjects, signalling for instance. In fact an A.T.C. Signals School was set up in London in 1942, which augmented the work done at the R.A.F. training centres.

The A.T.C. squadrons continued to provide training for those young men whose call-up into the R.A.F. was deferred. The usefulness of the training of cadet officers and hence cadets is best summed-up by Group-Captain Jordan, who said, 'Our A.T.C. training put the emphasis where it belonged – on things related to flying.' He added that the aviation training, along with the drill, was a great benefit to those going into the R.A.F.[131]

ANNUAL CAMPS

Camp accommodation for A.T.C. cadets, as for all cadets, was under canvas. There were six to a tent and each cadet had blankets and a palliasse (straw mattress). All cadets had to pay their own fare to and from camp, and contribute two shillings (10p) a day towards mess expenses. The most popular camps were those that provided flying. In 1941 His Majesty the King inspected the cadets at R.A.F. Halton (*Plate 20*). This was considered a great honour, particularly as the A.T.C. had been in existence for only a few months. The A.T.C. made effective use of the King's visit to make a timely complaint about the lack of flying. As a result the Air Council made particular efforts to include more flying where possible at all R.A.F. camps.[132]

The annual camp was the highlight of the year because it offered hands-on opportunity to use equipment not usually available, and the chance to train under active service conditions. The type of stations visited by A.T.C. cadets included:

> R.A.F. bomber, fighter, Tactical Air Force, coastal, Fleet Air Arm Stations, technical training schools, elementary flying training schools, operational training units, Air/Sea Rescue centres, gliding schools, combined service camps, etc.[133]

The type of training and subjects studied at the units appeared enticingly interesting for the future R.A.F. candidate. They are listed as:

> Airfield Control; Flare Path Duty; Dinghy Drill; Signals; Armaments; Range Firing; Meteorology; Briefing; Flying Control; Parachutes; Physical Training; W.T. Installation and Equipment; Gunnery; Photography; Navigation; Aircraft Recognition; Intelligence; Drill; Swimming and Gliding.[134]

How much was available to cadets depended on the 'state of alert' and security level, and the role of the particular station. At some stations there were added voluntary lectures on 'Leadership; Air Strategy; Fieldcraft and Navigation'. Each camp lasted for seven days and the first lecture was the prescribed talk on Security.

Flying was not the sole preserve of the R.A.F. A number of A.T.C. squadrons were affiliated to Fleet Air Arm stations, and in 1942 some 3,677 air cadets went to summer camp at Royal Naval Air Stations (R.N.A.S.). By 1944 over 100 squadrons were affiliated and more than 9,000 cadets attended training camps at R.N.A.S. The R.N.A.S. were able to offer some flying experience. A total of 215 hours flying time from aircraft carriers is recorded, 'including deck landings'.[135]

In 1942 approximately 5,000 cadets went to summer camps; by 1944 the number of air cadets attending camps with the R.A.F., the R.N.A.S. and with the Army had increased to 93,000.

CO-OPERATION, COMBINED OPS AND TRAINING

The first contact a cadet had with colleagues from another Service was often on the sports field. Sport was looked upon not only as a useful adjunct to physical training and fitness, but also as a means of engendering a sense of team spirit. There had always been a healthy rivalry between the army, the navy and the air force, and the cadets kept up this tradition in the sports arena. The amount of inter-service competition was limited by the war, and matches were therefore restricted to local encounters. It was not until after the war that national inter-service competition could be held. The A.C.F. and the A.T.C. held their boxing finals in the Albert Hall in 1943, and after the war this became the venue for the inter-services cadet boxing championships.

Physical fitness and hence physical training were of paramount importance in the training programme. The military authorities stressed that the physical fitness session should be an integral part of the cadet's training. Easily said! At unit level there was a shortage of P.T. instructors. The problem was alleviated when the army instituted P.T. Leaders courses (a basic assistant instructor's course) for cadets over 16. Initially they were for boys from the J.T.C. and A.C.F. units, and were run at several Command PT Schools. In 1943 the War Office produced a pamphlet specifically for the training of army cadets titled, *Pre-service Physical Training and Recreation for Army Cadets*.[136] In the same year the navy and the airforce began to run similar P.T. courses. The tests instituted by the army and used as part of the Certificate 'A' training programme became part of the standard training for all three cadet organisations. In fact, in 1945 the War Office produced a joint-service pamphlet called *Physical Efficiency Preparation for Service Cadets*.[137] As far as is known this is the only example of a training aid that was specifically for all the cadet organisations.

Physical Efficiency Standards for Service Cadets

Standard Nos.	Description	14–15 years Age Group Shoes	14–15 years Age Group Boots	15–16 years Age Group Shoes	15–16 years Age Group Boots	16–17 years Age Group Shoes	16–17 years Age Group Boots	Over 17 years Age Group Shoes	Over 17 years Age Group Boots
	AGILITY								
I	100 yards Sprint	15 secs.	16 secs.	14 secs.	15 secs.	13 secs.	14 secs.	13 secs.	14 secs.
II	Standing Long Jump	5 ft. 9 in.	5 ft. 3 in.	6 ft.	5 ft. 6 in.	6 ft. 6 in.	6 ft.	7 ft.	6 ft. 6 in
III	Running High Jump	3 ft. 6 in.	3 ft. 3 in.	3 ft. 9 in.	3 ft. 6 in.	4 ft.	3 ft. 9 in.	4 ft. 3 in.	4 ft.
IV	Running Vault	3 ft. 9 in.	No allowance	4 ft.	No allowance	4 ft. 3 in.	No allowance	4 ft. 6 in.	No allowance
	ENDURANCE								
V	1 Mile Run	7 mins.	7 mins. 45 secs.	6 mins. 30 secs.	7 mins. 15 secs.	6 mins. 20 secs.	7 mins. 5 secs.	6 mins. 10 secs.	6 mins. 55 secs.
VI	1 Hour Walk	3¾ miles	No allowance	4¼ miles	No allowance	5 miles	No allowance	5¼ miles	No allowance
	STRENGTH								
VII	Rope Climbing (15 ft.)	Once	{ No allowance for these tests as they can be done barefoot or while wearing socks. }	Once	{ No allowance for these tests as they can be done barefoot or while wearing socks. }	Twice	{ No allowance for these tests as they can be done barefoot or while wearing socks. }	Three Times	{ No allowance for these tests as they can be done barefoot or while wearing socks. }
VIII	Abdominal. From over-grasp hanging, raise both knees to touch undersides of apparatus with shins or insteps. (Pause between each raise.)	Once		Once		Twice		Three Times	
IX	Heaving. From alternate grasp hanging, facing beam, bar or stick, bend both arms to bring eyes to top level of apparatus. (Pause between each heave with arms stretched.)	Twice		Three Times		Four Times		Five Times	
	SWIMMING								
X	Swimming	30 yards		60 yards		80 yards		100 yards	

Followed in each case by remaining afloat, out of depth, for two minutes.

NOTE – The term 'shoes' includes both 'gym' shoes and leather soled shoes.

Fig. 5 – Physical Efficiency Standards for Service Cadets 1945 [H.M.S.O.]

The courses were held during school holidays and usually lasted for a week to 10 days. The one held at Western Command in 1943, for example, was for J.T.C. and A.C.F. cadets and included methods of instruction and training on the obstacle course, with assessment of the Physical Efficiency Standard tests. The course included the construction of improvised bridges and other obstacles using toggle ropes. This was particularly useful for those units that did not have access to a nearby military base and had to devise their own equipment.[138] The tests naturally took into account the difference in age groups. Boys were encouraged to wear boots when undertaking training, but not all could afford them and so, interestingly, there were two standards of test – one for those wearing plimsolls (or leather shoes) and another for those wearing boots. Some of the tests were more difficult when wearing boots and this was another reason for having two standards. The assessment included tests of strength, agility and endurance (*Fig. 5*). Probably the most useful service the cadet organisations afforded the military was to ensure that future servicemen were fit and ready for the rigours and training of wartime service life.

The three services have always co-operated for public parades and the cadet organisations were no different. It was not uncommon during the war to have a combined church parade on a Sunday, which included all cadets. At the Sunday church parades at Barnet the music was provided by the massed bands of the S.C.C. and the A.T.C. With most of the adult servicemen and women being overseas or on duty it sometimes fell to the cadets to provide all the uniformed personnel on public parades, whether this was on Remembrance Sunday or at the conclusion of a charity fund-raising drive. The wartime parades could include a poignant reminder of why the cadets were training. For example, in 1944 at Dundee a plaque was unveiled at the S.C.C. headquarters in memory of three former cadets who had died on active service. Units from the A.C.F. and the A.T.C. also attended the parade.[139]

Lt.-Cdr. F. W. Inns from the S.C.C., writing in the A.C.F. journal, said that as the cadet units of all three Services had so much in common it was in 'their interest – and, in fact, it is their duty – to collaborate as closely as possible in their activities'.[140] He went on to suggest that each district should appoint a Liaison Officer, and that a committee should meet regularly, to promote competitions and to co-ordinate parades and other joint ventures. There is no evidence to suggest that permanent committees were formed throughout the country, but there was a degree of liaison in many districts. There is certainly evidence of co-operation on a social level. It must be said that because the cadet units were all-male, many of the social activities, particularly those regarding dances and the putting on of shows, were with the Girls' Training Corps or other organisations that could provide the female element.

The degree of cadet co-operation went even further in the Hornsey district of London, where an inter-services cadet club was opened on 13 January 1943. Major-General The Viscount Bridgeman performed the official opening ceremony at the Welcome Club, Crouch End, under the chairmanship of the Mayor with support from by Vice-Admiral J. E. T. Harper and Air Chief Marshal Sir Robert Brooke-Popham.

The club was housed in a former cinema. It had a large hall suitable for dances, and rooms of various sizes for snooker, table tennis and so on. The Y.M.C.A. ran the canteen. The club had been open for just two months and already had a membership of 200 from the local Sea, Army and Air cadet units, who enjoyed the facilities for a monthly subscription of sixpence a head. A General Committee of officers from the three cadet services managed the enterprise.[141]

It would be fair to say that the alliance of the separately-uniformed cadet units sometimes engendered over-zealous competition rather than co-operation. However, the relationship was mostly good humoured and confrontation was usually confined to the sports field. A number of units shared accommodation and therefore a degree of co-operation was essential, if only for administrative reasons. In some districts units had separate facilities on the same site. At the R.A.F. station, Uxbridge, there was not only the expected A.T.C. squadron, but also an A.C.F. and a Girls' Training Corps unit. Here they took co-operation a stage further by planning and operating a syllabus that included joint training. The G.T.C. ran a communal canteen and the A.T.C. squadron raised £400 for the purchase of a joint-recreation hut. The cadets from the three organisations organised dances and other social functions, the profits from which went to war charities.

The co-operation in Uxbridge and West Middlesex extended to organising an inter-service boxing match, which included the local sea cadet unit. This was, by all accounts, a successful venture and it was reported that it helped to promote a 'happy feeling among the pre-Service units of the area'.[142]

From 1942 onwards many sea and air cadets who intended to join the forces and fly had attended joint annual camps at either R.A.F. or R.N.A.S. stations. The most important aspect was not a cadet's service affiliation but the need to give him practical aeronautical training. It also made sense from a logistical point of view to hold combined camps for all the three cadet services. Equipment and training areas were not readily available and so the sharing of facilities was a very practical approach.

The combined camps meant there could also be Combined Operations. North Western Command held a Combined Operations Camp at Blackpool in 1943. The camp was in operation for a period of 12 weeks and groups of cadets came for one week. In total 600 cadets (300 A.C.F., 200 A.T.C. and 100 S.C.C.) attended the camp. The culminating Combined Op was the highlight of the camp. At Blackpool the training areas included two large lakes with two islands. On one of the islands the A.T.C. acted as the enemy, and the A.C.F. held a garrison on the other. In the course of the ensuing battle, under cover of a smoke screen, the sea cadets landed 'a body of black-faced commandos [A.C.F. cadets] from "Montgomery Bay" . . . [and] to the accompaniment of thunder-flashes and yells the holding force was well and truly subdued'. Reinforcements rushed to the area and attempts were made to capture 'the radio-location station'. 'Very lights, smoke screens and squibs were among the effects during the hand-to-hand engagement that ended in the defeat of the enemy.'[143] The reporter makes no comment on the effects of the 'hand-to-hand' encounters, but merely states that it was 'all good and strenuous fun'. According to the S.C.C. report 1,700 cadets passed through the Combined Services Cadet Camps in 1943.[144] This does not seem very many in comparison with the numbers that attended the single-Service camps, but for those boys who were lucky enough to receive such training it must have been great fun. More importantly it gave them the chance to train with a variety of equipment.

In Devon, the Sea and Army Cadets held a joint camp that was organised by the Navy League and the National Association of Boys' Clubs. On at least one occasion the combined operations included boys from another youth organisation. Exercises included the evacuation of troops by rowing boat, and landing operations. The daylight air raids 'lent a spice of adventure to the training, and, on one occasion, two F.W.190s swooped down to bomb nearby barges while operations were in progress!'[145] A similar exercise was held on the banks of the River Wyre. This one involved the Sea and Army Cadet units from Fleetwood. The exercise required the sea cadets to transport an assault party across a river in five boats. The object was to capture the peninsula that was defended by an army cadet force. While the battle was in progress the cadets also had to deal with prisoners and wounded who had to be ferried to the sea cadet motor launch.

Every attempt was made to make these exercises as realistic and as challenging and exciting as possible. There was the obvious advantage to the boys of learning to co-operate and acquire new skills. At the same time combined operations must have helped the cadets to make better-informed choices about which arm of the Services they wanted to join for their subsequent active service.

Some school J.T.C. units had more than one branch of the Services represented and could provide inter-Service training on a more regular basis. The benefit of cadet training, as pointed out in every report, was first the learning of basic specialist skills – which was helpful to the individual and to the Services by cutting down the time spent on basic training. This also meant a significant saving in terms of cost. More importantly, perhaps, the training allowed cadets to attain a higher level of physical fitness, to gain an understanding of military discipline, and to experience working and living with others. These would be of long-lasting benefit to them, in the Services and in civilian life.

CHAPTER 5 REFERENCES

1 *The Sea Cadet* journal, April 1943
2 Minutes of the Navy League Sea Cadet Corps Committee, 15 May 1941
3 Ibid.
4 *The Sea Cadet* journal, November 1944
5 *The Sea Cadet* journal, Vol. 1, No. 12, 1944
6 *The Sea Cadet* journal, Vol. 1, No. 9, 1944
7 Ibid.
8 *The Sea Cadet* journal, Vol. 1, No. 2, 1943
9 *The Sea Cadet* journal, Vol. 2, No. 9, 1945
10 *The Sea Cadet* journal, Vol. 1, No. 2, 1943
11 *The Sea Cadet* journal, Vol. 1, No. 6, 1944
12 *The Sea Cadet* journal, Vol. 2, No. 9, 1945
13 *The Sea Cadet* journal, Vol. 1, No. 5, 1944
14 Taken from S.C.C. Certificate and Attendance Register of ex-Cadet Leading Seaman B. D. Clark of the Barnet Unit, 1942
15 *The Sea Cadet* journal, Vol. 1, No. 2, 1943
16 *The Sea Cadet* journal, Vol. 1, No. 11, 1944
17 *The Navy League* journal, June 1939
18 *The Navy League* journal, January 1940
19 Minutes of the Navy League S.C.C. Sub-Committee, 15 January 1942
20 Ibid.
21 *The Sea Cadet* journal, Vol. 1, No. 11, 1944
22 *The Navy League* journal, December 1941
23 Ibid.
24 *The Navy League* journal, January 1941
25 *The Navy League* journal, February 1941
26 Minutes of the Navy League S.C.C. Sub-Committee, 18 September 1941
27 Emergency meeting of Navy League S.C.C. Sub-Committee, 5 March 1942
28 Minutes of Navy League S.C.C. Sub-Committee, 8 October 1942
29 Ibid.
30 Ibid.
31 *The Sea Cadet* journal, Vol. 1, No. 4, 1943
32 *The Sea Cadet* journal, Vol. 1, No. 6, 1944
33 *The Sea Cadet* journal, Vol. 1, No. 4, 1943
34 *The Sea Cadet* journal, Vol. 1, No. 6, 1944
35 *The Sea Cadet* journal, Vol. 1, No. 11, 1944
36 Ibid.
37 Ibid.
38 *The Sea Cadet* journal, Vol. 1, No. 6, 1944
39 A. J. P. Taylor, *English History, 1914–45* [London: OUP, 1965], pp. 439–476

40 *The Sea Cadet* journal, Vol. 1, No. 6, 1944
41 *The Sea Cadet* journal, Vol. 1, No. 2, 1943
42 Ibid.
43 *The Sea Cadet* journal, Vol. 1, No. 4, 1943
44 *The Sea Cadet* journal, Vol. 1, No. 6, 1944
45 *The Navy League* journal, March 1940
46 *The Navy League* journal, February 1943
47 Minutes of Navy League S.C.C. Sub-Committee, 21 May 1941
48 *The Sea Cadet* journal, Vol. 1, No. 5, 1944
49 *The Sea Cadet* journal, Vol. 1, No. 1, 1943
50 Supplement to *The Sea Cadet* journal, 'Entry for Sea Cadets into Royal & Merchant Navy', July 1944. Appendix 13 to Chapter 2 of W. H. Lamond, *History of the Air Training Corps*.
51 A.C.F.A., *The Cadet Story, 1860–1980* [A.C.F.A.: London, 1982], p. 52
52 *The Cadet Journal*, Vol. IV, No. 3, 1942
53 War Office, *The Training of the Younger Cadet* [War Office: London, 1942], 26/GS publication/687, pp. 42–48
54 *The Cadet Journal*, Vol. IV, No. 5, 1942
55 Major C. R. Ward, *Section Training & Exercises* [Aldershot: Gale & Polden, 1941]
56 Brian M. Forrest T.D., *Drill & Weapon Training – guide to War Cert. 'A'* [Aldershot: Gale & Polden, 1945]
57 War Office, *Message Writing for Cadets*, Part V Training Manual War Cert. 'A' [War Office: London, 1945]
58 *The Cadet Journal*, November 1943
59 A.C.F.A., 'Instructions for candidates and Conduct of Certificate 'A' examinations [A.C.F.A. – 9/Cadets/5810 (M.T.Ac), December 1945]
60 Ibid.
61 *Chard & Ilminster News*, 14 March 1942
62 *The Cadet Review*, Vol. I, No. 1, 1945
63 *The Cadet Journal*, May 1943
64 *The Cadet Review*, Vol. I, No. 1, 1945
65 *The Cadet Journal*, Vol. IV, No. 4, 1942
66 Ibid.
67 A. Walker & M. B. Passmore M.A., *The Cadet Force at Bruton, 1910–1985* [Frome: Donald Press, 1985], pp. 15–20
68 Interview with Dr M. Plumtree ex-J.T.C. cadet
69 op. cit., Walker & Passmore
70 *The Cadet Journal*, Vol. IV, No. 1, 1941
71 *Shropshire Chronicle*, 10 August 1945
72 *The Cadet Review*, Vol. I, No. 1, 1945
73 Ibid.
74 *The Cadet Journal*, May 1942

75 *Chard & Ilminster News*, 1 November 1941
76 R. T. Graham, *Ilminster Grammar School, 1549–1949* [Ilminster School, 1991]
77 *The Cadet Journal*, October 1941
78 Ibid.
79 Captain L. J. Collins, M.A. Ph.D., 'Cadets at War, 1939–45' in *Army Cadet*, Vol. LVIII, January 1996
80 *The Cadet Journal*, October 1941
81 Ibid.
82 Hon. Col. F. E. Nagle, 'A Record of the A.C.F. in Counties Armagh and Down, 1943–1974' [C.T.C. Frimley Park Library, 1980], p. 4
83 *The Cadet Journal*, November 1943
84 Interview with Mr Paul Webber, ex-wartime J.T.C. Under-Officer
85 *Chard & Ilminster News*, 23 May 1942
86 *Shropshire Chronicle*, 19 May 1942
87 *The Salopian* [Shrewsbury School], Vol. LXI, No. 4, 1944
88 *The Salopian*, Vol. LXI, No. 17, October 1944
89 A.C.F.A., *The Cadet Story, 1860–1980* [London: A.C.F.A., 1982], p. 76
90 Ibid.
91 A.C.F.A., *A Camp Handbook for Officers, NCOs and Cadets* [London: A.C.F.A., 1947], p. 8
92 Col. F. W. Foley, C.B.E. D.S.O., *A Short History of the Frimley and Camberley Cadet Corps 1908–1948* [Aldershot: Gale & Polden, 1948], p. 32
93 op. cit., F. W. Foley, pp. 1–7
94 Unpublished notes from Lt-Col. Aubrey Chalmers A.C.F., 1997
95 *Shropshire Chronicle*, 4 August 1944
96 op. cit., L. J. Collins
97 *Chard & Ilminster News*, 30 January 1943
98 Letter from J. Bushell in unpublished files of Mr A. M. Robinson, 'Die Hards of the 40s' Association, 1997
99 A.C.F.A., *The Official Handbook of the A.C.F.A.* [London: A.C.F.A., 1949], p. 20
100 *A.D.C.C. Gazette*, Vol. I, No. 5, 1940
101 Mr Wolfenden, 'Air Ministry Bulletin No. 2850', No. 13 [BBC Broadcast], 23 January 1941
102 *Air Training Corps Gazette*, Vol. I, No. 1, 1941
103 *Air Training Corps Gazette*, December 1940
104 *Chard & Ilminster News*, 29 March 1941
105 *Air Training Corps Gazette*, Vol. I, No. 9, 1941
106 Wg. Cdr. H. W. Lamond R.A.F. (Retd), *History of the Air Training Corps – including the A.D.C.C. and the C.C.F. (R.A.F.)* [Unpublished: HQ A.T.C., R.A.F. Cranwell, 1984], p. 3-10
107 *Air Training Corps Gazette*, Special Supplement, Vol. III, No. 9, 1943

108 Group Captain R. (Lucky) Jordan, DFC AFC, *To Burma and Beyond* [London: James Publishing Co., 1995], pp1–5
109 op. cit., H. W. Lamond, p. 2-5
110 *Air Training Corps Rules & Regulations* [London: Air Ministry, 1941], p. 11
111 *Air Training Corps Gazette*, Vol. I, No. 6, 1941
112 op. cit., H. W. Lamond, p. 2-12
113 Ibid., p. 3-12
114 *Chard & Ilminster News*, 4 April 1942
115 *Air Training Corps Gazette*, Special Supplement, Vol. IV, No. 3, 1944
116 op. cit., H. W. Lamond, p. 3-8
117 Arthur Pearcy, *Aviation News*, 23 December–5 January 1989
118 Letter from Mr Mike Waddington, ex-wartime A.T.C. Cadet, 1997
119 Ibid.
120 *Air Training Corps Gazette*, Special Supplement, Vol. IV, No. 9, 1944
121 Letter from Mr Slater, ex-wartime A.T.C. Cadet, 1997
122 Souvenir Booklet: *Golden Jubilee of Air Cadets in the East Essex Wing 1941–1991* [Essex: Maldon Publishing Co., 1991], pp. 11 & 25
123 *Chard & Ilminster News*, 22 January 1944
124 op. cit., H. W. Lamond, p. 2-1
125 *Air Training Corps Gazette*, Vol. I, No. 6, 1941
126 *Chard & Ilminster News*, 26 April 1941
127 *Air Training Corps Gazette*, Special Supplement, Vol. III, No. 9, 1943
128 op. cit., Souvenir Booklet, pp. 7 & 19
129 *Air Training Corps Gazette*, Vol. I, No. 2, 1942
130 *Air Training Corps Gazette*, Vol. II, No. 5, 1942
131 op. cit., R. (Lucky) Jordan, pp. 1–5
132 op. cit., H. W. Lamond, p. 2-21
133 *Air Training Corps Gazette*, Special Supplement, Vol. IV, No. 4, 1944
134 Ibid.
135 op. cit., H. W. Lamond, p. 3-9
136 War Office, *Pre-service Physical Training and Recreation for Army Cadets* [London: H.M.S.O., 1943]
137 War Office, *Physical Efficiency Preparation for Service Cadets* [London: H.M.S.O., 1945]
138 *The Cadet Journal*, Vol. V, No. 1, 1943
139 *The Sea Cadet* journal, Vol. 1, No. 6, 1944
140 *The Cadet Journal*, Vol. IV, No. 3, 1942
141 *The Cadet Journal*, May 1943
142 *The Air Training Corps Gazette*, Special Supplement, Vol. I, No. 4, 1943
143 *The Sea Cadet* journal, Vol. 1, No. 3, 1943 and *The Air Training Corps Gazette*, Special Supplement, Vol. IV, No. 3, 1944
144 *The Sea Cadet* journal, Vol. 1, No. 2, 1943
145 *The Cadet Journal*, Vol. V, No. 1, 1943

CHAPTER 6 –
ASSISTING THE WAR EFFORT

THE CADET MOVEMENT was, ostensibly, another branch of the youth service. However, the aims of the Cadet Services, and the references in the newspapers to pre-service training, differentiated the J.T.C., S.C.C., A.C.F. and the A.T.C. from the other youth organisations. The cadet units saw themselves as directly serving the war effort, although the sense of involvement varied from unit to unit and from time to time. When they were away at annual camp and living in a military-style environment, any feelings of being part of the armed forces, and thereby contributing to the war effort, must have been heightened.

Involvement in the war effort could be on an *ad hoc*, temporary or permanent part-time basis. It could also be either civilian or military in nature and might involve individuals or whole units. The fact that cadets operated in units and were accustomed to taking orders meant that they could easily be organised into working parties. This was utilised most effectively by the farming community, particularly during the summer months.

HARVEST CAMPS

The Women's Land Army did much to make up for the deficit of manpower and to help the war effort, but during harvest time even more help was needed on the farms. Schools were co-opted to help and their cadet contingents were ideally suited to such agricultural endeavour. In 1940 the P.S.S.C.A. summer camp had to be cancelled, and so the following year Shaftesbury Grammar School Cadet Corps ran a Harvest Camp. The idea was to undertake cadet training on the days when the farmers did not need assistance, and to release the cadets for harvest work when required. The training programme was inevitably restricted and included mainly, 'map reading, knotting and lashing, and fieldcraft'. However, with the unavailability of army training areas, the combined harvest camp did mean that cadets could go away and undergo some concentrated practical training. Indeed, the enterprise was so successful that the farmers asked if they could run another and larger camp the next year.[1]

There were other advantages: for one thing, the War Agricultural Committee 'supplied a large dining tent free of charge, which also served for lectures during the rain – of which there was plenty – and also extra rations allowed for harvest workers were drawn'. The farmer could help in other ways by providing a place to store the cadets' bicycles, a place for them to cook and help with drying their clothes. There was a bonus for the cadets as the farmers paid them for their labour.[2] The fact that the boys were paid could be a liability as the harvest camp, at times, acted as a rival attraction to the annual training camp. At Shrewsbury School the boys were given a choice between harvest camp and training camp; at the former the boys were paid 6d a day, and this monetary reward proved a greater incentive to some of the boys.[3] This may account for the fact that in 1942, in addition to the training camp, the boys from Shrewsbury School 'devoted 5,433 hours to work on Shropshire farms during the summer term'. They also worked a total of 941 hours for the Ministry of Supply and Forestry.[4]

In August 1941 Major-General The Viscount Bridgeman – the man in charge of the Home Guard and the A.C.F. – visited the Shaftesbury School Camp in Dorset which combined military training with harvesting, and was impressed by what he saw: as a result the B.N.C.A. adopted the policy of encouraging the two kinds of practical war work. Help on the farms by boys from the public schools was not always confined to the holidays. At Sherborne it was unpopular when it clashed with a games afternoon in term time. It was not, however, allowed to interfere with cadet training.[5] At the Merchant Taylors' School the Cadet Corps ran a couple of 'agriculture camps that produced a total of 7000 hours of work!'[6] Schools and their Cadet Corps throughout Britain repeated this pattern during the summer months of the war.

The rural-based 'open' cadet units were also affected during the months of harvest, as many boys were required to work on the local farms in the evenings. The Minister of Labour did, at times, call upon A.T.C. personnel, who were on deferred service awaiting joining instructions from the R.A.F., to do farm work.[7] Harvest camps were not only for A.C.F. and A.T.C. cadets. In 1944 the Admiral Commanding Reserves issued a memorandum urging all officers and Sea Cadets to do their duty and play their 'full part as citizens in the vital work of gathering in the crops'.[8] Many cadets were engaged temporarily in agricultural work and were therefore helping to feed the country, which, of course, was a valuable contribution to the war effort.

FIRE WATCHING AND A.R.P. WORK

As in the First World War, school premises were adapted to meet wartime needs. This time, however, they were not converting playing fields into frontline trenches and simulating attacks against the foe, but constructing air-raid shelters to protect staff and pupils from enemy bombing. Parts of the playing fields were given over to the production of vegetables, and black drapes covered each window to ensure that no light was visible to enemy aircraft at night. Air raid drills, particularly in the cities, the industrial areas, the ports and along the eastern and southern regions of

England became a regular part of school life. At Chigwell School in Essex there was a ban on the ringing of the school bell to signify the end of lessons. Instead, a boy from the Corps blew on a bugle.[9] Presumably the bell was saved for giving warning of an air raid. Air raids could have unforeseen effects. Should an air raid occur during an exam the pupils, at least at Chigwell, were to descend to the basement and were put on their honour not to discuss the exam questions! On returning to the exam room the students had to write that the 'Paper [was] interrupted by air-raid warning for one hour twenty minutes,' or whatever the time had been.[10]

The dropping of bombs by the enemy could have much more serious consequences. Apart from injuries and loss of life, there was always the secondary hazard of fire. Students and teachers at the boarding schools were employed on fire watching duty. At the Merchant Taylors' School groups of senior boys took it in turns to sleep in the School and did a form of guard duty. They would listen for an air raid siren. Should the siren sound the pair on duty would rush to the roof and watch for any firebombs landing on the school. In the event of a missile actually crashing into the school the 'intrepid' boys had to waken the others in the party, alert the rest of the school and fight the fire! During the day, when the sirens at the local factories alerted everyone in the town and the surrounding area, the pupils would rush to the school air raid shelters. At each shelter 'there was a signals post manned by members of the Corps signals section, [who were] in touch by telephone or Morse with the other posts'.[11] Thus cadet training was put to good and effective use and reports of 'safe arrival', or of any 'incidents' or the 'all clear' could be passed on quickly.

J. G. Atherton, a boy from Manchester, described in his wartime diary what it was like to be an evacuee; he was also a member of the A.T.C. and the Home Guard. At his school there was a regular procedure for fire watching. At 1830 hours a section of three boys and a master in charge signed-in before placing portable lamps at strategic places, and wooden ladders in position. Then they would check the black-out curtains and ensure that hose pipes and stirrup pumps were ready. The section was accommodated in wooden bunks in classrooms and there they stayed until 0700, when they would rise and put away the ladders and lamps.[12] The duties of the fire watcher and the A.R.P. worker were not, of course, confined to the boarding school and their cadet contingents.

In 1939, the Government issued a pamphlet titled *National Service*, which was a guide 'to the ways in which the people of this country may give service'. It outlined the entry qualifications and the terms of service for the Armed Forces, Police, the Fire Service and other ancillary services, both full and part-time.[13] The pamphlet was issued during the period known as the 'phoney war' when hostilities were still only a threat, and so service with the cadets for boys and adults is not mentioned, and neither is the Home Guard. A boy of 17 could join the Infantry Supplementary Reserve or the Territorial Army, and both organisations would, of course, have been delighted to have senior cadets in their ranks. However, there was one type of defence work which could officially involve cadets and their instructors, and that was the Air Raid Precautions service (A.R.P.). The older cadets from the 'open' units would do fire watching duties as part of the A.R.P., although in 1943 it was announced in *The Sea Cadet* that S.C.C. officers 'are exempt from fireguard duties at business premises except during working hours'. In the area in which they lived they could be called upon to 'do duty only as a member of a street fire party'. The same exemptions applied to C.P.O. instructors and cadets in full-time employment, providing they attended the unit on three days a week.[14] This implies that by this time participation in the pre-service cadet organisations was considered a significant wartime duty.

PARADES, PERFORMANCES AND FUNDS FOR WAR
A person in uniform was a common sight during the war years as the military went about its essential business, although the full-time service personnel had little or no time for the civic side of military life. Public parades were left, in the main, to the Home Guard and the cadet organisations, and as most H.G. units did not have a band it was often the cadet services that provided the music. The Shrewsbury School J.T.C. Band, for example, was a regular and 'popular feature' at the Home Guard parades in the town.[15]

The size of many of the cadet units meant that their parades and inspections were held in spacious public places. As the regular forces had little time to parade in public the 'top brass' took advantage of these opportunities to inspect such large bodies of uniformed people. As already noted, cadets could be visited by His Majesty King George VI, or inspected by high-ranking military figures, such as the Chief of Naval Information, Rear-Admiral R. H. Dickson. The latter's visit is interesting in that the sea cadet unit at Horley in Surrey (*Plate 21*) are seen parading with fixed bayonets, a privilege usually given only to units that had been granted the 'freedom of the town or city'. Parades and displays would often include a drill display, or occasionally a more unusual and enterprising performance could be seen. The 258 Squadron (Coulsdon and Purley), for example, put on a 'Red Arrows' type display (*Plate 22*) in which the cyclists flew in formation before shooting down the enemy (*Plate 23*). This performance was for the benefit of King Haakon of Norway and the Crown Prince Olaf's visit to Purley in 1942.

Cadets were used to parading in public because of the pre-war Empire Day parades and the annual Remembrance Day services. Perhaps the most public of all the cadet parades was that held on Trafalgar Day in the famously eponymous London square. In 1945, when the war in Europe was finally over, the Sea Cadet Corps, under the auspices of the Navy League, celebrated the 140th anniversary of Nelson's greatest victory with a service and parade in Trafalgar Square. A month earlier the cadets of the 1st Cadet Bn. The Royal Inniskilling Fusiliers were part of a march-past in Londonderry on the occasion of the granting of the Freedom of the City to Field-Marshal Sir Bernard Montgomery. Thus it was that cadets performed a very real service on public occasions. Indeed, this continues today as most of the regular forces, for reasons of security, are not seen in uniform in public and often the only military-looking representatives in and around a town are the cadets.

The 1945 Trafalgar Day programme was completed with a Jubilee and Victory concert at the Coliseum, and a luncheon for Navy League representatives and V.I.P. guests at the Savoy Hotel at which the principal guest was Rt. Honorable A. V. Alexander, First Lord of the Admiralty. The proceeds from all the celebratory functions were used to swell the coffers of the Sea Cadet Corps. It was not unusual for fund-raising done by the pre-service cadet organisations to be carried out as part of organised entertainment. For example the entertainer, Henry Hall, when touring his 'Guest Night' concert party around the country, offered to put the best Army Cadet units in the locality on the stage.[16]

Single cadet units would raise funds for the members of their parent service. For example, in 1940 the sea cadets of York collected cash to buy 'comforts for the Navy'.[17] Also in 1940 the 1st Tyne S.C.C. unit at Hebburn organised dances and raised nearly £200 for the dependants of naval ratings killed in an air raid.[18] And in August 1940 the Air Defence Cadet Corps Committee set out, via its air cadet squadrons, to raise £5,000 to buy and present a Spitfire to the Royal Air Force.[19] More often than not the fund raising was a combined effort to which the whole community was expected to contribute, both in terms of time and money. In 1944 the Somerset town of Chard aimed to raise £100,000 – the estimated cost to keep, equip and maintain a company of the Somerset Light Infantry for a year. On this occasion the A.C.F. contributed by being part of a grand opening ceremony and parade, and by organising a dance at the Corn Exchange. It was a successful venture as the town's target was soon surpassed. The final total raised by the inhabitants of Chard was £124,143.[20]

Each year the Government launched a drive specifically to help raise money for one of the armed services. Town councils would publish a monetary target that they aimed to reach within a week. In 1941 there was War Weapons Week; in 1942 it was Warship Week, followed in 1943 by Wings for Victory; and in 1944 there was Salute the Soldier Week. To add incentive, prizes were given for the town that raised the most within each district; in Somerset there was the county 'Small Savings' flag for the more rural towns. As a result there was competition between Chard and neighbouring Ilminster. At the latter the A.C.F. organised a 'Gymkhana & Sports' on the grammar school playing fields.[21] It is impossible to say how much each cadet unit in the country raised as many efforts were combined with those of other organisations. However, it is known that the City of Salford Air Training Corps Wing raised £20,286. Not surprisingly the Northeast Surrey Air Training Corps Wing, 'centred on wealthy Wimbledon' raised over £50,000, 'of which over £1,000 was contributed by the cadets personally'.[22]

In London things were more elaborate. In 1943, Vera Hodgson, one of the Government's Mass Observation operatives, describes the efforts to raise money for the Wings for Victory campaign in Trafalgar Square. A Lancaster bomber was grandly placed on a high platform above the crowds, and there were, she wrote:

> Such crowds of people. Men selling flags and baubles. Music playing and soldiers in a jeep going round and round the square. I edged my way in and saw the big bomber O for Orange, a Lancaster . . . Presently I found some firemen selling odd stamps to put on the bomber, so I bought one . . . Then I worked my way to the fountain where some air cadets were shouting and enjoying themselves. I found they were trying to raise one million pennies to try and buy a Typhoon [fighter plane] for Westminster. They paddled around in a rubber dinghy such as wrecked airmen use and you threw pennies to them. Other lads were in rubbers wading about in search of pennies which had gone into the pool . . .[23]

The charitable assistance given by members of the cadet organisations was varied and could have a triple function. The first aim was, of course, to raise funds; the second aim could be to entertain, and thirdly it was a good public relations exercise. In April 1944, in aid of Salute the Soldiers Week, the A.C.F. Company in Hitchin, Hertfordshire joined a parade that included H.M. Forces and the U.S.A.F. Following the parade the A.C.F. Company put on a display in the Town Square. Each A.C.F. platoon featured a different aspect of training. There was rifle drill, P.T., a section attack, drill with a Sten sub-machine gun (*Plate 24*), and even an assault course competition (*Plate 25*). The Director of the Home Guard and the A.C.F., Lord Bridgeman, asked the people of Hitchin to salute 'the soldiers, the part-time soldiers of the Home Guard, and the soldiers of the future (the A.C.F.)' by giving generously. The target of '£250,000 was surpassed within a week'.[24]

SERVICE ON THE HOME FRONT

'Wartime service' for the cadets could take other forms. A Liverpool Grammar schoolboy remembers working with the Youth Service Volunteers cutting pit props at a summer camp. This he said, 'felt like war work'.[25] The wartime work could involve working directly with the military. Middlesex A.C.F. cadets, for example, were employed to fill sandbags, and to move barbed wire pickets as well as shift stores at the Greenford Depot, where they were helping the medically downgraded servicemen waiting to be transferred to the Pioneer Corps.[26]

The Royal Observer Corps was an obvious recruiter of A.T.C. talent. The two organisations used to compete against each other in aircraft recognition competitions, and the young cadet enthusiasts used to acquit themselves well. It was no surprise then, when the R.O.C. at Driffield in the East Riding of Yorkshire contacted the local A.T.C. unit and requested the services of two keen cadets. Reports indicate that the R.O.C. unit was unique, in that it was equipped with a Canadian (G.L.) gun-laying radar set which operated at night. More personnel were therefore needed for this operation, and so there were vacancies for daytime staff. The A.T.C. cadets chosen for daytime duty had to undergo the R.O.C. graded tests 'which included memorising wing spans' and learning how to operate the Micklethwaite height finder, and mastering the skill of finger plotting using a coin. They also had access to the list of aircraft still on the secret list.[27] This employment of A.T.C. cadets by the R.O.C. was not restricted to Yorkshire.

In 1939 the rules for National Service stipulated that youths under 18 'who can carry messages by motorbike, pedal-cycle or on foot' could work as part of the Communication Service for the A.R.P.[28] It was inevitable therefore that when the Local Defence Volunteers, later the Home Guard, was formed they too would make use of their junior cadet 'colleagues' for such work.

There was a great amount of aerial activity by the enemy, particularly in the eastern and southern areas of Britain, which meant that the Home Guard was constantly busy watching for enemy parachutes. The cadets from the A.T.C. assisted them in this task by acting as runners between the observation points.[29] It was the close relationship that the cadets, particularly the army cadets, had with the H.G. that provided the young men with a real opportunity of serving on the Home Front.

There were advantages in using cadets as messengers. First, the cadets were familiar with the local countryside; secondly, they had the necessary map reading skills; thirdly, they would be familiar with much of the military jargon, and, of course, they were terribly keen. 'The most interesting parts of our work are the night operations,' said a cadet from the Ayr Academy Cadet Corps, who had done 'some of these with the co-operation of Commando troops'.[30] The need was not just for H.G. units operating in the countryside; the urban-based H.G. units also required despatch riders. Members of the Princess Louise's Kensington Regt. Cadet Corps in London formed a detachment of 20 cadets to work as 'cyclist despatch riders'. They were attached to the 3rd London Battalion Home Guard, and they were specially trained for this work at Sunday morning sessions. On Monday evenings these despatch riders received instruction in unarmed combat to 'prepare them for anything they might be called upon to face should battle in the streets of London come about'.[31] One ex-cadet from the Middlesex A.C.F. remembers being given memory tests which entailed receiving a verbal message then 'doubling off' on a run and returning with sweat running into his eyes, puffing and panting and having to repeat the message 'word for word'.[32] There is no doubt that those cadet units which had H.G. instructors had the benefit of a more varied training programme, which could include bayonet fighting (*Plate 26*).

So prolific was the involvement of the army cadets in the work as messengers that the War Office published a training pamphlet in 1945 titled *Message Writing for Cadets*. This became a part of the War Certificate 'A' syllabus. Cadets had to learn how to take down messages clearly, and detachment commanders had, where necessary, to give the cadets lessons in 'memory practice' and handwriting. Among the skills the cadet messenger had to learn was the use of military abbreviations, and the method of describing positions, places and areas. They also had to learn how to use the Royal Corps of Signals Message Form, AFC2136.[33]

On 14 May 1940, following the B.B.C. news, the Secretary of State for War, Mr Anthony Eden, made his first speech to the nation, and it concerned the formation of the Local Defence Volunteers. He asked for volunteers. In the morning thousands of men 'signed-on' and by June membership had reached 1,456,000. However, it was not only men that volunteered. Within 24 hours of the minister's announcement all the London-based army cadet units offered the services of their cadets who were over 17, 'together with all the officers, most of whom had seen service in the last war'. Alas the offer was declined; instead cadets and officers could join as individuals.[34] By 1942 numbers in the Home Guard, as it was known by then, began to decline owing to the call-up of the younger volunteers into the army. The lessening threat of invasion also meant that fewer people were interested in joining.[35] Cadets were therefore needed to keep the numbers up, and with the appointment of Major-General Bridgeman as Director of the H.G. and the A.C.F. there ensued a different and closer relationship between the H.G. and the army cadets. The British National Cadet Association representative, writing in *The Cadet Journal*, spelt out the expected response of this closer relationship, saying:

> As a wartime measure ... the War Office has ... affiliated Cadet units to the local unit of the Home Guard, from which they are to receive ... assistance over training facilities.... All Cadets are expected to join this Home Guard unit on reaching the age of 17, since all young men of that age should be prepared actively to take up arms in the defence of their country ... and this applies to members of the Cadet Force even more than to others, since they have already been trained in the use of arms.[36]

At the same time the age at which a cadet could operate as a messenger for the Home Guard was lowered to 16, and the Army Cadet Force was openly referred to at the B.N.C.A.'s A.G.M. in late 1941 as the 'junior organisation' of the Home Guard.[37]

In May 1941 the Sea Cadet Corps Committee debated a proposal about a roster of 'Officers and Sea Cadets over the age of 17 who in the event of an invasion could be immediately called up and affiliated to the Home Guard as combatants'. The concern on the part of S.C.C. officers was that they would be regarded as 'nothing but civilians when it came to repelling the enemy', despite the fact that they gave up a considerable amount of their free time to train cadets for the services. The Sea Cadet units already gave local H.G. units assistance with regard to river patrols, and the Sea Cadet Corps Secretary said he would contact the Naval Authorities in charge of the River Patrol Service to see what more could be done.[38] However, as far as is known, no such list was drawn up (*Plate 27*).

The Air Training Corps was also concerned about membership of the Home Guard, but for different reasons. The A.T.C. argued that by 1941 the H.G. was established and therefore did not need A.T.C. members, and that 'the training of the youth of the country for R.A.F. duties, especially for air-crew work, is of paramount importance, and preference should be given to cadet work'. They did not go so far as to suggest that those who were members of both organisations should henceforth resign from the H.G., but that in future 'cadet work must have priority'.[39] A.T.C. units would still co-operate with the H.G. whether or not their staff or some of their cadets were members of the defence force. At Bishop Stortford in Hertfordshire, the cadets would often 'act as crashed German aircrew during [Home Guard] exercises'. On some exercises the cadets' task was to infiltrate the Home Guard's H.Q. (a pub called the Nag's Head), which apparently they were quite successful at doing.[40]

The Junior Training Corps contingents in the public schools appear to have been free from the regulatory constraints of their brother cadet organisations. Several schools signed up their J.T.C. units as part of the Local Defence Corps as soon as its formation was announced. In 1940, when invasion seemed likely, 60 cadets from the Bishop Wordsworth School in Dorset 'were formed into a second line of defence unit of the Local Defence Volunteers, later the Home Guard'.[41] At the Merchant Taylors' School in Hertfordshire cadet members became part of No. 3 Platoon of the 28th Company of a L.D.V. battalion centred in Rickmansworth. This school company was augmented by cadets from other nearby H.G. units. Weapons for the newly formed H.G. units were scarce, and many of the cadet units had to hand their Lee Enfield rifles over to the Home Guard. In 1940 the Rickmansworth H.G. had very few weapons and many of its members toted pikes. However, there was great excitement when the unit (with its cadets) went to see a demonstration of a new weapon in a field at nearby Northwood. It was a drainpipe which had a spike secured inside one end and two struts to hold it steady in the ground. It was, in effect, a very rudimentary mortar gun that was supposed to fire home-made 'shells' in the form of milk bottles filled with stones![42] Needless to say it was discarded. In 1942 the H.G. and the Cadets were issued with the new and cheap, but nevertheless effective, Sten sub-machine gun.

The amount of co-operation that existed between the cadet units and the Home Guard varied from district to district. In some areas where there was no cadet unit the H.G. was the only chance a youth had of getting into uniform prior to call-up. Occasionally A.C.F. cadet units would engage in combined operations with the H.G.; usually the cadets acted the role of the enemy. At other times the cadets acted as casualties that had to be dealt with medically and then evacuated from the battlefield. There were, however, cadet units that had a dual role as cadet contingent and as Home Guard platoon or company. One such was 'Z' Company of Shrewsbury School.

The function of the Shrewsbury School Home Guard Company in the event of an enemy invasion was printed in the Battalion's SECRET Operation Orders. Order No. 3 makes it clear where the threat(s) might come and precisely where 'Z' company would be deployed:

> Enemy. Enemy troops may attempt to enter SHREWSBURY
> (a) on foot and possibly disguised
> (b) by vehicles, either enemy or commandeered
> (c) by landing from the air by plane, glider or parachutes.[43]

Five of Shrewsbury town's H.G. companies were deployed in pre-arranged positions in and around the town, with a further two companies in mobile battle positions. The School – 'Z' Coy – shared the responsibility for the defence of the Shrewsbury railway station. The School H.G. contingent, working in a rota system with other companies, did six-hour night shifts; one section of the company was on duty from 2230 to 0130 followed by the second section from 0130 to 0430. During the day the station was under the control of the railway employees.

The officer commanding 'Z' company drew up a detailed plan of the area of the station, which included an analysis of its vulnerable points, and concluded that it was impossible to defend the whole area, which stretched over a mile. He therefore decided to have standing patrols (sentries) at vital strategic points: that is, they would defend the two junction areas, the signal box, and both the Severn and the English Bridge, but there was a mobile patrol around the pumping station area. Sentries would be in pairs and were armed with rifles and fixed bayonets. Sentries were to challenge all unauthorised persons by shouting 'HALT'. If the person challenged was unable to give a satisfactory explanation he or she was to be detained and the police to be notified. It was stipulated, and no doubt to the annoyance of railway employees, that any 'trainmen using unauthorised routes ... must be directed to the proper route'.[44]

Shrewsbury School was by no means the only J.T.C. or A.C.F. unit to be integrated into the Home Guard defence plans, but it gives an example of how older cadets could be and were involved in actively defending the country. Apart from the feeling of doing a 'proper defence job' the cadet who joined the H.G. prior to 1942 was issued with a battledress, gaiters and modern webbing equipment, whereas the ordinary army cadet was still wearing First World War uniform. There was therefore an added incentive for joining the Home Guard. Later in the war when weapons became more widely available it was not unusual for older cadets, who were also in the H.G., to take rifles and ammunition home. Indeed, as several ex-cadets and H.G. members will recall, they could even take the odd grenade home; some even remember taking a Bren Light Machine-gun home so that they could spend time cleaning it![45]

When campaign medals were distributed at the end of the war, the Defence Medal was awarded to all members of the armed forces and civilian defence organisations who had served for three years. Major Ted Warrick, who served with the Gloucester Home Guard Battalion and Cheltenham College Cadet Corps was awarded the Defence Medal: thus he partly earned his medal whilst still at school![46]

CHAPTER 6 REFERENCES

1. *The Cadet Journal*, Vol. IV, No. 2, 1941
2. Ibid.
3. Interview with Dr M. Plumtree, J.T.C. cadet, 1942–45
4. *Shropshire Chronicle*, 14 August 1942
5. Lt.Col. J. P. Riley M.P., 'The History of the Sherborne School Cadet Force, 1883–1988' in *Sherborne in Uniform* [Sherborne: Shelly, 1988], pp. 67–69
6. Cdr. R. B. Hawkey R.N.R. C.C.F., 'History of the Merchant Taylors' School, 1900–1982' [Rickmansworth: George & Roberts, 1981], p. 40
7. *Air Training Corps Gazette*, Vol. II, No. 9, 1942
8. *The Sea Cadet*, Vol. I, No. 9, 1944
9. Jonathan Croall, 'Don't you know there's a war on?' in *The People's Voice, 1939–45* [London: Hutchinson, 1988], p. 104
10. Ibid., p. 108
11. op. cit., R. B. Hawkey, pp. 39 & 40.
12. J. G. Atherton, 'Home and Away' and 'Home to Stay', the diary of a wartime evacuee from Stretford, near Manchester, 3 Sept 1939–April 1940, IWM
13. H.M.S.O., *National Service*, 1939, pp. 1–5
14. *The Sea Cadet*, Vol. I, No. 2, 1943
15. *Shropshire Chronicle*, 7 February 1941
16. *The Cadet Journal*, No. 1, February 1944
17. *The Navy*, April 1940
18. *The Navy*, February 1940
19. Wg. Cdr. H. W. Lamond R.A.F. (Retd), *History of the Air Training Corps – including the A.D.C.C. and the C.C.F. (R.A.F.)* [Unpublished: H.Q. A.T.C., R.A.F. Cranwell, 1984], p. 1-9
20. *The Chard & Ilminster News*, 29 April 1944
21. *The Chard & Ilminster News*, 3 June 1944
22. *Air Training Corps Gazette*, Special Supplement, Vol. III, No. 7, 1943
23. Leonard Moseley, *Backs to the Wall – London Under Fire, 1940–1945* [London: Weidenfeld, 1971], p. 300/1
24. *Hertfordshire Pictorial*, 18 April 1944
25. Correspondence with Mr Arthur Duggan – ex-A.T.C. cadet, 1943–45
26. A. M. Robinson unpublished archives, 'Die Hards of the 40s', Middlesex Army Cadets
27. Arthur Pearcy, 'Venture Adventure', in *Aviation News*, 23 December 1988 and 5 January 1989
28. op. cit., H.M.S.O., *National Service*, p. 16
29. Flt. Lt. D. R. Mason R.A.F.VR(T), 1096 Bishop Stortford Sqn., *Golden Jubilee of Air Cadets in the East Essex Wing, 1941–1991* [Maldon Printing Co., 1991]

30 *The Cadet Journal*, Vol. IV, No. 4, 1942
31 *The Cadet Journal*, Vol. IV, No. 5, 1942
32 op. cit., letter from C. K. Earthey, in A. M. Robinson's files
33 War Office, *Message Writing for Cadets*, May 1945
34 *The Cadet Journal*, Vol. IV, No. 1, 1941
35 S. P. MacKenzie, *The Home Guard* [OUP, 1995], pp. 34–90
36 *The Cadet Journal*, Vol. IV, No. 2, 1941
37 *The Cadet Journal*, January 1942
38 Minutes of the Sea Cadet Corps Committee, 15 May 1941
39 *Air Training Corps Gazette*, Vol. 1, No. 4, 1941
40 op. cit., D. R. Mason
41 Bishop Wordsworth School, handout sent to Wing Cdr West, H.Q. C.C.F. (R.A.F.) & A.T.C., R.A.F. Cranwell
42 op. cit., R. B. Hawkey, pp. 40–42
43 No. 1 Battalion Home Guard (Shropshire Zone) SECRET Operation Order No. 3, Shrewsbury School Archives, 1940 c
44 L.D.V. Force (Railway Section) 'Z' Coy Shrewsbury Standing Orders, Shrewsbury School Archives, 1940 c
45 Correspondence with Maj. E. M. Warrick RE (Retd) – J.T.C. member 1940–45 and Home Guard member 1941–45

CHAPTER 7 – REWARDS AND AWARDS, AND LOOKING TO THE FUTURE

MOST CADETS ENTERED the armed services on a full-time basis when they reached the age of seventeen-and-a-half. The majority of cadets who were members of the Home Guard did not, therefore, serve the three years necessary to qualify for the Defence Medal. Adults, particularly those not liable for call-up – such as older schoolmasters and those cadets who had left school and were in restricted occupations – could qualify for the Defence Medal via service with the Home Guard.

The Defence Medal was available to all, but officers were eligible for other decorations as well. When the public school contingents were designated as Officer Training Corps units their officers received T.A. commissions: thus their officers could receive the Territorial Decoration (T.D.) medal for long and efficient service. Officers of the Territorial Cadet Force, later the A.C.F., had no such recognition. On 9 April 1934, the imbalance had been partly redressed when the then Prince of Wales, the Patron of the British National Cadet Association, approved the institution of the Long Service Badge. This was granted for 15 years' commissioned service. It was not a King's medal and the badge and ribbon 'coloured red and dark green' had to be worn on the right breast. Similarly, the S.C.C. Admiralty-appointed officer who did not have the King's Commission could not qualify for a military long-service medal. The Board of the Admiralty stipulated that 'no Honorary unpaid Commissions could be given in the future [from 1941] in the R.N.V.R. to Officers unless those officers were in permanent full-time employment under the Admiralty'.[1]

During the Second World War the older established school contingents were re-designated Junior Training Corps. Thus there was a distinction between them and the Officer Training Units in the universities. Nevertheless, there continued to be a difference between the status of officers in the J.T.C. units in schools and that of officers in the rest of the Cadet Movement. The number of officers serving with the J.T.C. was relatively small, as membership was restricted to 30,000 cadets during the war. Any school forming a cadet unit after 1941 had to do so as part of the A.C.F. or the A.T.C.

The officers of the A.C.F. and the A.T.C. were rewarded for their valuable war-work in 1942 when they were granted the King's Commission. After the war the school units were combined in 1948 to embrace cadets from all three Services and they thus became known as the Combined Cadet Force, and the award of the T.D. did not henceforth apply to newly-appointed officers. The present award of the Cadet Forces

Medal – granted for 12 years' service with good conduct – was instituted in 1950, and is for officers and senior N.C.O. instructors of all the cadet organisations.

Although the creation of the Cadet Forces Medal did not occur until some five years after the war, it may be viewed, in part, as public recognition of the work done by the volunteer officers and instructors during the six years of conflict. It also erased the anomaly regarding different awards by recognising the contribution of the work done by all the cadet services.

War can be viewed as antithetical: it provides people with the opportunity to perform acts of cruelty and acts of courageous virtue. It is, of course, the latter that are encouraged, recognised and rewarded. Courage is not just the preserve of the officer or the adult. Cadets, particularly during the protracted period of conflict of a world war, had more chances than ever to put their training to full use, to demonstrate their resourcefulness and to perform courageous deeds that, at times, went beyond the call of duty. The Navy League, as if in anticipation of the forthcoming war, instituted the Navy League Cross 'For Gallantry' in 1938.

The Navy League Cross was struck as an expression of the direct desire of Lord Lloyd – then President of the Navy League – as a means of recognising 'outstanding feats of personal bravery on the part of individual members of the Sea Cadet Corps'.[2] Before the onset of war, only two cadets had been awarded the medal. By 1943, another 12 cadets had been awarded the Navy League Cross.

Most of the awards, at least at that time, were for rescuing younger boys and children from drowning. The most dramatic such incident appears to have been the rescue performed by Sea Cadet Signalman R Kahler from the Kingston (Steadfast) Unit who, while on a course at T.S. *Bounty* at Worcester in 1941, dived fully equipped and wearing a respirator into the river basin to effect 'a fine rescue'. Two other wartime related awards went to Cadet Petty Officers A. R. Howes and S. Nicholson of the Hull Unit who in 1941 went into a collapsed building and rescued 'a soldier, an elderly woman and two children before official help could arrive'. In May of the same year Cadet Harold Thompson of the St Clement Danes Unit helped to save a block of five shops in the Walworth area. During an air raid he made three journeys through falling debris to fetch the fire brigade.[3]

When the Admiralty took control of the Sea Cadet Corps training and much of the administration it was quick to acknowledge the value of the Navy League Cross for gallantry, although the assessment of the acts of bravery and responsibility for presentation remained the preserve of the

Navy League. The recipients could wear the Cross on the right breast when in Sea Cadet uniform, but it was not to be worn on other uniforms as it was not an official decoration approved by the Board of the Admiralty. However, not every act of bravery by a S.C.C. member qualified for the medal. If the act performed was brave, but not of the same order as that deemed worthy of a medal, the cadet would receive a letter of commendation from the Chairman of the Navy League.

This cadet awards system inaugurated prior to the Second World War is still in existence today, except that it is now a four-tier system. A Certificate of Commendation is 'For an act beyond the call of duty'. The next and higher award is a Gallantry Certificate. Above this is the Gallantry Medal, and the ultimate is the Gallantry Cross. The last is for saving life in circumstances of 'exceptional danger and personal risk to the salvor or salvors'.[4]

The Army Cadet Force did not have such an elaborate system of gallantry awards for its cadets, although there is evidence of a parchment certificate for an 'Act of Gallantry' being awarded to Cadet Eliezer Derrick from Carmarthenshire A.C.F. for saving a boy from drowning at a camp near Chepstow in 1945.[5] There were no doubt other recipients of the award, but records have not survived and so there is no evidence of how many were presented.

The Air Defence Cadet Corps (forerunner of the A.T.C.) copied the S.C.C. and instituted a Gallantry Medal for cadets. One of the first people to receive the award was Cadet Roy Clark of No. 171 (Christchurch) Squadron who, during a daylight-bombing raid in 1940 and despite injuries to himself, continued to render assistance to the official rescue squad.[6] Most of the awards were for courageous work done during air raids. Lance Corporal (the A.D.C.C. used army ranks) Cyril Wilson of No. 88 (St. Pancras) A.D.C.C. Squadron was doubly rewarded for his bravery in 1941 when he helped a policeman rescue 12 people from a bombed house. He was awarded the A.T.C. Gallantry Medal and received a cheque for £3 from the Mayor of the Borough.[7] In 1940 a group of cadets, Lance Corporal G. Saggers Wade from No. 20 (Ilford) A.D.C.C. Squadron and Corporal N. Davies and Lance Corporal F. Edwards from No. 4 (Ilford) A.D.C.C. Squadron twice went into action. On the first occasion they put out incendiary bombs which had fallen on a local Co-operative store and, later, in September 1940, repeated the act by rescuing people from a burning building.[8]

Any organisation that deals with weapons and explosives has to have the highest standards of safety. However, accidents will, inevitably, occur, albeit rarely. During the war more ordnance was dealt with and doubtless greater risks were taken. Research reported in televised programmes in 1998 has shown that standards of safety were not always so high in times of war. Occasionally cadets helped servicemen in 'bombing up' aeroplanes and assisted them in moving stores of ammunition and explosives; how many of the accidents incurred doing these tasks which involved cadets is unknown. It is recorded that nearly 800 civilians and Home Guard members died as a result of accidents with equipment and by what is euphemistically called 'friendly fire'. A substantial number of H.G. members were also cadets, and one can assume cadets were involved on occasions.

Incidents involving aircraft were logged and it is therefore easier to quantify them. There were 35 recorded accidents involving A.T.C. deaths in R.A.F. aircraft during the years 1942 to 45. In total 50 A.T.C. cadets were killed. Another fatality involved a German aircraft. This was in 1945 when an R.A.F. lorry, which was taking cadets home from a boxing match at R.A.F. Bircham Newton, was attacked by a Messerschmitt 110: one cadet died from 'a shrapnel ricochet from the burst of cannon fire [which] hit him in the chest'. The highest loss of life in any one accident occurred on 8 September 1943. Cadets P. Bond, D. J. Fox and E. L. Hall from 1180 (Buxton) Squadron were on a cross-country flight in Lancaster JB153. At 1320 hours the aircraft crashed two miles south-east of Wymeswold airfield. A further three cadets were killed when a R.A.F. lorry was involved in a collision in 1944, also from R.A.F. Wymeswold.[9] Most of the A.T.C. deaths occurred as a result of aircraft breaking up in flight and crashing into the ground or into the sea (*Plate 28*).

Interestingly the Sea Cadet Corps made provision for the injured amongst its ranks. In 1936 the Sun Hill Court Convalescent Home was established at Worthing on the south coast. It accommodated 30 boys and looked out over the Channel. The Service authorities and the Ministry of Health granted free medical treatment for members of the S.C.C. By 1945 it was agreed that 'treatment for an injury sustained during S.C.C. training should be given to a conclusion and not merely, as formerly, until the patient was able to travel home'.[10] The arrangement also applied to officers, C.P.O. instructors and enrolled civilian instructors as well as cadets.

Very occasionally a cadet's bravery went beyond the bounds of the Service's gallantry award, and the act of courage was recognised nationally. In 1942 Cadet Corporal Robert McCallum of No. 49F (Greenock) Squadron went to Buckingham Palace to receive the British Empire Medal from the King. He was the first A.T.C. cadet to be honoured in this way. Corporal McCallum was awarded the B.E.M. for gallantry and devotion to duty in an air raid. He continued, despite falling bombs and debris to carry messages by bicycle 'or rather a number of bicycles, because several accidents occurred rendering the machine he was riding unserviceable'. When his machine was damaged he continued on foot until he could get hold of another bike.[11]

Another A.T.C. recipient of the B.E.M. was Corporal B. E. Gill of No. 200 (Torquay) Squadron. While on duty in 1944 as a messenger for the Civil Defence, and along with a British soldier and an American sailor, he rescued two victims from a bombed basement. The task was dangerous as there was a strong smell of escaping gas, which meant there was a chance of a second explosion.[12] Cadet Leonard Wells from No. 244 (Scafell) Squadron, who rescued a pilot from a burning aircraft that had crashed, was another recipient of the BEM.[13]

No account of the Cadets and War would be complete without a mention of Cadet Corporal David Lazarus of the Army Cadet Force who was awarded the George Medal in February 1941. The award was announced in the *London Gazette*:

> During an air raid on London Volunteer Lazarus, aged 17, was on his way to report for duty when a bomb fell on a block of tenement flats. The building was reduced to ruins. Masonry and other debris was falling continuously, but Lazarus entered the ruins and began to remove quantities of wreckage with his hands in order to get to four people who were imprisoned. He managed to bring them out, despite the fact that he had already sustained injury himself. He then attempted to rescue a fifth occupant of the flats, but a wall collapsed and buried him. He was taken to hospital suffering from multiple injuries to the head, arms and body.[14]

There is no doubt that numerous acts of courage displayed by members of the Cadet Movement remain unknown and unrecognised to this day.

THE WAR ENDS AND THE CADET MOVEMENT LOOKS TO THE FUTURE

On 4 May 1945, the German forces in northwest Germany surrendered to Field-Marshal Montgomery. Three days later on 7 May, the Germans signed the instrument of unconditional surrender in the presence of General Eisenhower. This ended the fighting in Europe.

The dropping of the second atomic bomb at Nagasaki on 9 August signalled the end of the war in the Far East. The American General MacArthur received the formal capitulation of all Japanese forces on 2 September, and 10 days later in Singapore the Admiral in charge of the British Forces in the Far East, Lord Louis Mountbatten, received the Japanese surrender of south-east Asia. At last, the war was finally over.

The country celebrated. The blackout was ended. The lights were turned on and church bells were rung for the first time for years. There were church services and parades in towns and cities throughout Britain. The A.T.C. planned a rally to be centred on the England v. Scotland football match at the Tottenham Hotspur ground and at the A.T.C. Boxing Championships at the Albert Hall. This happily coincided with the end of the war in Europe and it became a Victory celebration. Two thousand cadets representing every A.T.C. unit in the country assembled in London, where they had a church service and march-past in Hyde Park. All the cadets were accommodated in an underground shelter in Camden Town – originally a tube railway station – which was fitted out with three-tier beds. The week from 15 to 22 of September was designated by the Government as 'Thanksgiving Week' – it also signified the anniversary of The Battle of Britain – and formal parades, church services and celebrations were held in London; all of these culminated in a 'Youth and Future Day'. On the final day, 22 September 1945, there was a ceremony celebrating youth in Trafalgar Square, followed by displays presented in Hyde Park by units of the Pre-Service Cadet Corps and National Youth Organisations. The following year, on 6 April 1946, army cadets from all over Britain and Northern Ireland took part in a Victory Parade in Hyde Park. This was the culmination of a nation-wide three-day recruiting drive. There was a march-past of 6,000 cadets, with the salute being taken by Princess Elizabeth, the future Queen Elizabeth II. There were also special services in Westminster Abbey and Westminster Cathedral.

The war had a profound effect on the cadet organisations; numbers had never been larger, recognition so formally acknowledged and their importance so obviously valued. The cadet organisations had become an integral part of the armed forces. The cadet organisations' function was outlined in the unofficial nomenclature – they had become known as the pre-service cadet corps. But now the war was over, what was their function? Were they still needed?

National Service for men in the armed forces was still in operation; indeed, it was to remain so until 1962. This meant that any boy wishing to prepare himself for military service prior to his 18th birthday could do so via the cadet organisations. The armed services and the Merchant Navy were always grateful to receive recruits that were already partly trained. In fact in 1948, in a debate in Parliament, the Labour Secretary of State for War, Mr Emanuel Shinwell, underlined the importance of cadet training to the Army when he stated:

> ... ex-cadets of the Junior Training Corps and Army Cadet Force, after undergoing selection processes, and after open competition, secured 80 per cent. of the vacancies in the January 1948, intake into the Royal Military Academy; ex-cadets secured 75 per cent. of the

vacancies in a recent intake into Officer Cadet Training Units; twenty out of every twenty-one cadets with Certificate 'A' who join the Army are either under training as officers or have earned promotion as non-commissioned officers within a few months of joining. The benefits of cadet training do not cease at the age of 18 . . .[15]

Despite the advantage of cadet training to the Armed Services, numbers in the Cadet Movement fell once the crisis of war was over and the youths, not unnaturally, concentrated on their civilian careers. In 1944 the numbers in the A.T.C. had fallen to 170,000[16]; by 1946 this was further reduced to 57,000.[17] The A.C.F. total was reduced to 100,000, although the J.T.C. membership remained at around 30,000.[18] The S.C.C. total membership was halved, and by 1947 was less than 22,000.[19]

Much of the temporary accommodation used by the cadet organisations reverted to its original use, and there was concern that, along with the reduction in the armed forces and the shut down of wartime establishments, there would be a shortage of accommodation for the cadet units. In July 1945 the Navy League S.C.C. Committee was already planning for the future, and there were proposals to open four permanent training camps. These were to function as conference centres, Area Officers' headquarters and adventure training centres.[20] The S.C.C. had been re-organised with a central administration and with a single head acting as the Superintendent of the S.C.C. One of his and his committee's tasks was to ensure that every unit was accommodated in its own 'stone frigate'. The British National Cadet Association, now re-named the Army Cadet Force Association to distinguish it properly from the other cadet organisations, was concerned with re-establishing its links with the Territorial Army once the Home Guard had been disbanded. The A.C.F. was also mindful of the possibility that the Government, in its rebuilding programme and proposed construction of new towns with facilities for the whole community, would overlook the needs of the A.C.F.[21] The A.T.C., also concerned about the loss of facilities, was assured by the joint Under-Secretary of State for Air that units 'badly in need of accommodation for training purposes, and which cannot provide it, will in certain circumstances have huts provided for them'.[22]

In spite of the expected reduction in numbers, the Cadet Movement had come of age during the period of the Second World War. It was obvious to all interested parties that the cadet organisations should not be allowed to suffer the fate experienced by the A.C.F. after the First World War. All cadet services had become more involved in, and were more valued by, their parent adult service. They had become more sophisticated in their operation. Training was now of a much higher standard, thanks to the assistance and the demands of the Armed Forces. However, the nature and emphasis of the training had to change. The country was no longer on a war footing and so cadet training had to be concerned with more than just military training.

The Government and the Army Council repeated what the both the Sea Cadet Corps and the Air Training Corps had always practised via their civilian welfare committees: namely, that the administration of a cadet organisation 'must be welded into the life of the community on the one hand, and that of its [parent Service] on the other'.[23] The A.C.F. was aware of what had happened after the First World War when, through mismanagement and a reluctance to change, those in charge did not adapt to the peacetime environment and the A.C.F., in the eyes of the Government, ceased to exist in the late 1920s.

The training programmes had to be modified and the emphasis had to be equally shared between the military requirements and the social and recreational development of the cadets. The social and recreational objectives were recognised by the grants that cadet units could receive from the Ministry of Education for administration, and by the financial help from the Local Education Authority for welfare purposes. The Armed Services continued to help by providing training facilities, adult instructors, and by continuing to provide some paid professional assistance, which afforded the volunteer staff some measure of relief in administrative matters. The capitation grants, chargeable to the Service's Government grant, were to continue – indeed the joint Under-Secretary of State for Air said in 1945 that there would be a 25 per cent increase and the grant was raised to a maximum rate of £1.[24]

The experience of the war highlighted not only the necessity for trained personnel but also the need for good leaders. The training of cadets would continue to foster and to stress the importance of civic duty. It has to be said that under wartime conditions many juveniles received less supervision and opportunities for committing petty crimes increased. The Government recognised the role played by youth organisations and in particular by the pre-service cadet corps in providing boys with discipline and a 'sense of direction'. This was realised as early as the beginning of 1940, and as a result Circular 1577/41, with its aim of promoting a form of National Service for youth, was introduced. The war in fact provided the cadet organisations with the opportunity for making a tremendous contribution in voluntary service to the community: an opportunity they grasped with both hands. Apart from the military objectives the cadets could be involved in collecting salvage, clearing bomb sites, serving in canteens or helping with evacuation. To live in wartime Britain meant to live at a time when the country came first, when the needs of others were often more important than one's own. The Cadet Movement aimed to capitalise on and continue this sense of corporate spirit and civic duty. This was in line with the thinking and aims of the Youth Advisory Council as outlined in its 1945 report entitled *The Purpose and Content of the Youth Service*.[25] As a result of this a new phrase came into cadet training, that of 'citizenship training'. Citizenship, and all that it implies, became an integral part of the philosophy of the Cadet Movement. Not long after, in 1947, the new Royal Warrant of the A.T.C. included 'training in citizenship' among its aims. The Sea Cadet Corps incorporated a similar aim in their re-worded Charter in 1947. In fact the S.C.C. was to link this aim with the intention of reverting to the lower, pre-war age of enrolment, which was 12. The Navy League S.C.C. Committee reasoned that it was 'necessary to "catch the boy" before he reaches the age at which he becomes one of those who herd on the streets after school hours'.[26] This lowering of the age of entry served to differentiate the Sea Cadet Corps from the Army Cadet Force and the Air Training Corps who preferred to maintain the status quo and enrol youths at the age of 14.

The Admiralty again, as in 1942, offered to take over the Sea Cadet Corps but as before, the Navy League rejected the offer, and instead a system of co-sponsorship was embodied in an agreement with the Admiralty. The A.C.F., alternatively, was busy re-establishing its links with the T.A. and was looking for officers and instructors with recent military experience to come and serve with the A.C.F. The A.T.C. did not want to go back to the pre-war days of the A.D.C.C., and in 1946 the A.T.C. was pleased to become a part of the R.A.F. Reserve Command. Both the A.C.F. and the A.T.C. were looking to strengthen their links with their parent service, whereas the S.C.C. appeared to favour a more independent approach.

The Cadet Movement would go through further changes, some of them radical, in the next few years. The Junior Training Corps for the training of army cadets in the public schools was soon to disappear. In 1948 the Combined Cadet Force, which was an amalgamation of the three cadet services that operated in the schools, would replace the J.T.C.

Changes in the recreational and physical fitness programmes had already been put into effect during the war, with a greater emphasis being placed on physical fitness and sport. Later, in the 1950s, came the introduction of the Duke of Edinburgh's Award scheme. And even later still, a greater revolution was to take place, and that was the much welcomed but extremely belated introduction of girls into the Cadet Movement in the early 1980s.

Never before in the history of youth organisations had so many teenagers donned uniform in preparation for the defence of their country. From that point of view the Second World War is an important landmark in the study of youth. And 1942 can be regarded as the watershed in the development of military youth organisations. This was when the Armed Forces become directly involved in the Cadet Movement and determined the standard of training and the direction training was to take. It was also a time when more facilities than ever before were opened to the cadet services, and when the separate cadet organisations became big enough and felt confident enough to publish their own magazines.

The future of the Cadet Movement post-war was foreseen as early as 24 February 1942 by the Rt. Hon. R. A. Butler, President of the Board of Education when, in a foreword in *The Cadet Journal*, he wrote:

> This is not a world in which we can sit back or rely on other people . . . It is the Government's policy to organise openings for you which will train and prepare you for the adventure of the future. Membership of a Cadet unit gives [cadets] opportunities for maturing in spirit, mind and body, so that they may play their full part as soldier-citizens.
>
> I write from the Board of Education because we have been entrusted by the Government with the task of encouraging boys to take up whatever training and national service suits them best. I know that the Cadet units will appeal to a very large number of boys. There is something in the word 'Cadet' which suits the new world. It means that all boys will have as equal a chance as possible and will train themselves from as young an age as possible. Make the best of this chance and you will be making the best of yourselves.[27]

It was a mark of achievement for those running the Cadet Movement when His Majesty King George VI agreed to become the Admiral of the Sea Cadet Corps, Colonel in Chief of the Army Cadet Force and Air-Commodore in Chief of the Air Training Corps, during the Second World War. The status of the Cadets was again confirmed after the war, in the House of Commons when the Rt. Honorable A. V. Alexander, the Minister of Defence, made an important statement on 2 July 1947. He reiterated the wholehearted support of the Government for the cadet organisations as initially voiced by Lord Munster in the House of Lords in 1943. He affirmed the fact that the cadets, 'had been finally lifted out of the realm of controversial politics, and were now accepted as a part of the Youth Service and defence system of the country'.[28]

The cadets serving between 1939 and 1945 were following a tradition started in 1860 when organised companies of youths first answered the call and volunteered to help repel a threatened invasion. At the turn of the century youth again responded to the call to arms, with some of them actually volunteering to go to South Africa and engaging in combat. The

First World War saw a phenomenal rise in numbers. How many cadets falsified their age between 1914 and 1918 and went into battle prematurely, and suffered the ultimate sacrifice cannot be known. The repercussions following the horrors of the Great War, with the universal distaste for anything military and the belief that war on that scale could not happen again was understandable. Yet come the hour, so too came the youth, once again in 1939. From 1941 onwards there was, at any one time, nearly half a million boys in military uniform undergoing preparatory training for war. Some of them, in the course of their duty, bravely distinguished themselves. The total number of those cadets, instructors and officers who lost their lives in the course of training and flying accidents or in service with the Home Guard, or Civil Defence will never be known. Others, of which there were hundreds of thousands, went on to utilise the training they had received as cadets and to acquire specialist skills in the Armed Forces before acquitting themselves well in theatres of war around the world. The study of the history of warfare has, strangely, ignored the contribution made by the Cadet Services. It is hoped that this account has redressed that omission and shown that British youth, via the cadets, and with the assistance of their volunteer leaders, has fulfilled a significant function and played an important role in times of war, as well as in the interim periods of peace.

Chapter 7 References

1. S.C.C. Committee, Minutes of the Meeting, 23 June 1941
2. *The Sea Cadet* journal, Vol. 4, No. 3, 1943
3. Ibid.
4. S.C.C. Regulations 1202, 'Gallantry Awards', January 1992, p. 12-1
5. *The Cadet Journal*, Vol. VII, No. 8, 1945
6. *Highcliffe & New Milton Advertiser*, 30 November 1940
7. *Air Training Corps Gazette*, Vol. II, No. 6, 1941
8. *Air Training Corps Gazette*, Vol. I, No. 1, 1941
9. *Air Cadet Review*, Vol. 22, No. 4, 1992
10. *The Sea Cadet* journal, Vol. V, No. 10, 1945
11. *Air Training Corps Gazette*, Vol. II, No. 5, 1942
12. *Air Training Corps News*, Special Supplement, February 1945
13. Wg. Cdr. H. W. Lamond R.A.F. (Retd), *History of the Air Training Corps – including the A.D.C.C. and the C.C.F. (R.A.F.)* [Unpublished: H.Q. A.T.C., R.A.F. Cranwell, 1984], p. 3-20
14. *London Gazette*, February 1941
15. *The Cadet Review* (extracts from Hansard), Vol. III, No. 3, 1948
16. Douglas Cooke, M.C. M.A. (Gen. ed.), *Youth Organisations of Great Britain, 1944–45* [London: Jordan & Sons, 1944], p. 191
17. *Air Cadet Facts*, No. 1, January 1983, AC/27351/PR(ED3)
18. A.C.F.A., *The Official Handbook of the A.C.F.* [London: A.C.F.A., 1949]
19. M.A.O. 8, Annexe A to Chapter 1, *History of the Sea Cadet Corps*, January 1992, p. 1A-1
20. The S.C.C. Sub-Committee Report, 16 July 1945
21. *The Cadet Review*, Vol. 1, No. 3, 1946
22. *Air Training Corps Gazette*, Special Supplement, Vol. V, No. 4, 1945
23. Ibid.
24. Ibid.
25. H.M.S.O., *The Purpose and Content of the Youth Service* [H.M.S.O.: The Youth Advisory Council, 1945]
26. S.C.C. Sub-Committee Minutes of the Navy League, 18 November 1946 and Appendix of Minutes of 3 March 1947
27. *The Cadet Journal*, Vol. IV, No. 6, 1942
26. Hansard, 2 July 1947

POST-WAR POSTSCRIPT

IT WAS DURING the Second World War that the Cadet Movement experienced its greatest expansion. It was also a time when the liaison between the separate organisations and their parent Service was at its closest; and, paradoxically, it was a time that witnessed an increased involvement with the local community.

The Sea Cadet Corps expanded by 75 per cent, the Army Cadets by 80 per cent and expansion of the Air Training Corps, by virtue of its formation, equalled 100 per cent. The need and enthusiasm for military service inevitably diminished when the war ended and membership of all military youth organisations declined, but the continuation of National Service ensured that boys could see the advantage of undergoing some pre-service training, at least until its cessation in 1962.

The closer co-operation and the realisation, on the part of the Royal Navy, of the benefits of the Sea Cadet Corps resulted in a 'Sea Cadet Charter' being drawn up in 1947 that formalised the logistical, administrative and training assistance given by the Admiralty to the Sea Cadet Corps via the Navy League. Training for the cadets, the adult petty officers and officers of the S.C.C. was henceforth provided at H.M.S. *Ganges*, and at other naval establishments, and also on board some of H.M.'s ships.

With the loss of officers and adult instructors due to the call-up for war service, it became increasingly clear that the need for training adult leaders was a priority. The War Office, like the Admiralty, and following the recommendations of the Amery Report in 1957 – whose task it was, under Julian Amery M.P., to re-assess the C.C.F. and A.C.F.'s needs – planned to provide a national training centre. In 1959, the Cadet Training Centre was set up at Frimley Park in Hampshire. Today regular army personnel staff the C.T.C. and the centre caters for adult A.C.F. leaders and runs leadership courses for senior cadets from the S.C.C., and A.T.C., as well as the C.C.F., and A.C.F. The R.A.F. also provides training specifically for the R.A.F.V.R. (T) officer and A.T.C., adult instructors at R.A.F. Cranwell. Courses are run at other locations that deal with subjects, such as those involving waterborne activities, shooting and flying. Thus all branches of the Cadet Movement receive specific training from their parent service.

The Royal Marines, who had cadet units at their training depots, were becoming increasingly aware that unlike other branches of the military they lacked a 'volunteer youth image'. It was not practical for the Royal Marines to start their own nation-wide Corps, but in 1955 the Commandant General of the Royal Marines asked permission to form a

Marine Cadet Section as part of the existing Sea Cadet Corps. Permission was granted in 1955 and within 10 years the very small number of units that had Marine Cadets increased to 90.

In 1942 girls, or rather women, not wishing to be excluded from contributing to the war effort formed equivalent uniformed organisations for girls. Thus the Girls' Naval Training Corps, the Girls' Training Corps and Women's Junior Air Corps, each with its distinct cadet-service orientation, were formed. They were not, however, part of the Cadet Movement but were affiliated to the youth service and what assistance they receive came from the Ministry of Education. In 1962, due mainly to dwindling numbers, it was suggested that the three girls' associations should amalgamate. The girls of the Naval Training Corps, according to the S.C.C. recoiled in horror. They, in line with the tradition of the boys' organisation, wanted complete separation from the influence of others and aligned themselves with the Navy League and the S.C.C. The lady Superintendent moved into the S.C.C. headquarters and a closer partnership between the Girls' Naval Training Corps and the S.C.C. was formed.

Those in charge of the Army Cadet Force stuck their heads in the sand, ostensibly for logistical reasons, and disassociated themselves from the girls' organisations. Thus the G.T.C. and Women's Junior Air Corps amalgamated to form the air-orientated Girls' Venture Corps.

On 31 March 1980, the Ministry of Defence (Navy) approved the admission of girls into the Sea Cadet Corps. The S.C.C. was already the main provider for the Girls' Naval Training Corps and so a take-over was both simple and inevitable: from that time on the various Girls' Training Corps ceased to exist. The following year the Air Training Corps allowed 22 selected squadrons to recruit girls. The scheme was an immediate success and it has now been extended. The Army Cadet Force eventually acceded to the inevitable and permitted girls to join the A.C.F. in 1983 and today approximately one third of all Cadet Movement membership is female.

Sport has always been seen as a natural adjunct of fitness training in the Cadet Movement and during the war inter-service competition, at least at the local level, was used as a means of encouraging friendly rivalry and co-operation between the cadet services.

After the war, despite financial difficulties, the cadet organisation began to organise sport on a regional and then on a national basis. In 1946 *The Star* newspaper proposed to organise a Youth Organisation Championship incorporating the pre-service organisations and the National Association of Boys' Clubs. The events were to be boxing and soccer, with the first finals being held at Wembley. Eventually boxing was dropped from the sporting curriculum of the Cadet Movement; this was in line with the cessation of boxing in schools. The football competition continued for a further two years before it too came to an end.

Today inter-service sporting rivalry is limited to shooting and swimming. With the reduction in numbers of today's Armed Forces and their accommodation the opportunity to temporarily house large cadet teams became increasingly difficult; besides the feeding and transportation of such teams can be an overly expensive undertaking. Both these factors must be taken into consideration when viewing the decline of inter-service sport on a national basis. Indeed, as an example, the A.C.F. have found it necessary to separate Scotland from England and Wales regarding national sporting championships because of the difficulties mentioned.

Sport has long been an integral part of the independent sector of education and is a separate school activity and not part of the Combined Cadet Force programme. Needless to say, because of the differences between the 'open' and 'closed' cadet units the sports competitions are held separately. In rifle shooting, however, there is both separate and combined competitions, as indeed there is in the inter-contingent military skills contests.

Adventurous training can include: climbing, abseiling, parachuting, paragliding, canoeing, sailing, rowing, caving, camping and hill walking. In the C.C.F. these pursuits may well be done as part of the schools' P.E. programme. With regards to the S.C.C., A.C.F. and A.T.C. these challenging pursuits are regarded as an essential part of cadet training and a considerable amount of time is spent at weekends or at annual camps doing adventurous training activities. This is proportional to the amount of importance the Armed Services now put on such challenging pursuits as a means of instilling confidence, and promoting self-reliance.

Going on expeditions in wild and mountainous country, whether at home or abroad – and increasingly it is in another country – is often undertaken as part of the Duke of Edinburgh's Award scheme. The latter, first introduced into the Cadet Movement in the later 1950s – is a universally recognised and accepted method of providing youth with worthwhile leisure activities that promotes individual development and encourages participation in voluntary service: something the Cadet Movement has been doing for over a century. Today, through the scheme, standards and procedures for all organisations dealing with youth have been universally accepted and standardised.

Throughout the history of the Cadet Movement, and particularly during the Second World War, the cadets have been involved in the community. Today this is no less true. Cadets in the 'open' units of the S.C.C., A.C.F.

and A.T.C. are positively encouraged to participate in the local civic events. Indeed, one of the aims of the Cadet Movement, as initially proposed by the nineteenth-century reformer and army cadet organiser Octavia Hill, is the promotion of a sense of community and the acquisition of social skills: in short, citizenship. Cadets are often engaged in raising funds for the Royal British Legion Poppy Appeal, the local hospice appeals or other good causes, but equally they could be assisting with an environmental project.

Involvement in civilian projects is one thing but some members of the Cadet Movement are concerned that there is an increasing and incipient trend towards justifying the cadet forces in terms of 'outside' criteria. This is reflected in the inclusion of civilian qualifications, such as National Vocational Qualifications, in parts of the organisations. The proponents of this trend argue that the gaining of additional qualifications is to the advantage of the individual, and no doubt this is true in some cases, but the majority of cadets and adults join the Cadets to participate in military-type activities. And they view these as an end in themselves. There is a connection between what the cadets do at school and what is done at the unit: the latter should complement the former, but essentially the training done with cadets is seen as being different from that undertaken at school, college or at work.

There is a second and important category of civilian qualifications that have a direct bearing on what training is carried out within the cadet units; and these include first aid certificates, sport and adventurous training qualifications. As cadet training includes more adventure training pursuits, these qualifications are deemed essential for both adult and cadet.

Any foreign travel done by the organisations is not confined to expeditions in mountainous regions, although the annual combined-service cadet exchange with the Canada Cadet Corps is primarily concerned with training in the Rocky Mountains. Each cadet organisation, under the auspices of their parent service, send cadets abroad to military stations in Germany and Cyprus. There are also combined-service cadet exchanges with India, Pakistan, Australia and other Commonwealth countries. Naturally the cadets selected to go on such overseas training trips are among the best and a process of selection is employed, and with the aid of sponsorship the opportunity to travel is increasing.

It is impossible to be precise about numbers in the various cadet organisations, as cadets are joining and leaving all the time but it is estimated that there are about 2,500 C.C.F. cadets in 242 schools. The Sea Cadet Corps has 15,550 cadets in 400 units; the Army Cadet Force has recently increased to 44,000 in 1,600 detachments, and the Air Training Corps numbers are in the region of 41,000 in 1,500 squadrons. Therefore, in total the figure equates to approximately 103,000 cadets. There are about 21,000 officers, instructors and administrators serving in the 'open' units of the S.C.C., A.C.F. and A.T.C., with approximately 650 school teachers operating with the C.C.F. In addition the S.C.C., A.C.F. and A.T.C. organisations have voluntary civilian committee members who, to varying degrees, assist with welfare, sport and essential fund-raising.

Each of the cadet organisations is a separate entity for the purpose of funding. Suffice to say they receive a degree of financial and resource assistance from the M.O.D. This, however, is insufficient to cover all costs. Therefore, a considerable amount of self-financing has to be done, and in the case of the S.C.C., which is supported but not sponsored directly by its parent service, this amounts to about 50 per cent of expenditure.

Although the Cadet Movement is ostensibly a voluntary organisation, there is some remuneratory reward for officers and instructors. It is understood that the majority of serving adults, in order to fulfil the commitment asked of them, have to take time away from their employment. The M.O.D., in recognition of this, allowed a number of pay-days per year; this was to cover the period spent at annual camp or on a training course and a few weekends. This arrangement is under review and the remunerative pay allowance looks set to be cut.

The cadet 'youth service' cannot perforce be near the top of the M.O.D.'s list of priorities and in an age of financial constraint it is inevitable that savings have to be made. At a time when less and less adults are prepared to engage in part-time voluntary service, and many teenagers are discernibly less physically active; when youth crime is on the increase; when the Army in particular is under strength, it would seem, by many, that cutting back on the financial support required by volunteers is counter-productive. Besides which, about 30 per cent of the Armed Forces come from the ranks of the Cadet Movement. The volunteer adult officers and senior N.C.O.s are the backbone of the Cadet Movement and without them the Cadet Movement would cease to function and both society and the Armed Services would be disadvantaged.

History has shown that the Cadet Movement has played a dual role in both peace and war. Today, thankfully, its function is confined to the former. The aims of the different cadet service organisations may be worded differently but essentially they are identical.

All have the shared aim of promoting and encouraging an interest in their particular branch of the Armed Services. By virtue of the type of instruction given, each cadet organisation provides both training and an experience that will be practically valuable to any youngster considering a career in the Regular or Reserve Forces. This 'pre-service training', as it was called during the Second World War, is valuable to both the individual and the military. It helps the cadet to decide whether or not to pursue a career in the Armed Forces and, at the same time, provides the youngster with an added advantage should he or she choose to do so.

The Sea Cadets Corps talk of 'helping young people towards responsible adulthood'; and the Combined Cadet Force, the Army Cadet Force and the Air Training Corps state that one of their aims is the 'development of good citizenship'. The Cadet Movement is not unique in this endeavour as other youth organisations share this aim. However, time spent on developing a cadet's sense of civic duty is evidence that the Cadet Movement is not just concerned with military training and is not, as some outsiders believe, merely a recruiting ground for the Regular Forces.

Today with the absence of conscription fewer people have any interest in, or experience of, the Armed Forces. From an educative point of view the Cadet Movement has a useful purpose, as time with the cadets provides a basic knowledge of at least one branch of the Services. It is also a fact that to many of the public the cadets are the only physical sign or evidence of the Armed Forces they will encounter.

Where the cadet organisations differ from other youth organisations is in their unequivocal encouragement and development of a young person's powers of practical leadership, within a progressive and challenging physical environment. A noble aim founded on the needs of wartime Britain as the history of the Cadet Movement clearly shows. The pursuance of these aims with the support of the Royal Navy, the Army and the Royal Air Force and the time and expertise of so many dedicated volunteer adult officers and instructors, should ensure that the Cadet Movement continues to fulfil a useful purpose in the service of youth in Britain.

BIBLIOGRAPHY

PERIODICALS

Air Defence Corps Gazette
Air Pictorial
Air Training Corps Gazette
Army Cadet
Aviation News
The Army Cadet Journal & Gazette
The Britannic Magazine
The Boys' Own Magazine
The Cadet Revue

London Gazette
The Navy
The Navy League
Popular Flying
Radio Times
The Salopian
The Sea Cadet
Times Educational Supplement
The Yeovillian

NEWSPAPERS

The Times
Sunday Times
The New York Times
Harrogate Advertiser
Shropshire Chronicle
Western Gazette

Hayes Gazette
The Chard and Ilminster News
Highcliffe & New Milton Advertiser
Hertfordshire Pictorial
Sunday Pictorial

REPORTS, DIARIES AND REGULATIONS

H.M.S.O., 'Interdependence Committee on Physical Deterioration', 1904

H.M.S.O., 'Regulations Governing the Formation, Organisation and Administration of Cadet Units by County Association', Army Order No. 197, 1910

H.M.S.O., 'Syllabus of Physical Training for Schools' (Board of Education), 1919

H.M.S.O., 'Syllabus of Physical Training for Schools' (Board of Education), 1933

H.M.S.O., 'Air Raid Precautions Handbook No. 8' (Home Office), 1938

H.M.S.O., 'National Service', 1939

H.M.S.O., 'The Purpose and Content of the Youth Service' (Youth Advisory Council), 1945

P.P. No. 329, 'Progress of Merchant Shipping', 1902

Atherton, J. G., 'Home and Away' and 'Home to Stay', evacuee's diary, 1939–1940, Imperial War Museum

Horsfall [ed.], 'Proceedings of the Conference of Education on Health' [Manchester: Heywood, 1885]

1st Cadet Bn., 'The Queen's, Royal West Surrey Regiment Enrolment Book', May 1889 to June 1891

A.C.F.A., 'Instructions for candidates and Conduct of Certificate 'A' examinations', A.C.F.A. – 9/Cadets/580 (M.T.Ac), 1945

Nagle, Hon. Col. F. E., 'A Record of the A.C.F. in Counties Armagh and Down', 1943–1974 [Cadet Training Centre, Frimley Park], 1980

M.A.O. 8 (S.C.C.), 'History of the Cadet Movement'
M.A.O. 10 (S.C.C.), 'Rank and Status of Officers'
Navy League and S.C.C. Sub-Committee Minutes. S.C.C. H.Q. files, Lambeth, London
Capper R.N., Lieut. H. D. (Compiler), Royal Navy 'Warrant Officers' Manual', 1910
Air Ministry Bulletin No. 2850, No. 13 (BBC, Mr Wolfenden's address) 23/1/1941
Air Ministry Order No. A484, 1940
Air Ministry, 'Air Training Corps Rules & Regulations', 1941
H.Q. Air Cadets, 'Air Cadets Facts', No. 1, January 1983
Lamond R.A.F. (Retd), Wg. Cdr. H. W. 'The History of the Air training Corps 1938–1983' [H.Q. A.T.C. & C.C.F. (R.A.F.), R.A.F. Cranwell], 1984
Souvenir pamphlet, 'Golden Jubilee of Air Cadets in the East Essex Wing, 1914–1991' [East Essex Wing A.T.C.: Maldon], 1991
W.O. 'The training of the younger cadets' 26/GS publications/687, 1942
W.O. 'Pre-Service Physical Training and Recreation for Army Cadets', 1943
W.O. 'Message writing for cadets', part V, 1945
W.O. 'Physical Efficiency Preparation for Pre-Service Cadets, 1945

BOOKS

A.C.F.A., *A Camp Handbook for Officers, NCOs and Cadets* [London: A.C.F.A., 1947]
A.C.F.A., *The Official Handbook of the A.C.F.A.* [London: A.C.F.A., 1949]
A.C.F.A., *The Army Cadet Force Handbook* [London: A.C.F.A., 1955]
A.C.F.A., *The Army Cadet Force Handbook* [London: A.C.F.A., 1962]
A.C.F.A., *The Cadet Story 1860–1980* [London: A.C.F.A., 1982]
Beckett, Ian & Simpson, Keith [eds.] *A Nation in Arms* [London: Donovan, 1990]
Beresford Ellis, Peter, William Piers, *By Jove Biggles! The Life of W. E. Johns* [London: W. H. Allen, 1981]
Blackie, Agnes C., *Blackie & Son: a short History of the Firm* [London & Glasgow: Blackies, 1959]
Bond, Brian, *War and Society in Europe, 1870–1970* [London: Fontana, 1984]
Chandler, David & Beckett, Ian [eds.] *The Oxford History of the British Army* [Oxford: OUP, 1996]
Cockerill, A. W., *Sons of the Brave* [London: Leo Cooper, 1984]
Collins, L. J., *Theatre at War, 1914–18* [Basingstoke: Macmillan, 1998]
Cooke M.C. M.A., Douglas [ed.], *Youth Organisations of Great Britain, 1944–45* [London: Jordan, 1945]
Croall, Jonathan, *Don't You Know There's a War On?* [London: Hutchinson, 1988]
Cunningham, Hugh, *The Volunteer Force* [London: Croom Helm, 1975]
Currie, Lt-Col. Bill, *The King's Cadets* [King Edward's: Bath, 1994]
Darley, Gillian, *Octavia Hill – A Life* [London: Constable, 1990]

Doyle, Brian [ed.], *The Who's Who of Children's Literature* [London: Evelyn, 1969]

Foley C.B.E. D.S.O., Col. F. W. *A Short History of the Frimley and Camberley Cadet Corps 1908-1948* [Aldershot: Gale & Polden, 1948]

Forrest T.D., Brian, *Drill & Weapon Training - a guide to War Cert. 'A'* [Aldershot: Gale & Polden, 1945]

Golding, Harry [ed.], *Wonder Book of Soldiers* [London, 1919]

Graham, R. T., *Ilminster Grammar School 1549-1949* [Ilminster School, 1991]

Hamilton, Ian, *National Life and National Training* [London: King & Sons, 1913]

Harris, Lt.-Col., *Rugby School Corps 1860-1960* [London: Brown, Knight & Truscott, 1960]

Hill, Octavia, *Our Common Land and other short essays* [London: Sydenham, 1877]

Hill, Octavia, *Letters to My Fellow Workers* [London: Martin, 1910]

Hughes T.D. M.A., Lt.-Col., *The Army Cadets of Surrey, 1860-1960* [London: Owen Spyer, 1960]

Hawkey R.N.R. (C.C.F.), Cdr. R. B., *History of the Corps at Merchant Taylors' 1900-1981* [Rickmansworth: George & Roberts, 1981]

Johns, W. E., *The Rescue Flight* [Oxford: OUP, 1938]

Johns, W. E., *Biggles Goes to War* [Oxford: OUP, 1938]

Johns, W. E., *Biggles Defies the Swastika* [Oxford: OUP, 1941]

Johns, W. E., *Worrals Flies Again* [London: Hodder & Stoughton, 1942]

Johns, W. E., *Spitfire Parade* [Oxford: OUP, 1942]

Johns, W. E., *Gimlet Goes Again* [Oxford: OUP, 1944]

Jordan DFC AFC, Group Capt., *To Burma and Beyond* [London: James, 1995]

Kemp, Peter K., *The British Sailor - a social history of the Lower Deck* [London: Dent, 1970]

Kipling, Rudyard, *The Five Nations* [London: Methuen, 1949]

Lewis, Michael, *The Navy in Transition* [London: Hodder & Stoughton, 1965]

MacKenzie, John M., *Propaganda and Empire - the manipulation of British public opinion, 1880-1960* [Manchester: MUP, 1986]

MacKenzie, J. M., *Imperialism and Culture* [Manchester: MUP, 1986]

MacKenzie, S. P., *The Home Guard* [Oxford: OUP, 1995]

Mangan, J. A., *Athleticism in the Victorian and Edwardian Public Schools* [Cambridge: CUP, 1982]

Marwick, Arthur, *The Deluge - British Society and the First World War* [Basingstoke: Macmillan, 1986]

Marwick, Arthur, *The Home Front - the British and the Second World War* [London: Thames & Hudson, 1976]

McIntosh, Peter C., *Physical Education in England since 1800* [London: Bell, 1968]

Morris, Alan, *First of the Many - the story of the independent force, R.A.F.* [London: Jarrods, 1968]

Morrish, Ivor, *Education Since 1800* [London: Allen & Unwin, 1970]
Moss, Mrs H. W., *Moss of Shrewsbury* [London: Sheldon, 1932]
Moseley, Leonard, *Backs to the Wall* [London: Weidenfield & Nicholson, 1971]
Oldham M.A., J. Basil, *A History of Shrewsbury School, 1852–1952* [London: Blackwell, 1952]
Percival, Alicia, *Youth Will Be Led – the story of the youth organisations* [London: Collins, 1957]
Philpott, Brian, *Challenge in the Air* [Hemel Hempstead: Models & Allied, 1971]
Pimlott, J. A. R., *Toynbee Hall: fifty years of social progress, 1889–1934* [London: Dent, 1935]
Riley M.A., Lt.-Col. J. P., *Sherborne in Uniform* [Sherborne: Shelly, 1988]
Sainsbury T.D., Lt.-Col. J. D., *The Hertfordshire Yeomanry – an illustrated history, 1794–1920* [Welwyn: Hart Books, 1994]
Simon B. & Bradley I. [eds.], *The Victorian Public Schools* [London: Gill & Macmillan, 1975]
Smith, W. David, *Stretching Their Bodies – the history of physical education* [Newton Abbot: David & Charles, 1974]
Springall, Fraser & Hoare, *Sure and Steadfast – a history of the Boys' Brigade 1883–1983* [London & Glasgow: Collins, 1993]
Springall, J., *Youth, Empire and Society* [London: Croom Helm, 1977]
Stevenson, John, *British Society, 1914–45* [Harmondsworth: Penguin, 1984]
Taylor, A. J. P., *English History, 1914–45* [London: OUP, 1965]
Thomas, Imogen, *Haileybury* [Hertford: Haileybury Society, 1987]
Walker A. & Passmore M., *The Cadet Force at Bruton, 1910–1985* [Frome: Donald Press, 1985]
Wells C.B.E. D.S.C. R.N., Capt. J., *The Royal Navy – An Illustrated History, 1870–1982* [Stroud: Sutton, 1994]
Westlake, R. A., *A Register of Territorial Force Cadet Units, 1910–1922* [Wembley: Westlake, 1984]

A

Act of Enlistment: 1.
Admiralty: 2, 11–12, 22, 34, 40, 45–46, 53, 56, 80, 82–84, 101, 108, 110–111, 113, 117, 167–169, 175, 181.
Air Council: 90, 136, 142.
Air Defence Cadet Corps: 1, 57–58, 73, 75–76, 89–91, 157, 169.
A.D.C.C.: 59–60, 90–92, 132–133, 135, 138, 175.
Air League: 57–60, 73.
Air Ministry: 39, 58, 60, 73, 75, 87, 90–91, 133–134, 136, 139.
Air Raid Precautions: 116, 156.
A.R.P.: 127, 155–156, 159.
Air Raid Wardens: 2.
Air Scouts: 92, 134.
Air Training Corps: 3–4, 39, 73, 75, 87, 91, 92, 115, 118, 132–133, 161, 174–176, 181–182, 184–185.
A.T.C. Signals School: 142.
A.T.C.: 76, 79, 87, 90–95, 110, 118, 125, 127, 132–138, 140–143, 145–147, 153–155, 159, 161, 167, 169, 170–173, 175, 181, 183, 184.
Air/Sea Rescue: 142.
Aircraft:
  Avro Anson: 58, 138–139.
  B-17 Fortress: 132.
  B-24 Liberators: 132.
  Blenheim: 58.
  Bulldog: 58.
  Dagling: 139.
  Dakota: 138.
  F.W.190s: 147.
  Fairey Battle: 138.
  Halifax: 138.
  Hind: 58.
  Kronfield ground-trainer: 139.
  Lancaster: 158, 170.
  Lowe-Wilde glider: 139.
  Marauders: 139.
  Messerschmitt 110: 170.
  Oxford: 138.
  Slingsby Kirby Cadet Glider: 139.
  Sopwith Camel: 74.
  Spitfire: 72, 157.
  Stirling Mk. V: 138.
  Typhoon: 158.
  Vimy: 72.
  Wellington: 138.

193

Flight Lieutenant John Alcock: 72.
Richard Aldington, Author: 48.
Right Honorable A. V. Alexander: 85, 157, 176.
Field-Marshal Lord Allenby: 52–53.
Amateur Swimming Association: 137.
Amery Report: 181.
Julian Amery, M.P.: 181.
Sir Alan Anderson: 55.
Archbishop of Canterbury: 70.
Archbishop of Westminster: 70.
Army Cadet Association: 53.
Army Cadet Corps: 23, 85.
Army Cadet Force: 3–4, 7, 24, 51, 87, 89, 92, 127, 161, 169, 171–172, 175–176, 182, 184–185.
A.C.F.: 79, 86–89, 91, 93–94, 110, 119–121, 124–132, 140, 143, 145–147, 153–154, 157–158, 161–163, 167, 173–175, 181–184.
A.C.F.A: 54.
Army Cadet Force Association: 3, 173.
Army Cadets: 58, 94, 120, 123, 125, 147, 157, 181.
Army Council: 174.
Ashburton Shield: 15, 21.
Association of Scottish Cadets: 53.
J. G. Atherton, ex-A.T.C. Cadet: 155.
Rear-Admiral Attwood: 110.
Auxiliary Air Force: 2, 60.
Awards and Decorations:
    A.T.C. Gallantry Medal: 169.
    V.C.: 40.
    M.C: 40.
    D.S.C.: 40.
    British Empire Medal: 170.
    B.E.M.: 171.
    Cadet Forces Medal: 167, 168.
    Cadet Mechanic's Badge: 111.
    Certificate of Commendation: 169.
    Defence Medal: 163, 167.
    Duke of Edinburgh's Award: 175, 183.
    Gallantry Certificate: 169.
    Gallantry Cross: 169.
    Gallantry Medal: 169.
    General National Trophy: 121.
    George Medal: 171.
    Green Efficiency Star: 120.
    Long Service Badge: 167.
    Navy League Cross: 168–169.

parchment certificate: 169.
Rifle Brigade Trophy: 121.
Territorial Decoration: 167.
T.D.: 167.
Territorial Efficiency Medal: 20.

B

General Sir Robert Baden-Powell: 8, 24–25, 33, 40, 70, 78.
Balfour Act of 1902: 14.
Captain H. H. Balfour, M.P.: 132, 141.
Marquess of Bath: 87, 131.
Battle of Britain: 75, 87, 90, 93, 133, 172.
Admiral Lord Charles Beresford: 22.
Bevin Boys' Scheme: 95.
Ernest Bevin, Minister of Labour and National Service: 79, 86.
James Bigglesworth: 74.
Biggles: 73–76.
'Blue Book': 136.
Edmund Blunden, Author: 48.
Board of Education: 78, 140, 176.
Boer War: 3, 14–19, 35, 41, 64, 66, 68, 74, 77.
Boers: 12–13, 15.
Air Cadet P. Bond: 170.
Bounty Scheme: 94, 109–111, 118.
Boy Scouts Movement: 8.
    Boy Scouts Commissioner: 9, 40.
    Boy Scouts Association: 45, 70, 134.
    Boy Scouts: 24–25, 32, 49.
    Scouts: 40, 135.
Boys' Brigade: 23–25, 31, 40, 45, 47, 49, 68, 72, 88.
Boys' Empire League: 68.
Boys' Life Brigade: 1, 23.
Boys' Naval Brigade: 1, 7, 11–13, 23–24, 33, 40, 45–46.
Whitby Boys' Naval Brigade: 11.
Boys' Training-Brigs: 9.
Reginald Brabazon, the Earl of Meath, Diplomat: 70.
Edward J. Brett, Publisher: 64.
General Lord Bridgeman: 89, 119–120, 131, 146, 154, 158, 161.
British Boys' Training Corps: 33.
British Expeditionary Force: 34,–35.
B.N.C.A.: 53, 86, 89, 119–121, 154, 161.
British National Cadet Association: 52, 119–120, 161, 167, 173.
British Sailors' Society: 45, 84.
Sir George Broadbridge: 55.

195

William Ingham Brooke, Youth Leader: 10.
Air Chief Marshal Sir Robert Brooke-Popham: 146.
'Buff Book': 136.
Rt. Hon. R. A. Butler, President of the Board of Education: 176.

C

Cadet Battalions:
   1st (London) Cadet Battalion of the Queen's Regiment: 10.
   1st and 2nd Bn. King's Shropshire Light Infantry Cadets: 126.
   1st Cadet Battalion of the Royal West Surrey Regiment: 10.
   1st Cadet Battalion the King's Royal Rifle Corps: 14, 21, 66.
   1st Cadet Battalion, The Manchester Regiment: 9.
   1st Cadet Bn. Royal Irish Fusiliers: 131.
   1st Cadet Bn. The Royal Fusiliers (City of London Regt.): 126.
   1st Cadet Bn. The Royal Inniskilling Fusiliers: 157.
   1st Essex Cadet Battalion: 36.
   2nd Cadet Battalion, East Surrey Regiment: 46.
   2nd Cadet Bn: 89.
   2nd Canterbury Cadet C.L.B. Battalion: 45.
   3rd Cadet Bn. Royal Ulster Rifles: 130.
   3rd Cadet Bn. The Royal Ulster Rifles: 88.
   Cheshire Cadet Battalion: 31.
   City of Sheffield Battalion: 87.
   Huddersfield Volunteer Battalion: 8.
   King's Royal Rifle Corps Cadet Battalion: 37.
   The 1st Cadet Bn. The Royal Irish Fusiliers: 89.
Cadet Corps: 1, 154.
   1st Somerset Naval Cadet Corps: 33, 45.
   2nd Cadets, King's Royal Rifle Corps: 86.
   3rd Cardiff Non-school Cadet Corps: 88.
   Ardeer Factory: 88.
   Armagh Royal School: 131.
   Ayr Academy Cadet Corps: 86, 160.
   Ayrshire Docks: 37.
   Ballynahinch: 88.
   Brightlingsea: 141.
   British League of Cadet Corps: 8.
   Burntisland Shipbuilding Company: 88.
   Cadet Corps: 1, 8.
   Campbell College: 131.
   Carmarthenshire A.C.F.: 169.
   Chard: 124, 134, 140.

Chard A.C.F.: 129.
Cheltenham College Cadet Corp: 163.
Clacton: 141.
Company of Juvenile Volunteers: 8.
Corps for Junior Clerks: 15.
County of London Cadets: 130.
Doncaster Cadet Corps: 86.
East London: 9–10.
Frimley and Camberley Cadet Corps: 36–37, 130.
Greenwich Naval Cadet Unit: 45.
Haileybury House: 96.
Hertford Cadet Company 2nd (Watford Scouts): 33.
Holywood: 88.
Killyleagh: 88.
King's School: 125.
King's Shropshire Light Infantry A.C.F.: 131.
Latymer Upper School Cadet Corps: 126.
London Irish Rifles: 125.
London Rifle Corps: 65.
Middlesex A.C.F.: 159–160.
Middlesex Regiment: 125.
Newport Sea Cadet Corps: 45.
Newtonards: 88.
Oundle School J.T.C.: 131.
Pre-Service Cadet Corps: 172.
Princess Louise's Kensington Regt. Cadet Corps: 160.
R.M. Depot Cadet Corps: 46.
R.M. Light Infantry Cadets: 46.
Regent House School: 88.
Richmond Boys' Naval Cadets: 46.
Sedbergh School J.T.C.: 122.
Shaftesbury Grammar School Cadet Corps: 153.
Shrewsbury School J.T.C. Band: 156.
Shropshire A.C.F.: 129.
Sleaford Grammar School Cadet Corps: 51.
St Albans School J.T.C.: 120.
Warwickshire A.C.F.: 125.
Westminster Scottish Cadets: 125.
Weybridge Scout Cadets: 33.
Cadet Movement: 1–4, 9–12, 26, 31, 32, 78, 80, 85, 95–96, 119, 129, 153, 167, 171, 173–176, 181–183, 185–186.
Cadet Squadrons: 90–91.
1078 Squadron: 140.

109 (Port Glasgow, Greenock and Kilmalcolm) Squadron: 138.
1096 (Bishop Stortford) Squadron: 139.
1180 (Buxton) Squadron: 170.
1474 (Wickford) Squadron: 141.
1476 (Rayleigh) Squadron: 139.
1904 Squadron: 141.
258 Squadron (Coulsdon and Purley): 156.
308 Squadron: 141.
414 (Epping) Squadron: 137.
Air Squadrons of the J.T.C.: 91.
City of Salford Air Training Corps Wing: 158.
Lambeth: 59.
No. 88 (St. Pancras) A.D.C.C. Squadron: 169.
No. 1 (City of Leicester) Squadron: 59.
No. 1119 Squadron: 92.
No. 1440 (Shoreham) Squadron: 139.
No. 171 (Christchurch) Squadron: 169.
No. 2 (Watford) Squadron: 59.
No. 20 (Ilford) A.D.C.C. Squadron: 169.
No. 200 (Torquay) Squadron: 171.
No. 244 (Scafell) Squadron: 171.
No. 315 (Didsbury) Squadron: 139.
No. 4 (Ilford) A.D.C.C. Squadron: 169.
No. 4 Squadron: 59.
No. 49F (Greenock) Squadron: 170.
Northeast Surrey Air Training Corps Wing: 158.
Nottingham Squadron: 59.
University Air Squadrons: 91–92, 133, 136.
Watford: 59.
Cadet Training Centre: 181.
C.T.C.: 181.
Cadet War Emergency Committee: 119.
Sir Julian Cahn: 51.
Canada Cadet Corps: 184.
Colonel Sir Philip Carlebach: 53, 119.
Catholic Cadet Units: 47.
C.C.T.A.: 52.
Central Council of the Territorial Associations: 50–51.
Certificate 'A': 19, 38, 50, 55, 84, 87, 89, 120–123, 126, 128, 130, 143, 160, 173.
Cert. 'A': 19, 128.
Certificate 'B': 19.
Certificate 'T': 125.

Neville Chamberlain, Prime Minister: 81.
Air Commodore J. A. Chamier, Secretary-General of the Air League: 58–59, 73, 133.
Church Lads' Brigade: 9, 22–23, 32–33, 37, 40, 45, 47–48, 52, 54, 66, 68, 72.
   Folkestone Church Lads' Brigade: 45.
   Maindee Church Lads' Brigade: 45.
   Newport Church Lads' Naval Brigade: 45.
London Diocesan Church Lads' Brigade: 33.
Winston Churchill, M.P., First Sea Lord: 70, 81.
Circular 1516: 78.
Circular 1577: 79.
Civil Defence: 2, 171, 177.
Civil Service Commission: 113.
Air Cadet Roy Clark: 169.
Harry Collingwood: 63. See Lancaster, W.J.C.
Combined Cadet Force: 1, 7, 167, 175, 182, 185.
C.C.F.: 181, 183–184.
Combined Services Cadet Camps: 147.
Committee of Physical Deterioration: 16.
Earl of Cork and Orrery: 55.
Counties:
   Antrim: 89.
   Bedfordshire: 105.
   Dorset: 116, 154, 162.
   Essex: 85, 92, 105, 155.
   Fermanagh: 89.
   Fife: 88.
   Glamorgan: 88.
   Gloucestershire: 102.
   Hampshire: 124.
   Hertfordshire: 54, 88, 105, 158, 161–162.
   Kent: 14.
   Leicestershire: 122, 131.
   Middlesex: 146.
   Monmouth: 88.
   Northamptonshire: 131.
   Northumberland: 40.
   Oxfordshire: 68.
   Rutland: 131.
   Shropshire: 36, 88, 154.
   Somerset: 13, 85, 88, 92, 94, 124, 129, 134, 140, 157–158.
   Surrey: 8, 21, 37, 67, 88, 156.

Tyrone: 89.
Worcestershire: 84, 104.
Yorkshire: 8, 90–91, 138–139, 159.
County Associations: 1, 20, 25, 31.
County Territorial Associations: 19, 49.
Crimean War: 1, 7, 9, 66.
Lord Croft: 131.
Earl of Cromer: 70.
Lord Curzon: 70.

D

D-Day: 94.
Air Cadet Corporal N. Davies: 169.
Al Deere, Air Ace: 93.
Air Cadet Eliezer Derrick: 169.
Rear-Admiral R. H. Dickson: 156.
Sir Arthur Conan Doyle, Author: 68.

E

Admiral Eardley-Wilmot: 67.
Mr Anthony Eden, Secretary of State for War: 160.
Education Act of 1870: 64.
Air Lance Corporal F. Edwards: 169.
General Dwight D. Eisenhower: 171.
Ellis and Williams, Biographers: 74.
Empire Day Movement: 70.
   Empire Day: 70–71, 73.
Squadron Leader Enoch: 141.
Viscount Esher: 70.

F

Miss Gracie Fields, Entertainer: 101.
First World War: 3, 19, 34, 37, 45–46, 51, 57, 63, 66, 69, 73–74, 77, 79, 87, 89, 119, 127, 154, 163, 173–174, 177.
Great War: 45, 71, 177.
Admiral Lord Fisher: 12, 16, 22.
Fleet Air Arm: 57, 73, 115, 118, 137, 142–143.
Rear-Admiral Fleet: 13.
Colonel Ford: 33.
Cecil Scott Forester, Author: 76–77.
Air Cadet D. J. Fox: 170.

Admiral Sir Sydney Fremantle: 83.
Furness Withy, Sponsors: 56.

G

Garibaldi, Politician: 65.
Sir Eric Geddes, M.P.: 48.
Colonel Gibbon, A.C.F.: 88.
Captain Charles Gibson, Author: 74.
Air Cadet Corporal B. E. Gill: 171.
Girl Guides: 24.
Girl Scouts: 24.
Girls' Life Brigade: 24.
Girls' Naval Training Corps: 79, 181–182.
Girls' Training Corps: 1, 79, 146, 181–182.
Girls' Venture Corps: 182.
Robert Graves, Poet: 48.
Captain George Groves, A.C.F.: 127.

H

Hackney Wick Mission: 10.
Rt. Hon. Viscount Richard Haldane: 18, 25, 36, 94.
Air Cadet E. L. Hall: 170.
Henry Hall, Band Leader: 157.
Admiral Sir Lionel Halsey: 82.
Sir Ian Hamilton: 33.
Jonas Hanway, Philanthropist: 2.
The Right Honourable The Earl of Harewood: 91.
Vice-Admiral J. E. T. Harper: 146.
George Alfred Henty, Author: 65.
Octavia Hill, Reformer: 10, 24, 31, 49, 183.
Hitler Jungend: 119.
Hitler Youth: 119.
Hitler: 55, 74, 86.
Home Guard: 2, 79, 86, 89, 120–121, 127–129, 140, 154–156, 158–163, 167, 170, 173, 177.
   3rd (Yeovil) Company Somerset Home Guard: 86.
   3rd London Battalion Home Guard: 160.
   46th W.R. [Doncaster] Bn. Home Guard: 86.
   Gloucester Home Guard Battalion: 163.
   Shrewsbury School Home Guard Company: 162.
Horatio Hornblower R.N: 76–77.
Sea Cadet Petty Officer A. R. Howes: 168.
Colonel J. Huck: 119.

201

I

Imperial Cadet Yeomanry: 39.
Imperial Defence League: 14.
Imperial Federation League: 68.
Infantry Supplementary Reserve: 156.
Lieutenant Commander F. W. Inns: 145.
Sir Thomas Inskip: 55.
Inter-Services Cadet Committee: 87, 94.
Commander J. Irving: 56.

J

Admiral Lord Jellicoe: 52.
Lieutenant-General Sir Hugh Jeudwine: 53.
Jewish Lads' Brigade: 47–48, 52.
Captain W. E. Johns, Author: 72–76, 94, 137, 141.
Amy Johnson, Aviator: 73.
Johnnie Johnson, Air Ace: 93.
Group Captain Jordan: 135, 142.
Junior Training Corps: 4, 55, 84–85, 120, 129, 162, 167, 172, 175.
J.T.C.: 89, 92, 121, 125–126, 129–131, 143, 145, 148, 153, 162–163, 167, 173, 175.

K

Sea Cadet Signalman R Kahler: 168.
Captain Lorrington King: 76.
'Gimlet': 76.
William Kingston, Author: 64.
Rudyard Kipling, Author: 17.
Field-Marshal Lord Kitchener: 35.

L

Ginger Lacey, Air Ace: 93.
Lads' Brigade: 7, 23.
Lads' Drill Association: 68, 70.
Lady West Memorial Shield: 51.
Wing Commander Lamond: 137.
W. J. C. Lancaster: Alias Collingwood, Harry. See 63.
Dr J. Lang, Archbishop of Canterbury: 52.
Army Cadet Corporal David Lazarus: 171.
League of Empire: 68, 70.

League of Nations: 55.
Legion of Frontiersmen: 70.
Charles Lindbergh, Aviator: 73.
Lord Lloyd: 55–57, 168.
Lloyds Bank: 56.
Local Defence Corps: 162.
Local Defence Volunteers: 159–160, 162.
Locarno Treaties: 55.
Betty 'Frecks' Lovell.: 75.
Lucas Tooth Foundation: 51.

M

General D. MacArthur: 171.
Mansion House Advisory Committee of Associations for Boys: 33.
Marine Society: 2, 12, 45, 116.
Air Cadet Corporal Robert McCallum: 170.
Merchant Navy: 11, 13, 32, 71, 80, 85, 104, 107, 113–114, 116, 172.
Merchant Fleet: 2, 56, 81, 94, 110.
Bernard Miles, Actor: 94.
Military Units:
    1st A.A. Divisional Signals Regiment: 125.
    1st Cadet Battalion, the Queen's Royal Regiment (West Surrey): 54.
    1st Cadet Bn. Oxfordshire and Buckinghamshire Light Infantry: 85.
    1st Cadet Volunteer Battalion, Somerset Light Infantry: 13.
    1st Lanarkshire Rifle Volunteers: 24.
    1st Royal Marine Light Infantry Company: 46.
    1st Surrey Rifle Volunteers: 8.
    1st Volunteer Battalion King's Shropshire Light Infantry: 13.
    2nd Cadet Battalion, East Surrey Regiment: 33.
    2nd Hertford Battery R.F.A.: 33.
    3rd Battalion Warwickshire Rifle Volunteers: 8.
    3rd City of Edinburgh Rifle Volunteer Corps: 8.
    5th Battalion King's Shropshire Light Infantry: 37.
    6th Battalion, East Surrey Regiment: 33.
    70th Bn. The London Irish Rifles: 125.
    7th Bn. Somerset Light Infantry: 86.
    8th Bn. Surrey Volunteer Regiment: 46.
    Air Battalion: 57.
    Army Ordnance Corps: 39.
    City Imperial Volunteer Battalion: 14.
    Coldstream Guards: 128.
    Free French Forces: 130.

Honorable Artillery Company: 1, 39.
King's Own Yorkshire Light Infantry: 86.
No. 18 Squadron R.A.F.: 58.
Norfolk Yeomanry: 73.
Northumberland Division: 25.
Paddington Rifles: 22.
Pioneer Corps: 159.
Queen's Westminster Rifle Volunteers: 8.
R.E.M.E.: 125, 126.
Royal Corps of Signals: 122, 126, 160.
Royal Engineers: 57.
Royal Observer Corps: 2, 159.
Royal West Kent Regiment: 46.
Somerset Light Infantry: 157.
The Rifle Brigade Association Club: 121.
The Royal Inniskilling Fusiliers: 89.
The Royal Ulster Rifles: 89.
Welsh Guards: 126.
Minister of Defence: 176.
Ministry of Defence: 182.
M.O.D.: 184–185.
Minister of Labour: 154.
Ministry of Labour: 79, 94.
Ministry of Education: 79, 174, 181.
Ministry of Health: 170.
Ministry of Information: 94.
Ministry of Supply and Forestry: 154.
Ministry of War: 113.
Monarchs:
  Crown Prince Olaf: 156.
  Edward VII: 14, 54.
  The Prince of Wales (Edward VII): 65.
  The Prince of Wales (Edward VIII): 37, 53, 167.
  Elizabeth II: 172.
  George III: 1.
  George V: 14.
  George VI: 54, 82, 142, 156, 176.
  King: 89, 170.
  Haakon of Norway: 156.
  James I: 1.
  Kaiser Wilhelm II: 14.
  Kaiser: 15.
  Victoria: 8, 73.

Field-Marshal Sir Bernard Montgomery: 157, 171.
Morgan Grenfell, Bankers: 56.
Henry Whithead Moss, Headmaster of Shrewsbury School: 17.
Lord Louis Mountbatten: 171.
Lord Munster: 176.
Museums:
    Imperial War Museum: 4.
    Maritime Museum: 4.
    National Army Museum: 4.
    R.A.F. Museum: 4.

N

General Sir Robert Napier: 65.
Napoleon III: 7.
National Advisory Youth Council: 78.
National Association of Boys' Clubs: 147, 182.
National Cadet Association: 57.
National Fire Service: 95.
Fire Service: 2, 155.
National Sea Training: 40, 45.
National Service Act: 83.
National Service League: 68, 70.
National Vocational Qualifications: 183.
National Youth Organisations: 172.
Naval Brigades: 13, 34.
    Wandsworth Boys' Naval Brigade: 46.
    Wimbledon Naval Brigade: 46.
Naval Brigs: 13.
Naval Training Corps: 181.
Navy League: 4, 10–14, 21–23, 26, 31–32, 34–35, 40, 45–46, 53, 55–59, 66–68, 70–71, 80, 82–83, 101, 109–110, 117, 147, 157, 168–169, 173, 175, 181.
    N.L.S.C.C.: 119.
    Navy League Sea Cadet Officers: 46–47.
London Training Brig Fund: 23.
Boys' Club: 22.
Navy League Home: 12.
Sea Cadet Petty Officer S. Nicholson: 168.
Lord Northcliffe: 69.
Lord Nuffield: 56–57, 59, 72.

O

Officer Cadet Training Units: 128, 173.
Officer Training Corps: 18, 24, 47, 54, 119, 167.
O.T.C.: 19, 20, 25, 31, 35–36, 38–39, 48, 55, 85.
Lieutenant Olney, S.C.C.: 109.
George Orwell, Author: 71.

P

P.Q.17: 114.
The Maharaja of Patiala: 56.
Ex-Air Cadet Arthur Pearcy: 138.
Periodicals:
   A.C.F. journal: 145.
   A.D.C.C. Gazette: 132.
   Air Cadet Gazette: 93.
   Air Defence Cadet Corps Gazette: 75.
   Air Training Corps Gazette: 137.
   Amalgamated Press: 69.
   Army Cadet Journal: 120.
   Aviation News: 138.
   Boys of England: 64.
   Boys of the Empire: 64.
   Boys' Own Magazine: 65.
   Boys' Own Paper: 64, 75.
   Chard and Ilminster News: 137.
   Daily Telegraph: 69.
   Girls' Own Paper: 75.
   Hayes Gazette: 86.
   London Gazette: 171.
   Morning Post: 70.
   Popular Flying: 74–75.
   Shrewsbury Chronicle: 79.
   Sons of Britannia: 64.
   Sunday Times: 49.
   The A.T.C. Gazette: 133, 140–141.
   The Boys' Friend: 64.
   The Cadet Journal: 127, 129, 161, 176.
   The Modern Boy: 74.
   The Navy League: 23, 68.
   The Navy Today: 78.
   The New York Times: 77.

The Salopian: 130.
The Sea Cadet: 94, 105–107, 111, 113, 156.
The Star: 182.
The Times: 11, 83.
The Young Briton: 64.
The Young Englishman: 64.
Times Educational Supplement: 76.
Union Jack: 64.
Bains E. Peto, M.P.: 45.
Prince of Wales's Shield: 51.
Public and Secondary School Cadet Association: 40, 52, 54, 130.
P.S.S.C.A.: 130, 153.

R

R.A.F. Bircham Newton: 170.
R.A.F. Church Fenton: 138.
R.A.F. Cranwell: 181.
R.A.F. Debden: 139.
R.A.F. Driffield: 138.
R.A.F. Halton: 142.
R.A.F. North Weald: 137.
R.A.F. Wymeswold: 170.
E. M. Remarque, Playwright: 48.
River Patrol Service: 161.
Field-Marshal Lord Roberts: 14, 68.
Royal Air Force: 57, 74, 90–91, 118, 132–133, 157.
R.A.F.V.R.: 91, 141.
R.A.F.V.R. (T): 141, 181.
R.A.F.: 58, 60, 72–73, 75–76, 84, 87, 90–91, 93–94, 114, 125, 132, 135–138, 141–143, 146, 154, 161, 170, 175.
Royal British Legion: 183.
Royal Flying Corps: 57, 73–74.
Royal Life-Saving Society: 137.
Royal Mail: 56.
Royal Marines: 46, 118, 126, 181.
Royal Military Academy: 172.
Royal Naval Air Service: 57, 74.
Royal Naval Air Stations: 115, 143.
R.N.A.S.: 143, 146.
Royal Navy: 2, 7, 11–12, 16–17, 32, 34, 40, 55–57, 60, 65, 68, 71, 80–81, 83–85, 93–94, 107–111, 113–114, 116, 118, 137, 141, 181.
Dartmouth cadets: 34.

R.N. Barracks Boys' Brigade: 13, 45.
R.N. Cadet Corps: 13.
Royal Naval Cadet Corps: 45.
R.N.V.R. Special Branch: 47.
Royal Navy Volunteer Reserve: 34, 82.
R.N.V.R.: 46, 81, 116, 117, 167.
Royal United Services' Institute: 18.

S

Salisbury Plain: 57.
Colonel Albert Salmond: 10.
Salute the Soldier Week: 158.
Salvation Army: 50.
Siegfried Sassoon, Poet: 48.
Scarborough Education Committee: 45.
Jacques Schneider: 72.
   Schneider trophy: 72, 73.
Schools, Colleges etc:
   Abingdon: 22.
   Bath College: 23.
   Bedford: 14.
   Berkhamstead: 60.
   Birmingham: 125, 129.
   Bishop Wordsworth: 162.
   Bradfield: 14.
   Burton: 67.
   Campbell College: 88.
   Canton High: 88.
   Chard: 85, 124.
   Charterhouse: 8, 36.
   Chigwell: 85, 155.
   Clifton: 17.
   Colchester: 141.
   Coventry: 125.
   Croydon High: 54.
   Dulwich College: 9.
   Ellesmere College: 13.
   Eton: 7, 10, 18, 24, 36, 38, 39.
   Felsted: 7.
   G.W.R. School: 17.
   Haileybury: 14, 54, 60.
   Harrow: 7, 38, 60, 84.

Honorable East India Company's Military College: 8.
Hurstpierpoint: 7.
Ilminster Grammar: 127.
Ilminster: 129.
King Edward: 38.
King's School: 126.
Lancing College: 131.
Latymer House: 86.
Liverpool Grammar: 159.
London District P.T. School: 126.
Loughborough College: 136.
Loughborough Summer School: 141.
Marlborough: 36, 58.
Merchant Taylors': 35, 47, 54, 154–155, 162.
Naval Physical Training School: 16.
Newcastle-under-Lyme: 15, 35, 38, 92.
No. 49 Gliding School: 139.
Oakham: 38.
Oratory: 38.
Oundle: 38.
Outward Bound School: 116.
Pangbourne Nautical College: 115.
Radley: 58.
Reigate Grammar: 54.
Rossall: 7.
Royal Naval College: 1, 65, 116.
Rugby: 7, 8, 21, 35, 38, 58, 60.
Shaftesbury: 38, 154.
Sherborne: 14, 35, 84, 154.
Shrewsbury: 1, 7, 13, 17–18, 37–38, 126, 129, 154, 162–163.
Slough Grammar: 85.
Southampton University: 115.
Stowe: 137.
Stratford-upon-Avon Technical College: 125.
Toynbee Hall University Settlement: 9.
Uppingham: 15, 38, 133.
Watts Naval Training School.: 45.
Yeovil: 86.
Scout-Brigades: 33.
Scout-Cadets: 40.
Sea Cadet Corps: 2–4, 10, 12–13, 23–24, 33, 45–46, 55–57, 80–85, 87, 92, 101, 108–109, 111, 114, 117–118, 137, 145, 147, 154, 157, 161, 168, 170, 174–176, 181–182, 184–185.

1st Tyne S.C.C.: 157.
Ballyholme: 114.
Beckenham: 84.
Belfast: 114.
Birmingham: 101–111.
Bournemouth: 80.
Brighton: 80.
Bristol: 80.
Bromley: 85, 104.
Canterbury: 80, 108.
Cardiff: 108.
Cheltenham: 80, 84.
Colwyn Bay: 105.
Croydon (West): 104.
Dulwich: 117.
Dundee: 108.
East Cowes: 108, 117.
Elham Valley: 108.
Evesham: 83, 104.
Falkirk: 105, 114.
Farnham: 102.
Gateshead: 101.
Glasgow: 114.
Hackney: 83.
Halifax: 81, 114.
Hoylake: 114.
Hull Unit: 168.
Kingston (Steadfast) Unit: 168.
Kingston-upon-Thames: 85.
Littlehampton: 102.
Liverpool: 114.
Lowestoft: 113.
Newport: 117.
Northampton: 105.
Norwich: 108.
Paisley: 84.
Poole: 116.
Southend: 85, 114.
St Clement Danes Unit: 168.
Stoke Newington: 114.
Streatham: 104.
Stroud: 102.
Sunderland: 114.

Sutton Coldfield: 84.
Swansea: 81.
Wallsend: 113.
Whitstable: 102, 108.
Wimbledon: 102.
Winchester: 101.
Windsor: 24.
Wisbech: 102.
Worcester: 85, 109.
Worthing: 81.
S.C.C.: 60, 87, 91, 94–95, 107–110, 113–114, 118–119, 147, 153, 156, 167, 169, 170, 173, 175, 182–184.
Sea Cadet Lieutenants: 46.
Sea Cadet Training Centre: 115.
Sea Scouts: 33.
Sea Training Home for Poor Boys: 22.
Second World War: 2–4, 54, 71–72, 74, 80, 84, 89, 167, 169, 173, 175–176, 181, 183, 185.
Senior Training Corps: 55.
Tom Shaw, M.P.: 49.
R. C. Sherriff, Playwright: 48.
Mr Emanuel Shinwell, M.P.: 172.
Ships and Training Stations:
Bismarck: 85.
Britannia: 11.
Duguay Trouin: 111.
Folkestone T.S.: 95.
H.M.S. Aboukir: 34.
H.M.S. Chrysanthemum II: 109.
H.M.S. Duke of York: 114.
H.M.S. Foudroyant: 111, 117.
H.M.S. Ganges: 181.
H.M.S. Implacable: 111, 117.
H.M.S. Nelson: 13, 45.
H.M.S. Nightjar: 115.
H.M.S. President: 108–109.
HMS Invincible: 71.
Indefatigable: 12.
Mercury: 12.
Paddington Brig: 22–23, 31.
Reading Brig: 12–13, 22.
Scharnhorst: 85, 114.
Stroud Packet: 109.

211

T.S. Undaunted: 104.
T.S. Bounty: 109–111, 168.
T.S. Gold Seal: 117.
T.S. Jervis Bay: 83.
T.S. Queen: 111.
T.S. Resolute: 45.
T.S. Severn: 104.
T.S. Windsor: 12.
Windsor: 22.
Tirpitz: 85, 114.
Warspite: 12.
Zaza: 115.
Sir William Smith: 24.
Duke of Somerset: 45.
Special Constabulary: 2.
Squadrons:
  No. 266 Squadron: 74.
Duke of Sutherland: 58.

T

Tactical Air Force: 142.
Technical Training Scheme: 124.
Territorial and Forces Act: 19.
Territorial Forces Bill: 20.
Territorial Army: 19–20, 32, 53–54, 156, 173.
T.A.: 53, 120, 167, 175.
Territorial Army Cadet Force: 24, 57, 69.
Territorial Army Reserve: 129.
Territorial Cadet Force: 19–21, 24–25, 32–33, 35–37, 39–40, 45–49, 52, 54, 66, 68–69, 167.
T.C.F.: 21, 26, 38, 53–54, 60, 72.
Territorial Force: 18, 25.
Territorial Force Association: 19, 32, 37, 39.
Territorial Association: 52.
Sea Cadet Harold Thompson: 168.
Lieutenant Jack Thornback: 13.
Towns, Cities etc:
  Aberdovey: 116.
  Abingdon: 22.
  Acton: 113.
  Addiscombe: 8.
  Aldershot: 14.

Axminster: 92.
Barnet: 145.
Barrington: 132.
Belfast: 12.
Birmingham: 38–39.
Bishop Stortford: 161.
Bisley: 15.
Bitteswell Park: 131.
Blackpool: 147.
Bournemouth: 57.
Bridgnorth: 13, 36.
Bristol: 66–67, 109.
Bruton: 125–126.
Camden Town: 172.
Cardiff: 88.
Chard: 92, 157–158.
Chatham: 46.
Chelsea: 4.
Chepstow: 169.
Church Stretton: 131.
Coventry: 108.
Crayford: 36.
Dartmouth: 81.
Derby: 15.
Devizes: 125.
Didcot: 39.
Doncaster: 8.
Driffield: 159.
Dryffyn-on-Sea: 126.
Dundee: 145.
Dunkirk: 81, 83, 121, 126.
Dunstable: 139.
Dunstan Beach: 131.
Falkirk: 105.
Feltham: 113.
Fleetwood: 147.
Folkestone: 95.
Geneva: 55.
Glasgow: 59, 84, 88.
Greenford: 159.
Greenwich: 4, 65, 116, 117.
Hammersmith: 45.
Harrogate: 56–57.

213

Hayes: 113.
Hebburn: 157.
Hendon: 4, 72, 126.
Hertford: 73.
Heybridge: 105.
Hitchin: 158.
Hoddesdon: 54.
Holyhead: 130.
Horley: 156.
Hornsey: 146.
Huddersfield: 8.
Ilford: 59.
Ilminster: 92, 158.
Inskip: 115.
Kensington: 22–23, 45.
Kidsgrove: 92.
Kingston: 113.
Kinmel Park: 129.
Kirkbymoorside: 139.
Leeds: 138.
Liscard: 12.
Liverpool: 12, 59, 66, 79, 113.
London: 4, 10, 14–15, 38, 55, 59–60, 86, 96, 108–109, 113, 146, 157–158, 160, 172.
Londonderry: 157.
Malvern: 128.
Manchester: 9, 16–17, 155.
Merthyr Tydfil: 95.
Nagasaki: 171.
New York: 73.
Newcastle: 92.
Northwood: 162.
Overstone: 131.
Oxford: 22, 128.
Paddington: 22.
Paris: 73.
Pirbright: 128.
Plymouth: 108.
Port Eynon: 115.
Portsmouth: 1, 13, 45, 108, 111.
Preston: 115.
Purley: 156.
Reading: 12.

Richmond: 37–38, 113.
Rickmansworth: 162.
Rochford Airfield: 139.
Shrewsbury: 13, 36, 79, 90, 92, 130, 162–163.
Slough: 110–111.
Southampton: 12.
Southwark: 10.
Stansted: 140.
Stepney: 96.
Stockport: 31.
Swindon: 17.
Tidworth: 35.
Twickenham: 113.
Upper Hayford, near Oxford: 58.
Uxbridge: 146.
Wallasey: 113–114.
Walworth: 168.
Westerham: 14.
Whitchurch: 36.
Whitstable: 7.
Wimbledon: 33, 37, 158.
Windermere: 111.
Windsor: 12–13.
Worcester: 111, 168.
Worthing: 170.
York: 157.
Trafalgar: 63, 71.
Trafalgar Day: 22, 67, 71, 83, 157.
Marshal of the Royal Air Force the Viscount Trenchard: 58.

U

U.S.A.F.: 132, 158.
Ernst Udet, German Air Ace: 73.
United Service Training Corps: 94.
United States Air Base: 139.

V

Sir Francis Fletcher Vane: 9.
Versailles Treaty: 55.
Messrs. Vickers, Engineers: 56.
Victorian League: 68.
Rear-Admiral J G P Vivian: 83, 101.

215

Volunteer Corps: 7, 15.
Volunteer Cadet Corps: 9–10, 16.
Old Boys' Volunteer Company: 15.

W

W.V.S.: 2.
Air Cadet Lance Corporal G. Saggers Wade: 169.
Lord W.W. Wakefield: 56, 141.
War Agricultural Committee: 153.
War Office: 8, 10, 19–20, 25, 35, 49–50, 53–55, 76–77, 85, 120, 122–126, 128–129, 143, 160–161, 181.
War Weapons Week: 158.
Sir E. W. D. Ward: 15.
Edmund Warre, Headmaster, Eton College: 18, 24.
Warship Week: 158.
Major Ted Warrick: 163.
Waterloo: 63.
Captain Wells: 81.
Air Cadet Leonard Wells: 171.
Western Front: 74.
Major-General J. A. C. Whitaker: 123, 129.
General Sir George White: 14.
Flight Lieutenant Arthur Whitton-Brown: 72.
Admiral Sir William Whitworth: 109.
Air Cadet Lance Corporal Cyril Wilson: 169.
Wings for Victory: 158.
J.F. Wolfenden, Director of Pre-Entry Training, A.T.C.: 91, 132–133, 140–141.
Viscount Wolseley: 10.
Women's Auxiliary Air Force: 75.
Women's Junior Air Corps: 79, 181–182.
Women's Land Army: 2, 153.
Joan Worralson: 75.
Lieutenant Harold Wyllie, R.N.V.R.: 117.

Y

'Y' Scheme: 118, 137.
'Yellow Book': 136.
Y.M.C.A.: 131, 146.
Young Airmen's League: 57.
Youth Advisory Council: 175.
Youth Organisation Championship: 182.
Youth Service: 78, 80, 159, 176.